CW01369699

THE healed STATE

Published By
Wolff Publishing UK

ISBN : 978-1-3999-5419-8

Copyright Christianne Wolff 2023

The right of Christianne Wolff to be recognised as the author of this work has been asserted by her in accordance with the Designs and Copyrights act 1988.

The work may not be copied in any way without prior written permission of the publishers.

Disclaimer

Before using the advice in The Healed State book, you may wish to seek medical advice and permission from a medical doctor. The instruction and information in The Healed State book does not replace any medical procedure. Christianne Wolff disclaims any liability, or loss.

I DEDICATE THE HEALED STATE TO MY LOVING HUSBAND ROBBIE, WHO HAS HELPED ME HEAL.

IN LOVING MEMORY OF JON DARVELL WHO INSPIRED EVERY WORD IN THIS BOOK

With special thanks to my sister Marie-Francoise, my assistant Gina and my Aunty Christine for reading through the book and inspiring me along the way.

My husband Robbie Wood for learning to become a photographer especially for this book and taking some amazing shots.

Lou Banks for creating beautiful graphics and Peter Fox for editing The Healed State.

My past clients who have given me greater insight than anyone else I know.

And to all my past, present and future mentors, thank you for your wisdom.

CONTENTS

Introduction	5

Stage 0 - The Apathetic State — 15
What are you resisting? Before healing comes grief. — 16
If my body could speak, what would it tell me now? — 17
What apathy or resistance do you have towards healing? — 17
Are you in the safety zone? — 17
Where is my energy at? — 18

Stage 1 - The Destructive State — 21
Tune into what pain you have — 22
Listen to your body — 25
What are you destroying — 26
What do you need healing — 26

Stage 2 - The Artificial State — 33
What do we actually need to quit? — 34
The senses — 39
Releasing the chains — 42
Dopamine and addiction — 45
You have the power to destroy and to heal — 49
Self Sabotage/Safe — 54
Victim — 55
Hygiene — 57

Stage 3 - The Raw State — 73
Who am I — are you ready to receive healing? — 74
Authentic self — 75
Create a new setting — 83
Surrendering and forgiveness — 89
Understanding what healing is — 96
Process for being ready to heal — 98
Meditation — 103
Reconnect and listen — 105
Essence of you — 107
Journaling — 111

Stage 4 - The Healing State — 115
Routine — 117
Allowing yourself pleasure — 120
Living in colour — 131
Mindfulness — 133
Flow state — 136
Charge with Nature — 143
Micro biome — 152
Water — 172
Ceremony — 181
Smudging — 182
Vibration- your words. — 189
Sound healing — 189
Triggers — 193

Stage 5 - The Heightened Healing State — 197
Physical
  Breath — 198
  Vagus Nerve — 209
  Exercise — yoga — 229
  Sleep — 236
  Nutrients — 244
Mental — 268
  How to rewire your brain — 270
  Motivation versus routine — 273
Emotional
  Trapped emotion — 276
  Placebo and Nocebo — 280
  Playfulness, joy and wonder — 283
Spiritual
  Heightened Flow State — 289
  Goddess energy — 295

Stage 6 - The Healed State — 301
Recap — 302
Process of being healed — 303
Acknowledgement list — 307
Pain as a motivator — 313
The Healed State Barometer — 315
STARRBEAM — 319
STARRBEAM chart — 320

the healed state

INTRODUCTION

To heal is to touch with love that which we previously touched with fear

Stephen Levine

The healed state has been within me since I was a little girl.

At school, I would often stare at the teachers, admiring their auras, their energy and sensing their inner turmoil. I became so lost in their world that sometimes I couldn't hear their actual words until they would shout my name with a question, and shake me back to a conscious state whilst a kind friend would whisper the answer to me.

As soon as I got home from school, I was in nature as much as I possibly could be - climbing trees, speaking to our animals, speaking to plants, and speaking to the angelic world.

For me, healing was reciprocal between me, my pets and the trees I climbed, but my first experience of healing a person happened in 1989 whilst on holiday with my Granny. It was a strange set of circumstances that led to me healing her swollen knee on a beautiful beach in the Algarve, and since then, healing has been a big part of my life to this day.

That morning I picked up a book on my Granny's book shelf entitled "The Naked Ape" by Desmond Morris. I remember reading a particular chapter about how intelligent the octopus is; how it can solve intricate mazes and how it can recognise people.

I was engrossed in the book until lunch time when my Granny announced that we would go to the 'Rickety Rackety' beach; our nickname for Quinta do Lago as it had a long, wobbly footbridge to cross to get to the ocean. My Granny adorned herself in a gold turban and matching gold-heeled shoes. As she clobbered along the bridge, she was a strange combination of high glam and spiritual earth. The wobbly bridge held many treasures of beautiful wildlife beneath it. I often saw crabs, egrets, and turtles, among others. But, never had I seen an octopus until that very day, a few hours after I'd read about their high intelligence. I yelped with excitement at the sight, thrust my arm forward as I pointed at the alien with its orchestra of legs, grabbing my Granny's wrist to share this joyful moment with her. We were both so excited to watch it in the shallow waters of the Ria Formosa, swimming almost in a dance with itself.

However, my squeals of delight started to attract an audience on the bridge and our excitement soon turned to utter horror when a man jumped off the bridge with a bucket, grabbed a large broken branch and hit the octopus on the head. That wondrous creature had just become his family's supper.

My elation quickly turned to sadness and anger. I felt a burning high energy married with an explosion of disappointment, and all I could do was dive into the sea and let its arms comfort my sorrow. At that point, I noticed that this charge I had inside me left me experiencing a huge magnet of energy between my hands.

When I got out of the sea I shared this strange new energy with my Granny and she suggested I place my hands on her knee as it had been causing her a lot of pain (I don't think walking in gold heels on an unstable bridge helped). This was my introduction to healing another person. On that day, I came to know the healing power of the sea and experienced the transmuting energy, charging pain and anger with something positive... love.

I knew I could heal. I could heal myself and heal others, and I presumed everyone else could too.

the healed state

I still do... but I realise now that many people have not been shown how. So writing this book is my opportunity to reveal the incredible, vast healing powers that we all have at our fingertips through what we eat, how we move, how we think and how we connect.

> **the healed state** is about taking responsibility for your health in making changes to heal yourself.

I started writing **the healed state** at the height of the first lockdown in April 2020. The world seemed to have gone crazy, everyone seemed frozen in fear, polarities of opinion were spreading and I felt compelled to put pen to paper to show that our bodies still had the power to heal.

During lockdown we had the perfect moment to make more home cooked meals, slow down our fast-paced lives, and enjoy more family time. This should have improved our health, yet other problems arose, especially issues affecting mental health.

It could have been an opportunity to boost our immunity, lower our stress levels and improve our physical fitness, but for the majority of people, the reverse was the case. In my 27 years of running a wellbeing business, it was the busiest I had ever been. I had thousands of people go through my signature programme, The Body Rescue Plan, as a result of the dramatic effect the pandemic had on their weight, health and wellbeing, This was not caused by Covid-19, but by fear and people needed help more than ever before.

Many people did not know how to manage their fears, addictions, moods, lack of sleep and what seemed to be uncontrollable weight gain.

According to international statistics, anxiety and stress levels rose by 25% worldwide and weight gain rose by 53% in those suffering from depression. Aside from the effects of Covid-19, many became the unhealthiest they had ever been purely as a result of their behaviours.

Your behaviour has been scientifically proven to have incredible healing effects on your mind and body. You only have to look at how placebo trials work to realise this. Your mindset also has the power to kill you, given half a chance. It's up to us to harness the incredible power of the mind for good.

In the healed state, you will learn from many proven scientific studies that behaviour plays a key role in healing. For instance...

- Forgiveness improves your immunity
- Altruism improves memory
- Optimism decreases your chance of death from disease by 40%
- Being happy means you are less likely to catch a cold
- Contentment means you experience less physical pain

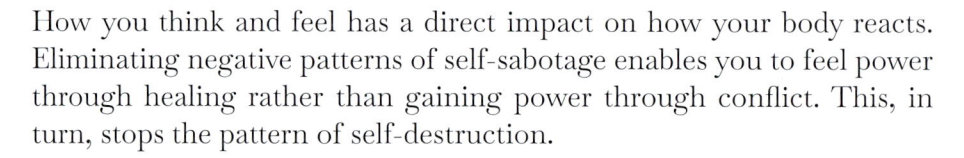

How you think and feel has a direct impact on how your body reacts. Eliminating negative patterns of self-sabotage enables you to feel power through healing rather than gaining power through conflict. This, in turn, stops the pattern of self-destruction.

You reveal the blocks and you heal them.

I will also show you how to heal through the activities you perform daily, how to experience many modalities of healing, and even how to heal in your sleep.

If you have a disease, are in pain, or are struggling with depression and stress, this book will show you the pathway to health.

The path is a simple one, as simple as turning away from screens and into nature. You will learn how nature deprivation is associated with depression, and how the more screen time you have, the higher the risk of ill health you have. Simply changing these behaviours can bring you healing.

Healing is a constant process. Just as you brush your teeth and shower each day, your focus on living in a healed state should also be a daily practice.

We are constantly exposed to many toxins through stress, harmful microbes, toxic people and even pollution, and as a result, we are in a constant state of repair and healing. Our being works autonomically for us in fighting disease, but stress and overwhelm can take over, which can then lead to an onslaught of issues for the body, mind and soul. This book reveals many ways to release stress. In fact, I show you a method that enables you to lower your cortisol levels in just one minute!

True healing brings physical, mental and emotional renewal, allowing the wisdom from your struggles to remain and the pain to be released.

In this journey of the healed state, we will explore the following five states of healing:

Physically   **Mentally**   **Spiritually**

Emotionally   **Environmentally**

These will enable you recover, regenerate and be whole. We also ask what your life would look like if you don't find healing.

You would feel:

Lost   **Unhealthy**

Impaired   **Unwell**

Sometimes, we get so accustomed to being in a permanent state of pain, anxiety or stress that we are unaware of what being healed looks and feels like. Creating pain can easily become a habit, and it often feels much safer to be in pain– because that's what we know.

What if you didn't have to endure pain, trauma and health problems?

We layer ourselves up with so many protective cushions to escape this pain, through excess food, sugar, caffeine and alcohol, and through harmful habits like smoking and doing drugs.

There is a better way. The purpose of this book is to help us understand why we don't heal and why we block healing, and to then peel back these comfort cushions so that we can heal daily in a simple but very effective way.

It is a complex issue but it is also a very simple one, at some point in your life you started building up layers of protection.

THE HEALED STATE

This book is not about not experiencing stress. We all have to endure stress for one reason or another, and in fact stress can be very useful given the right conditions.

However, most of us stay in a suspended state of stress for far too long without even realising it. In this book, I offer ideas on how to bounce back quicker by living in a Healed State rather than a stressed out state!

What's the point of being in a healed state?

- It boosts your immunity
- It lowers stress levels
- It helps you live in the present
- It lowers depression
- It makes you happier
- It gives you a more fulfilled life
- It prevents addictive behaviour
- It enables you to achieve whatever you want
- It stops you from self-sabotaging
- It gives you self-worth
- It gives you strength
- It allows you to receive and give love
- It stops self-harm
- It allows you to live harmoniously

In contrast, from the moment we wake up, we can spend our day dulling our senses through caffeine, sugar, alcohol, cigarettes, drugs and stress.

Dulling our senses puts us in a reactive state and we become:

- Reactive and stressed, or
- Reactive and servile to others.

Who are you in this drugged up, stressed, reactive served state?

Who are you and who do you want to be?

I've written many award-winning books in The Body Rescue Plan series, and have been a healer and trainer for more than 30 years. I share stories about clients who have been on their healing journeys and have eliminated disease, stress, depression, sleep issues and fatigue. They are now reconnected to the core essence of who they really are, and are thriving. Prior to their healing, these people had built up fat, toxins, disease, stress and anger like protective layers hiding their core essence from themselves and the world. Does this apply to you?

In this book, I also share how I was able to uncover some personal issues which required healing.

You will learn that unveiling these toxic and negative blocks allows light to stream through you, turning your vulnerability into a super power.

The alternative is continuing the vicious cycle of pushing those core infestations under water only for them to resurface to pull our energy down and lure us into placing more protective layers around ourselves.

The healing process can be as simple as focusing on your breath– the inhale is healing and the exhale is releasing.

the healed state takes you back to the time when you were once a free spirit, floating in nature, humming like a bird, sparkling like the phosphorescence in the sea. It is finding the core person you were before you were taught anything, before you were poisoned, before you were let down, before you were made to feel anything but who you should be.

the healed state is finding the brightest shining star in you and growing outwards again from this place of birth to connect to your greatest experience in life.

Regardless of what it is, you let it in. You accept it in full force and you feel no guilt. You feel it with all your senses and you open up like a flower absorbing sunlight.

the healed state is finding who you are without pain, without sacrifice, without suffering, without self-sabotage, without neglect, without hate. It is taking a raw look at the angelic body which has been bestowed upon you– a body which no one told you about.

It is finding this without the need to have any external affirmation or acceptance. This is internal work and no one needs to understand or validate you. Your core being is perfect. You only need to clear out the blockages that have stopped you from finding yourself.

We are all made up of matter and all matter vibrates. How we vibrate is everything. When we allow our bodies to vibrate on a higher frequency, a positive energy illuminates us from within. However, when we fuel our bodies with toxins we become ill and our vibration dulls.

The healed state is when your body has the consistent harmony of flowing energy it needs to heal you physically, mentally, and emotionally. The moment this harmony is blocked, we become unwell.

Let's get to work on removing those energy blocks with simple, proven and exciting methods that work so you can live in a healed state.

*This is an intimate journey with yourself.
Take your time with each chapter.*

the healed state

STAGE 0
THE APATHETIC STATE

*What you resist,
persists.*
C. G. Jung

1. Before healing comes grief. What are you resisting?

2. If my body could speak, what would it tell me now?

3. What apathy or resistance do you have towards healing?

4. Are you in the safety zone?

5. Where is my energy at?

> **Before healing comes grief. What are you resisting?**

The apathetic state of Stage Zero is being the antagonist to healing. It is not so much creating a conscious negative environment for healing, but more a resistance, an apathetic one.

It's the 'before' photo.

Stage 0 is the start of your healing journey.

Before you tune into what you want to heal in Stage 1, it's important to understand where you are right now. It's not what you want or how you will go about fixing it, but getting to understand your general energy and how you got to this point.

Your apathy and resistance to change to create healing is a big part of how you got here.

And that is absolutely fine– sit with that and connect to who you are.

Before healing comes grief.

This may be your time to allow that grief to surface. Feel your resistance to change and sit with how you got to this space.

In Stage 2 we enter an artificial state. We break down the layers of whatever you haven't given up that has made you sick. But, right now, at Stage Zero, we are sitting with ourselves, observing who we are without any pressure to change. This stage is about understanding the journey which has led you to this point.

In the forthcoming stages of healing, I will ask you a series of questions to help you get through each milestone. The first question on this healing journey is:

> ### If my body could speak, what would it tell me now?

This isn't addressing the issue of what needs healing, but it's simply sitting in the presence of you and observing who you are.

What got you here?

This is important to know, because how you arrived at this point is not how you want to continue. As Sigmund Freud put it, *"The definition of madness is to repeat the same mistakes over and over again and expect different results."*

You arrived at this point through a series of thoughts, habits and actions. Some of these will need to be adjusted or changed, and I will show you how during the healing stages.

Stage 0 is not about changing your actions. It's about observing and understanding who you are.

The second question in Stage 0 is:

> ### what apathy or resistance do you have towards healing?

Are you in the safety zone?

Your ego will keep wanting to repeat old patterns of thought, habit and action over and over again.

That's because it is far easier for you to work on autopilot with all the sub-conditioned beliefs and subconscious thoughts and actions being on a loop. You, as a person, are happier staying in a loop because change requires conscious effort, and conscious effort means you are messing your ego and its comfort zone.

During the healing stages, you will listen to a series of meditations that will help you rewire the subconscious patterns you have built up. You created most of these past patterns without being aware of it, using them as a form of protection to get by in the world.

Unfortunately, this can put you in a very confused state as our body desperately wants to heal, but you as a construct may want to stay put.

Meditation is such a powerful tool for our journey to healing because it can help us subtly change our sub-conditioned behaviours without fear of success, or fear of failure.

Do you have a fear of success? Do you have a fear of failure?

The apathetic state is your safety zone. However, this is not where you will either be happiest or the most fulfilled, and it cannot be where you get healed.

Where is my energy at?

For instance, if you are currently overweight and want to lose weight, the energy going in is more than the energy going out (You are eating more than you are burning). There should be less energy going in than is going out – or less toxic, and more healthy and loving.

If you find yourself always in need of more money, it could be because there's more energy going out than is coming in (ie you are overspending and not earning enough to cope).

If you want more love, where is your energy at? If you want more joy, where is your energy at?

In other words, where is your focus, and what decisions are you making based on that focus?

To be healed, the energy going in should be more than that going out.

To help you get started on this journey, please listen to the first meditation here.

Take a seed meditation and then go to Stage 1 - Tuning Into What You Want to Heal.

the healed state

STAGE 1
THE DESTRUCTIVE STATE

Holding on to anger is like grasping a hot coal with the intent of throwing it at someone else; you are the one who gets burned.

Buddha

1. **Tune into the pain you have**

2. **Listen to your body**

3. **What are you destroying?**

4. **What do you need healing?**

Tune into What you Want to Heal

In Stage 0 of **the healed state,** we observed who we are in our apathetic state, what we do on autopilot day in and day out, and how we got to this position.

In Stage 1, we will now be focusing on what we want to heal.

Right now, look in the mirror and see who you are and what pain you have.

We often hear people saying that disease is cruel. Yet the biggest cruelty is not giving our body exactly what it needs to heal.

Somewhere, something is not working for you– internally, externally, in your environment, in your life.

Patterns of negative behaviour are constantly repeating themselves ending in either the same results, or in even more negative outcomes. The good news is that we have the power to change this. We have the power to replace these negative behaviours and layers that have built up over time, which we can replace with injections of healing energy instead.

In stage 1 of this journey, we need to tune into whatever it is that needs to be healed in our lives.

Asking what needs healing can run deep, and that's because the symptom you feel might not tell you actually needs to be treated.

Let me explain... When I was 11, I had long, thick hair, down to my bottom. I was on holiday at my Aunty Claire's house in France and one morning, I excitedly sprung out of bed in anticipation of our holiday. To get ready for the day, I started brushing my hair when suddenly, I couldn't move my shoulder. Yup, I had pulled a muscle brushing my hair and it was painful. I couldn't move my neck or my arms. My nerves were enjoying a good old party of spasms in my back, and I had to lie down in complete stillness until it subsided.

Since then, there has been my weak spot in my back. Every now and then, I feel pain in my neck, but actually the muscle knots are in my lower back. I spent years doing neck stretches and mobility exercises for my shoulders, when it was actually my lower torso that needed all the work. Once I knew this, I could prevent a reoccurrence of the same back issue. I developed a routine of core stability exercises and yoga postures, and as a result, I don't suffer nearly as many moments stuck in a spasm frenzy, and don't have to be sedentary for an entire day anymore.

We often don't realise the core of whatever it is we need help with because it has manifested into something else. We see the symptom but not the cause.

For instance...

- It could be that you aren't attracting your loved one because you are insecure about your looks.
- It could be that the insecurity relates to a skin condition caused by an intolerance to a certain food - let's say sugar
- It could be that you are addicted to that certain food because you have a parasite living in you - let's say candida
- It could be that you have candida because you have had a lot of antibiotics for persistent bladder infections
- It could be you had a lot of bladder infections because you endured a trauma
- It could be you experienced trauma because...

The process of finding out what needs healing can go deep. It is often connected to a traumatic experience from our past which is now manifesting into something else because we haven't dealt with it.

If it has manifested into something else, it may not stop but could just get bigger.

There are several ways we can confront the broken stem which needs fixing, and I have created a beautiful meditation below to help you analyse what is broken in you.

Remember, this is not about how you need to fix it. For now, it's just identifying what needs fixing.

If you feel you need external, professional support on any part of the healing journey or if it's too traumatic for you to manage alone, seek advice from your Medical Practitioner straightaway.

This is intended to start you on your healing journey, so that you can live in a healed state and revert to this healed state in future times of stress.

Our bodies can scream out at us for help. They can begin to tell us gently what is needed, but most of the time, we ignore them. Eventually the pain in us gets bigger and bigger until we finally hear and connect what is going wrong. Perhaps this is where you are now.

We are living in a dopamine culture where we constantly try to numb the pain we feel in the hope that it will disappear. But, all our body wants is the tools it can use for healing and for health.

Our body will still work for us, no matter what we throw at it. But at some point, it can become severely fatigued and if ignored, will eventually run out of energy completely.

Throughout **the healed state**, I will ask you to listen more closely to its needs. With each question I ask, you will take a deeper dive into your mind, body and soul to understand their needs and find a pathway to reaching your healed state.

Ask yourself these questions:

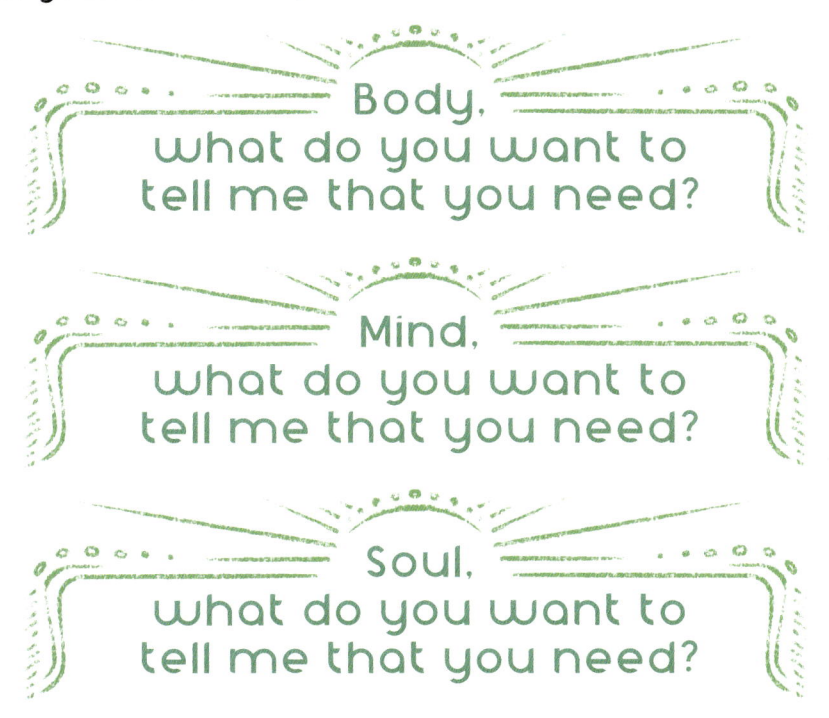

Body, what do you want to tell me that you need?

Mind, what do you want to tell me that you need?

Soul, what do you want to tell me that you need?

What positive changes would I like to see in my life?

Is there anything you don't want to heal because you feel it will make you weaker?

Sometimes, it can be difficult to focus on what you need to heal because it may be a whole host of things, or it could be that you are very disconnected from who you are.

Sometimes, we become alienated from ourselves because we are unwilling to give up what makes us sick (We will cover this in Stage 2).

Another way you could ask yourself what needs healing is to look at what isn't working in your life.

I call this 'The destructive state' because at the moment, you are destroying the pockets of happiness you could have.

So another question for you is:

> **What are you destroying in your life?
> Or What is going wrong?**

When we see the negatives, we can then just flip the answer around. For example:

Answer
I am destroying my body.

Question
Where are you destroying your body?

Answer
My stomach.

Question
What do you want to tune into for healing?

Answer
I want to heal my stomach.

For Stages 0 and 1, we are not focusing on the 'how' (that will come). We are trying to identify the what and the where, and understanding a little of the backstory helps us determine how deep the healing needs to go.

> **What and Where do I need healing?**

You could break up this process by reflecting on different parts of your body and your life to help you unearth wounds that have not healed.

Let's break down the areas.

Your Face and Neck

- Eyes
- Ears
- Nose
- Mouth
- Tongue
- Teeth
- Cheekbones
- Forehead
- Skin
- Scalp
- Skull
- Brain
- Throat
- Neck

Your Arms

- Shoulders
- Collar bone
- Bicep
- Triceps
- Elbow
- Forearms
- Wrists
- Hands
- Fingers
- Thumbs
- Nails
- Skin

Your Torso

- Chest
- Shoulder Blades
- Spine
- Rib cage
- Pelvis
- Lungs
- Heart
- Spleen
- Gall bladder
- Stomach
- Colon
- Pancreas
- Liver
- Kidneys
- Bladder
- Vagina
- Pelvic floor
- Penis
- Blood
- Skin

Your Legs

- Quads
- Hamstrings
- Knees
- Shins
- Calves
- Ankles
- Heels
- Feet
- Toes
- Nails
- Skin
- General Fitness
- General Mobility
- General Flexibility

What do happiness and joy feel like in your body?

WHAT ARE YOU DESTROYING & WHAT DO YOU NEED HEALING?

Your Ethereal Body

Don't worry if you don't understand what a soul is. Or what your chakras or aura are. I will explain these in the meditations.

- Crown
- Third Eye
- Throat
- Heart
- Solar Plexus
- Sacral
- Root

What do happiness and joy feel like in your ethereal body?

STAGE 1 · THE DESTRUCTIVE STATE

What do happiness and joy feel like in your mind?

Your Mind

- Do you focus on the negative?
- Do you over think?
- Do you have control?
- Do you have a fear of losing control?
- Do you suffer with cognitive dissonance? (when your beliefs don't line up with your action)
- Do you feel unworthy?
- Do you feel unloved?
- Do you have self-care?
- Are you stressed?

Your Soul

- Is your soul crying?
- Is it being suffocated?
- Is it being stimulated?

What do happiness and joy in your soul feel like?

WHAT DO YOU NEED HEALING?

There are two meditations to listen to that take you through the ethereal body and the physical body/mind. It is a good idea to listen to these meditations a few times initially to go deep into the needs of your body.

After you've listened a few times, you can progress to practicing it regularly by doing a mental body scan when you wake up each morning. A body scan is what we do in the meditations as above, and it involves looking through our mind, body and soul to understand how their needs are to be met for that day. It ensures that your decision making will align with healing rather than against it.

You can also tune into where your body, mind and soul need healing every night before you sleep and ask for the needed healing as part of your nightly meditation. We learn how to do this in Stage 6.

Most of your healing happens while you are unaware of it. Most of it is an automatic process of your cells performing tasks to patch up what has gone wrong. But, if you make a conscious effort not to mess up their hard work, you then work as a team and the reward is that you will feel and look so much better. Remember, for Stage 1, we are just tuning in to what is wrong rather than how to fix it. That comes later.

Now listen to the meditation here to connect with what needs healing.

And then, write down what you feel after you have listened to it.

Remember, life is not linear.

You may need to do this process many times, as life throws us curve balls all the time- new areas of your body, your mind, your life may need healing.

Life happens; different things happen each day to our body in the form of accidents, illnesses and stress. Therefore, your body can change daily and that's fine. Your body is a work in process.

Just as you need to breathe, move, drink, eat, and clean regularly, you also have to create a practice of living in a healed state, and to get to that state, you have to understand what needs healing on a daily basis.

When we focus on what we want to heal, our decision making becomes better aligned with healing and with who we want to be.

You can also extend the desire for healing throughout your life:

- Your Work
- Your Income/money
- Your Relationships
- Your Friendships
- Your Family life
- Your Home
- Your Creativity
- Your Spirituality
- Your behaviours

If you feel you need to, take some time to reflect on these aspects of your life and ask yourself:

What do happiness and joy feel like in these areas?

In Stage 2, we will be leaving the destructive state and going into the artificial state. But, before we get there, ask yourself the following questions:

What is instructing you to not heal?
What are you protecting?

the healed state

STAGE 2
THE ARTIFICIAL STATE

Before you heal someone, ask him if he's willing to give up the things that make him sick.
Hippocrates

1. What do we actually need to quit?

2. The Senses

3. Releasing the chains

4. Dopamine and addiction

5. You have the power to destroy and to heal

6. Self-sabotage/Safe

7. Victim

8. Hygiene

What do we actually need to quit?

When we tune into healing our bodies, one of the most important questions we can ask ourselves is "What do we need to quit to heal our bodies and are we willing to quit it?"

The reason why this is important to start with is because it's identifying our own responsibility for the healing journey (rather than blaming someone else) which then enables a deeper understanding of how to heal ourselves.

What we think needs healing could simply be the manifestation or the symptom of what we need to work on healing.

This is often why medicinal drugs don't work for us holistically– they only treat the symptom and not the cause.

For instance...

- If you need healing with your weight problems, is it the fat that needs to be healed from your body? ...
- Or the series of actions that led to the fat build up? ...
- What caused those actions?
- Are you in an addictive cycle with food?
- And if you are in an addictive cycle with food, could it be because you are masking a pain?
- So, to heal an overweight body, first and foremost, you need to identify the pain you are masking.
- And then when you look at your habit of masking pain— with food/sugar/alcohol/drugs, you then have to ask, "Am I willing to give that up?"

- **What is worse?** The addictive behaviour that has made your body and mind ill, or the feeling of hopelessness around giving up that substance with which you mask your pain?

When people come to me with sugar addictions, or food addictions in general, that's the first question I ask- "What pain is sugar masking?"

Sugar is both physically and mentally addictive. This is why it is important to look at the mental and physical dimensions of addiction in order to achieve healing.

Over the years, I have run five-day sugar free challenges for thousands of people (sign up here if you want to join) and one of the first things the group will say is how nervous they are prior to starting.

They are not sure if they are willing to give up what is causing them to suffer because they are using that substance to relieve pain. It's a Catch 22.

In reality they are nervous because they will not have their 'go-to' numbing device anymore. I call this numbed state of living 'the artificial state'.

For this next step, you need to ask yourself whether you are willing to live in this artificial state?

And if so, why?

Why do you want to give up what is making you sick?

- Are you willing to give up the numbing device that is making you ill?
- Why are you willing to give that up?
- What do you want to feel instead?

This isn't the healed state, but it's allowing the beginning stages of healing to happen. The healed state is the end stage. Stage 0 is the apathetic state, then Stage 1 is the destructive state, followed by the artificial state and the raw state, leading to the healing state and the healed state.

When we are open and honest about all the layers upon layers of protection we have built up, we make ourselves ready for healing.

You can't get to a healed state if you are numbing pain with drugs, and that includes caffeine, sugar, alcohol, vast amounts of food, junk food, stress, sex, and any other dopamine highs (more on dopamine later).

The raw state (the next stage) can only begin when we give up what's making us sick.

What will you have to give up in order to not make yourself sick anymore?

When you have to give up something to heal yourself, to help you on your journey, you then have to find other ways to heal that pain. Ways that will help, not hinder you.

Sugar addiction is as an example of how people protect, numb, or give themselves a high with something as simple as sweet treats. Whilst sweet on the surface, sugar can become highly destructive when consumed in excess.

Processed sugar has a catastrophic effect on the body's ability to heal. It is highly inflammatory, causes pain in the joints, affects concentration, affects sleep and digestion which are both vital for the body's healing process, upsets hormonal balance, speeds up heart rate, raises blood sugar levels, increases blood pressure, affects the skin and causes disease. Honestly, I could go on.

I have run sugar free challenges for up to 7000 people at a time, three times a year for many years. What's incredible is that the body heals itself very quickly. In just a few days, participants report that their sleep, pain, skin, digestion and energy levels have dramatically improved. I remember one lady posted a video on the SFC group of her doing a thumbs up, moving her thumb up and down. Initially, I thought, "That's an odd video- what is she doing?" But when I read her comment on her post, I understood she had shared the video because it was the first time she had moved her thumb with ease in many months.

In Stage 1 of **the healed state**, I asked you to look in the mirror and analyse what needs healing in your life. We now have to understand what we need to give up in order to achieve this healing. Sometimes, it can be hard to know what to give up, especially if there are many things to consider. However, I would bet that sugar will be near the top of the list for most of us.

The funny thing about sugar is that when it's out of your life, even for as little as five days, you'll experience a positive shift. Your decision making, self-care, self-love, and energy for life will change because your senses become heightened. You don't necessarily have to analyse each part of your body because you become far more in tune with yourself.

When you dull your senses, you have no clue who you are and what you need. You are addicted to the thing that is dulling your senses. So, quitting sugar (or anything else that's detrimental to your healing) is a necessary step towards opening up the vessel of your body to what you actually need.

Remember, it's a cycle!

You are in pain (mental, emotional, physical). You need something to dull the pain and so, you take a drug. However, it only gives you a short-term relief while causing damage to you.

And, in additon to causing harm to you, it fails to get to the root cause of the pain you are suffering.

STAGE 2 · THE ARTIFICIAL STATE

The Senses

One of the reasons we get addicted to food, drugs, people, social media, sex, porn, etc, is that we don't actually feel anything. We chase the high, seeking more pleasure (to relieve pain usually), but it comes at a huge cost. The cost can be ultimately not feeling anything at all. Heightening your senses in a natural way (as opposed to in an addictive or artificial way) gives you a much more interesting, happy and fulfilled life.

I have had so many clients tell me they suddenly started feeling again while on their healing journey. It may be tasting simple foods, hearing the exquisite orchestras of nature, heightening the sensations from their fingertips, smelling the aromatic fragrances of nature and seeing all the beautiful colour around them instead of focusing on what they don't have and what they are missing out on.

Our 'Body Rescue' retreats are designed to reawaken the senses through a fun mix of yoga, meditation, fitness and clean eating. I remember that a few years ago, while teaching our 'Body Rescue' retreat in Ibiza, one of our clients, Fiona, began experiencing this reawakening. One day at breakfast, after three days of being on the retreat, she asked, "Have you changed anything about this yogurt? It tastes so delicious today?"
"No," I replied. "It's just plain yogurt"
"Oh wow! I can't believe how much more flavour it has."

Fiona had gone through a difficult time. Her husband, the owner of a successful eyewear business, had suffered a sudden stroke which left him paralysed and brain damaged. Not only did she have to deal with the terrible harm the stroke had done to her husband's body and care for him in his current state, she also had to deal with the stress of taking over a business she had previously not been involved in.

The process of reawakening was gradual for Fiona. After Day 1, she noticed she felt more relaxed and better rested after having turned in at 8:30pm the night before, which was unusual for her.

Here's the thing– we don't set the bedtime on our retreats, but we often find that without TV, alcohol, and excessive screen time, people naturally go to bed when their bodies tell them to. Sleep is when the body gets most of the healing it needs.

On the last day of the retreat, Fiona said something very amusing to my husband who offers fitness classes for participants– "Robbie, your trainers look so colourful and bright today! Have you been wearing them all week?"
"Yes," Robbie replied. "They're the only shoes I brought with me!"

Fiona was totally bemused by how her senses had become so alive in just four days. This was not only the result of consuming less sugar, caffeine and alcohol, but also of having four days of very good sleep, deep relaxation and exercise.

One of the reasons your senses come alive in such a short time while on our retreats is that by participating, you allow yourself to go more into homeostasis, you stimulate the vagus nerve (more on that in Stage 5!), and you balance your chakras.

Essentially, this means that you are able to achieve more balance in your mind and body, with less sensory overload, allowing your body to perform and function better, which gives you a richer life experience.

Fiona was in her 50's, generally healthy and not overweight. She also had a healthy diet, but the stress she had endured, the lack of sleep and lack of relaxation meant she wasn't seeing life clearly or fully through her sensory lenses which are:

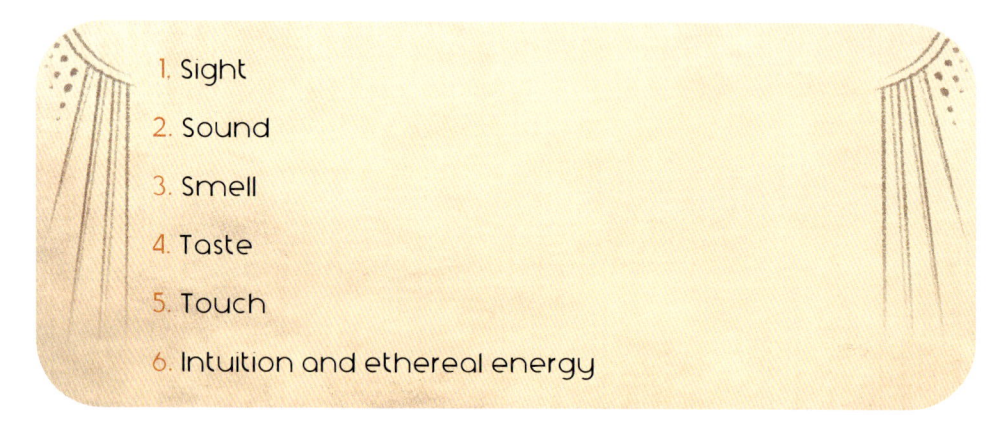

1. Sight
2. Sound
3. Smell
4. Taste
5. Touch
6. Intuition and ethereal energy

Stress was making her sick and she needed a solution.

FOMO – or the Fear Of Missing Out - plays a major role in our resistance to 'Having to give up something', but when you start focusing on what you gain, and allow that to come into your psyche, you realise how much better your life can be.

Instead of seeing this step as having to give up or lose something, see it as upgrading yourself.

I love playing the upgrade game! It can change your mindset and support your healing process. It can also lessen the depressing feeling that you are missing out.

So, if the question, "What do I have to give up because it's making my body sick?" doesn't resonate with you, think, "What can I do to upgrade my health?" Upgrading always means getting rid of something else, but it feels both exciting and joyous.

There is nothing boring about getting rid of something that makes you ill. You are already missing out. You are missing out on living the life you were meant to experience in the natural heightened state that your body was blessed with. Living in the artificial state is not living; it has no depth, no knowledge and no grounding. It's a high-pitched squeal that cannot give you a happy life. It just takes you to the high-pitched squeal again and again, till you become trapped there, never able to slow down and feel.

You are forever on this rollercoaster being spun around. At first, it is exciting and exhilarating, but ultimately, you want to get off as you can't see–everything is blurred, burdened and bereft.

The artificial state is a life depleting state.

You are now swapping the old with the new, the worn out with the fresh and shiny. You are creating a new you.

When you want to give up addictions or harmful habits, there are several processes you need to go through.

Initially, you may have a mental, emotional and physical addiction or a dependence on things that harm your wellbeing, and may require external help, depending on how deep your dependency goes (we are not only talking about addiction in this stage).

Although alcohol and drugs can lead to serious addictions, I have worked with thousands of people who have quit sugar, and as a result come off medication for depression, anxiety, pain, heart issues, cholesterol, Type 2 diabetes and HRT. Many have reversed diseases, rid obesity and many other diseases and health-related issues. In fact, every time I interview someone who has dramatically changed their life through either quitting or reducing their sugar intake, I am always surprised at how it changed their health and their life. Sugar is one of the most addictive drugs in our society. I will go out on a limb here and say it's worse than the usual class A drugs because it's everywhere, it is socially acceptable, and it is celebrated.

If you want help with quitting sugar, follow my sugar free challenge here.

Releasing the Chains

I have given healing to many people who were very sick with cancer, some with just months to live.

Some clients will do everything to heal their bodies, whilst many others have a general apathy towards the idea of giving up things that are damaging their bodies.

Sugar is one of the worst things you can consume if you have cancer or many other diseases. Yet, I often meet many clients who though very ill, loathe having to give up that one treat. It would seem that to them, that treat is more important than getting better.

THE SENSES

Quitting is not impossible though– far from it. I have met the most hardened addicts who were able to quit what was making them sick and have gone on to heal hideous, immobilising, life-threatening diseases, restoring their bodies and lives to health. I have also seen people die because they refused.

Now that you understand where you are suffering, and what you want to heal, you need to ask yourself whether you are willing to give up or replace that element of your life that is making you sick.

Now, this is a difficult decision to make because our addictive patterns of negative behaviour and our subconscious actions to constantly numb ourselves can convince us that it's impossible to break the habit.

We want to heal ourselves. We want to stop living in pain and fear, but the cycle of drugging our senses so we don't feel anything is deeply engrained. We drug ourselves with sex, porn, anger, food, drugs, booze– anything that lights up our dopamine receptors. The problem is that we end up chasing the dopamine high, whilst neglecting everything else that matters. We get sicker, our relationships fail, our creativity nosedives, and we get little joy out of life. We stop being able to feel anything, except perhaps the pain we continue to create in our bodies and the fear of losing our numbing devices.

Fear is a very powerful emotion. Whilst we need fear to help us navigate dangers and protect ourselves, it can also take over, be all consuming and even kill us. When we go through fear, real physiological changes happen within us. Our sympathetic nervous system switches on, fight-or-flight goes into overdrive, and if not suspended, it can make us very ill. Living in a prolonged state of fear also has the potential to lock us into an early demise.

Dopamine and Addiction

*Pleasure and pain come from
the same part of the brain!*

Dr Anna Lembke

Dopamine is a neurotransmitter hormone that is responsible for feelings of **pleasurable reward and motivation.**

When dopamine is out of balance, it can lead to several mental health and neurological diseases.

In her book, Dopamine Nation, Dr Anna Lembke explains that the pre-frontal cortex (PFC), the grey matter part of the brain around our forehead, is responsible for gratification, storytelling, future planning, considering future consequences, and the process of having a spiritual experience.

The PFC communicates with the lower stem regions of the brain that deal with reward pathways.

Keeping that communication flowing and strong is essential to a healthy brain. In other words, the non-addicted brain.

What happens in addiction is that the PFC stops communicating efficiently with the lower brain stem reward pathway and therefore, your pleasure/pain sequence starts to go out of balance.

When you are addicted, you are no longer able to accurately assess impact and future consequences because you are driven by your limbic brain which is your reward pathway.

Dr Lembke says:

> "When we experience pleasure, dopamine is released in our reward pathway; the more our balance tips (towards pleasure), and the faster it tips, the more pleasure we feel. But here is the important thing about the balance, it doesn't want to remain tipped to either side (pleasure or pain) for very long. It wants to remain level. Hence, every time the balance tips toward pleasure; powerful, self-regulating mechanisms kick into action to bring it level again. They just happen like a reflex."

Your brain wants to bring you to a state of equilibrium known as homeostasis.

The same part of the brain is responsible for pleasure and pain. Whether you are in pain or pleasure, the brain will eventually pull you back to the neutral state of homeostasis.

However, whilst trying to achieve homeostasis, the brain doesn't exactly float back to the neutral state and stay there. If we have swung far one way or the other (pleasure or pain), the pendulum will swing back but go into the other side first. So, if we are in pleasure, it will swing back to pain before going into the state of homeostasis.

This is where it becomes potentially dangerous for our addictive behaviour.

We don't want to be in pain. So, at that stage, we may get addicted to something potentially toxic because it can give us another high. Unfortunately, the things that give us the biggest and quickest dopamine hits are usually toxic for the body.

Imagine you gain your unnatural high from let's say processed sugar (I speak a lot about sugar as most of us can relate to it, and in my profession it's the thing which I help most people quit). Your brain then works its mechanisms to bring you back to the homeostasis state, but tips you into the pain side whilst it works its way to getting you back to neutral. You feel pain, i.e. a comedown, and you then instinctively crave the high again because you don't like this comedown feeling. So you consume more sugar to get out of pain, and the cycle begins.

Sugar will also mess with other parts of your body to replay this system of comedowns through your blood sugar levels dropping, and your body wanting them raised again as well as the fact that it oversaturates your tastebuds so nothing else tastes as good. Yet, all your body wants to do is heal you. It's not just the brain that wants to achieve a state of homeostasis, your body also wants to achieve homoeostasis by monitoring and maintaining internal states, such as your temperature and blood sugar levels.

When it comes to an addictive pattern, whether it's food, sex, porn, drugs, video games, etc, we are in a dopamine cycle, similar to a washing machine tossing laundry around and around.

The problem with dopamine is that its receptors become burnt out when overused. So, if you get a high from one bar of chocolate, after a while, one bar won't be enough. You will now need two, then three and so on, to get the same high you once got from just the one bar. It's why people go from soft drugs to hard drugs in succession, soft porn to hard porn, or from one cigarette to many.

When the satisfaction we can get from these things fades progressively with overindulgence, it is called 'tolerance'. At this point, we stop feeding our body what is good for it, and only feed it what gives us the dopamine high. We become numb, lifeless robots.

There are two ways you can prevent this burnout of dopamine addiction:

> Tolerate the pain barrier - until you can naturally get back to homeostasis.
>
> OR
>
> Avoid the extreme highs in the first place.
> (Quit what is making you sick)

Working with the vagus nerve is also a very powerful way of restoring homeostasis (more on this in Stage 5). Remember, here in Stage 2, we are still identifying what we need to give up in order to heal.

DOPAMINE AND ADDICTION

Whilst we all seek pleasure, having too many highly pleasurable experiences dulls our senses and stresses us out. This is particularly the case when the high comes from something unnatural and fast rather than the natural high experienced in nature.

We all know that spoilt child who wants more, more, more! Think Veruca Salt from the film Charlie and the Chocolate Factory; **"I want it all, and I want it right now!"** We have all been around parents who at Christmas, try to bring out presents a little at a time throughout the day so their child doesn't become overwhelmed, and we have all seen spoilt celebrity kids grow up to become drug addicts.

We all want riches, but the richest countries in the world are the ones that have the most suicide and pain. It appears the more we have, the more depressed we are.

In Stage 5, I will show you some powerful ways to restore the state of homeostasis. But for now, remember that dopamine makes us crave for things that will give us more dopamine highs. So, we should be mindful about what we crave and why we crave it.

And when you are in the pain side of the pendulum, just think, "This soon shall pass."

Do you need to give up your addictive cycle with the dopamine hit?

It's not just food, drugs and sex. It's also how social media works as well. The short videos, the likes and loves are all wired to trigger our dopamine response.

You have the power to destroy and heal

You might be reading this thinking, "But I'm not addicted to anything, and I don't need to give up anything that's made me sick. I just need a cure."

If this is you, then maybe you need to think more laterally.

Let me tell you about Paul. He was one of my healing clients who was diagnosed with cancer four years before he joined my programme. He had gone through all the conventional treatments without much success, and I was his last hope.

He had had many operations, many rounds of chemo, seen many healers and nutritionists. Yet not one of them had spoken to him about what he needed to give up in order to get better. Yes, they suggested a healthy diet and cutting down on alcohol and sugar, but diseases in our body manifest themselves in many ways. This is why in my opinion, it is a good idea to look at the mental and emotional side of things when starting treatment for a disease as serious as cancer.

As it turned out, it wasn't his unhealthy diet that Paul had to give up. It was also his way of holding onto anger and blaming others. He had a habit of holding grudges and could not see the power of this negative habit and how it was making his body sick.

Many people find it difficult to understand which actions of theirs– physical, psychological, emotional or spiritual– are healing or destroying their bodies.

You are a powerful manifester!

To help you understand this, here's an example.

If I were to ask you, "What could you do today to make yourself ill tomorrow?" What would come to mind?

Well, you might get the idea to drink a lot of alcohol, smoke cigarettes, eat junk food, get no sleep, get really angry, have a row with a loved one... what else?

What else could you do to make yourself feel physically unwell?

You could tense your body, lie in one position for too long, hold something till you feel pain, cause yourself an injury, be totally disorganised, not do any of your duties or daily tasks/routines, etc.

What else?

Not wash, not brush your teeth, wear smelly and dirty clothes, breathe in bad air, be around negative people, be mean, swear all day long, watch horror movies, and think of everyone and everything that makes you angry.

What else can you think of?

I think you get the picture!

Now I want you to read the following words and notice how you physically feel in reaction to them.

"You are a disgusting, fat, useless piece of crap and you should never have been born!"

Okay. Now we have got ourselves way past the healed state to the destructive state. We all do this- because it's so easy to do.

You can make yourself ill very easily. There's no doubt about it.

If you did all of the above in a 24 hour period, you would probably be unable to get out of bed, and you could quite easily manifest disease in your body.

This feeling of ill health and disease is a response to what you ate, what you drank, what energy you allowed around you, how you treated people, the air you breathed, the way you moved your body, the stress you experienced, and even the thoughts you had.

In other words, we can decide whether the things we do on a daily basis contribute to healing us or putting us in a destructive state.

The good news is now that you know you can easily manifest an unhealthy body, you also know you can manifest a healthy one.

All we have to do is reverse the above.

Maybe drink a lot of vegetable juice and water, eat healthy food, get good sleep, do things that make you feel calm, give someone a hug and tell them you love them... what else?

Ask yourself, "What can I do to make myself feel healthy and happy tomorrow?"

You could stretch or move your body, protect your body, be organised, do your duties or daily tasks/routines...

What else?

Wash, brush your teeth, wear clean and gorgeous clothes, breathe in good air in nature, connect with positive beings, sing and speak beautifully all day long, watch inspirational movies and think of all the wonderful things people have done for you.

What else can you think of?

Now I want you to read the following words and notice how you physically feel in reaction to them.

> **You are a beautiful, incredible human being and it's a miracle you were born!**

How does that physically make you feel?

Most people would feel uplifted, and that uplift is the beginning of allowing healing into the body.

Now that you understand more about how your actions and thoughts can destroy your body, what else do you need to quit in order to heal? It even goes down to how you talk about yourself and the language you use.

This is exactly how a placebo works. The power of your thought can heal or destroy your body.

This is called the Placebo Effect.

The Placebo Effect occurs in a situation where a patient is cured of a disease after being given an inactive substance (like a sugar pill) disguised as medicine.

There's a flip side to this phenomenon. For instance, in some cancer drug trials, a percentage of the patients who received the 'fake' chemotherapy drugs lost their hair! This is known as the Nocebo Effect, and it occurs when a patient experiences a negative outcome after a harmless substance is administered as treatment, usually as a result of their negative beliefs and expectations.

We can create our own Nocebo Effect with superstitions. For instance, believing that something bad will happen to you if you walk under a ladder, see a magpie and don't salute, or look into a smashed mirror, may cause you to experience the very thing you are afraid will happen.

Interestingly, the placebo effect tends to be stronger among optimists than for pessimists. In her book, Mind over Medicine, Dr Lissa Rankin discusses this:

"Studies found that optimists are more likely to respond to placebos than pessimists, and that people who score higher for emotional resilience and friendliness respond more readily to placebos."

In fact, during many double blind, placebo-controlled drugs trials, the optimists are often screened out before the actual official trial begins as they are considered to have excessive placebo responses. This is termed "The Washout" phase.

Dr Rankin further explains that 40-50% of people who have received placebo drugs or treatment for headaches, colitis, ulcer pain and hot flashes, completely get rid of their condition. It even works for fertility. As much as 40% of women with infertility issues become pregnant whilst taking placebo fertility drugs.

In fact, there is a database called the Spontaneous Remission Project, compiled by Caryle Hirshberg and Brendan O'Regan, where 3500 references document cases of inexplicable spontaneous disease remission. In other words, diseases defined as either terminal or incurable disappeared!

This has also been proven in the reverse. A new drug has been trialled on these 'washout phase' optimists to identify the effect of opioid blockers on their response to placebos. In effect, the opioid blockers were used to block the pathways in their brains responsible for optimism. Can you guess the outcome? Well, participants who were given opioid blockers did not experience the placebo effect.

I discuss intention setting and limiting beliefs a lot in my first book, The Body Rescue Plan. The evidence strongly suggests that expectation is fundamental to how the placebo works.

Rankin continues:

"This combination of expectation and conditioning creates measurable changes in brain activity, and neurochemistry. Scientists have shown that placebo effects rely on complex neurobiological mechanisms involving neurotransmitters (endorphins, cannabinoids, and dopamine) as well as the activation of the relevant areas of the brain. This suggests that anything we can do to mimic these neurobiological changes might alter perception of symptomatology."

Stress and pessimism leads to disease. Calm, positive optimism leads to good health.

Do you need to stop being cynical in order to heal?
Are you worrying yourself sick?

I have created a wonderful meditation for you on filling that void with healing energy. Please listen here.

Self-Sabotage

Why do we block the flow of good energy?

At this point, you are probably beginning to understand why you self-sabotage your 'good' behaviour. Perhaps in the past you were focused on quitting what made you sick in order to heal, but you threw in the towel. Perhaps you have done this many, many times in the past.

Dopamine can play a big part in that cycle and in Stages 3-5, we focus on how to allow healing energy in and methods to reduce and stop the self-sabotaging patterns.

In my book, The Body Rescue Plan, I introduced the concepts of trigger points and limiting beliefs as either leading away or towards self-sabotaging behaviours, particularly towards personal health and weight.

In Stage 2 of **the healed state**, we also identify triggers in order to know when to stop or avoid them. Being triggered or experiencing trigger points can make or break your effort to heal your body.

Typically, triggers can be brought on in moments of stress, such as when you're having a row with your partner, experiencing stress at work, feeling sad or bored, feeling disorganized, etc. This is where you feel some form of pain and because you don't like this, you relapse into old habits to feel better again.

The choice of how to take yourself out of pain can either be good or bad for your healing process. Often, the choices we make to escape pain are bad because as we learnt with how dopamine works, we tend to seek out the quickest and biggest pathway to the high, and that is usually something toxic.

However, self-sabotaging behaviour can also be brought on when our safety is threatened. It can be a pattern of conditioned responses from when we experienced trauma in the past. Maybe self-sabotage was how we self-soothed in difficult times, making it a habit and a dependent behaviour.

Being triggered isn't always about running away from pain. Holidays and celebrations can be triggers too throwing us off our routine or making us feel like we are missing out on something.

When we examine our self-sabotaging behaviours to try and identify what we need to stop doing, it is important for us to assess whether we need to quit safety-seeking behaviours. What we can do instead is found in Stages 3 - 5.

Victim

When looking at what we need to quit (or upgrade), in addition to food, substances or habits we have formed- we also need to look at the way we react to situations.

Playing the victim can be an extremely toxic and harmful repetitive cycle. It could be how we learned to gain attention, and it could be a state we perpetuate because we were a victim of something traumatic in the past. We can be triggered to retreat into victim mode when the behaviours of those around us remind us of when we were neglected. The typical victim reaction is to say, "It's not fair. Why me?" and then throw in the towel.

> **It is also a very easy way, and a very easy excuse, not to progress.**
>
> **I tried, but 'they' made me feel so awful, I gave up.**

Do you play victim? Is it always someone else's fault?

When helping people heal, one of the first things I assess with them is why or what created their ill health in the first place.

Many people blame it on others, whether present or past.

Yes, past traumatic events can be terribly painful, and can trigger us throughout our lives, but do we become slaves to them or do we regain our own power?

Remember, you are healing for you, and no one else. You are doing this for you, which means you can't blame anyone or anything for how you feel from now.

Do you need to quit living in victim mode?

YOUR NOTES

Hygiene

We all understand the premise of physical hygiene and its importance for our body's ability to heal. What fascinates me from my experience working with clients on an individual basis is seeing how people rarely maintain good hygiene in all areas of their lives. By 'all areas' I mean the people we surround ourselves with, the information we consume, the air we breathe, the environments in our homes, our body (skin, hair, etc), and our inner being (mental, emotional and spiritual).

I've known clients who are fastidiously tidy at home, but think nothing of eating junk food, or eating in excess.

I had one client Sarah, who told me she couldn't live with anyone and had to conduct all her intimate relationships outside of her home because of her extreme level of cleanliness. Yet, her body was a dumping ground for junk food.

Initially she couldn't connect the two, so we focused on cleansing her body first, and then her mind and spirit, to take her back to a healed state. After a series of sessions, she became much less concerned with the condition of her house because her internal environment felt much more balanced.

What I didn't want her to do was create another addiction or obsession with her body. Often obsessiveness with cleanliness can be a distraction of blocking or not wanting to be in communion with yourself.

In the western world, when we think of hygiene, we think of a sterile environment. Clean, bug free, shiny.

Wash your hands, use anti-bacterial solution, shower daily, use deodorant, wash your hair a few times a week, wash your face twice a day, brush your teeth twice a day, use mouth wash, clean your dishes, clean your home, wash your clothes, wash your car and use a ton of perfume in your home as well as on yourself and your clothes.

In the 1800s Florence Nightingale was hailed for discovering the dramatic effects of hygiene. Preventing disease and sanitary hygiene has been part of the western culture ever since.

Prior to her discovery, the western world was a lot less sanitary. Nightingale strongly advised that people open windows to maximise light and ventilation and release "stagnant, musty and corrupt" air. She also helped improve drainage to combat water-borne diseases like cholera and typhoid.

She wrote:

"Dirty carpets and unclean furniture pollute the air just as much as if there were a dung heap in the basement."

Nightingale went on to demonstrate the high proportion of soldiers' deaths caused by disease in comparison to battle wounds, and in 1858 became the first woman admitted to the London Statistical Society.

There's no doubt about it– hygiene is essential for a healthy body and environment… to an extent.

In 1847 a Hungarian physician, Ignaz Semmelweis, was one of the first to understand that dirty hands play a role in the transmission of disease. He ordered the obstetrical clinic in Vienna to use chlorinated lime solution for hand washing, and as a result, the death rate due to childbed fever lowered from 18% to 2%. In other words, the use of his solution meant you were 16% less likely to die just by lying in bed in the hospital.

However, the recommendation outside of hospitals is still good old-fashioned hand-washing. Hand sanitisers kill bacteria, but they don't remove dirt or anything else.

The first commercial antibacterial solution was Prontosil, created in the 1930s by the German biochemist, Gerhard Domagk, but antibacterial soaps and solutions are not all they're cracked up to be.

Triclosan was previously a common antibacterial ingredient found in liquid soaps and solutions, but its use was banned by the US Food and Drug Administration (FDA) in September 2017.

Children with prolonged exposure to Triclosan had a higher likelihood of developing allergies. Scientists suggested this could be as a result of reduced exposure to bacteria, which can be essential to developing a strong immune system.

Another study found evidence that Triclosan interfered with muscle contractions in human cells. The evidence then showed that the chemical can penetrate the skin and enter the bloodstream. A survey taken in 2008 found that Triclosan was in the urine of 75 percent of people tested.

In addition, a number of studies have also found that thyroid function can be affected by Triclosan, which could potentially lead to infertility, artificially-advanced early puberty, obesity and cancer.

Analyses of the health benefits fail to show that Triclosan can reduce the transmission of respiratory or gastrointestinal infections. This is probably because antibacterial soaps specifically target bacteria, but not the viruses that cause the majority of seasonal colds and flus.

Antibacterial soaps and solutions have the potential to create antibiotic-resistant bacteria and potentially cause health risks. They can also kill the good bacteria in your gut, which are essential for killing your bad bacteria and essential for your immune system and gut health.

Antibacterial soaps are also bad for the environment.

The US Geological Survey, the largest water, earth, biological science and civilian mapping agency, has found from many of its surveys that the chemicals from antibacterial soaps and solutions are frequently detected in streams and other bodies of water.

From all of this information, we can deduce that being overly hygienic isn't necessarily good for our health and our journey to healing.

Getting to the healed state means getting a flourishing microbiome, and a powerful immune system that can fight the diseases thrown at it.

Whilst external help is sometimes essential, taking care of our bodies and minds is ultimately what restores our good health.

More about microbiome later. But absolutely wash your hands!

Just as excessive use of antibacterial solutions is a potential health hazard, heavy use of antibiotics can also cause bacterial resistance.

The World Health Organization calls antimicrobial resistance a threat to global health security. Some bacteria are resistant to various drugs, which complicates the treatment of infections.

Dr. Stuart Levy, President of the Alliance for the Prudent Use of Antibiotics and a Professor of Molecular Biology at Tufts University School of Medicine in Boston, believes antibacterial soaps are dangerous.

"*Triclosan creates an environment where the resistant, mutated bacteria are more likely to survive,*" states Levy, who published a study on the germicide two years ago in the journal 'Nature'.

So what is the solution?

In my opinion, it is best to use antibacterial solutions and antibiotics sparingly, and prioritise improving your immune system and your health (Stage 5). You can buy plenty of non-chemical soaps or solutions from your health foods shop or make your own to use on your skin, in your house, for your clothes and even for your teeth. Any number of chemicals can make you sick.

So, the question to ask (which I asked at the start of Stage 2) is still "Will you give up whatever is making you sick?" You need to understand what is making you sick in the first place to know what to give up, and it might take some detective work to find out. It may not necessarily be something you are addicted to. It could be something as simple as being too sterile and not allowing your body to become its own healing hub.

Spiritual Hygiene

It is poor spiritual hygiene to give every one access to you. Access to you is a privilege
Mercy Johnson

In addition to physical hygiene, we also need to look at spiritual hygiene.

- Who are you letting in your space?
- What are you letting in your space?
- Who or what do you need to give up that is making you sick in your space?
- What habits are you creating to contribute to poor mental or spiritual hygiene?

This is also referred to as boundary setting!

Setting boundaries is not to restrict or create animosity with friends, family, loved ones or anyone else. It's to create better relationships and better vibes all round.

The classic negative habit that most of us have endured too much of is screen time, not just by the act of looking at your screen all day long but who or what you interact with and what content you are consuming. I have already spoken about dopamine and the reason this contributes to addictive cycles but, what energy are you letting in beyond that?

Who are you allowing to invade your space?

Being in the public eye, this was something I had to learn to deal with from the get-go. I am not an 'A' list celebrity, but I have trained many 'A' list celebrities and given healing to many film stars, pop stars, and high profile people. I have watched their behaviour around how they handle criticism, and the onslaught of negative attention. Some handle it well and some don't.

I remember the first time I was on the front cover of a newspaper. It was just a local one in my county with a readership of about 10,000. I felt a real shift in my energy, as if somehow more people had access to me. It was a strange and bewildering experience, but it obviously also had its benefits in spreading the word.

Negative comments from my own fanbase could hurt my ego, causing me to retreat into victim mode. However, I have a very simple way of dealing with negative attention.

Firstly, I register that I get a lot of very positive attention, BUT I don't absorb it. I don't let it inflate my ego and I don't rely on it for my self-worth. I feel this is not talked about enough. Many people in the public eye crave positive attention. So, any negative attention drains them. We all seek attention everywhere we go. If you are on social media, you are in the public arena anyway, even if on a smaller scale. You can feel validated when your comment is 'liked.'

We are a nation of validation seekers, and it does not help us heal. In fact, it keeps us in the seek state, which leads to the dopamine highs and addictive patterns.

We rely on validation for our happiness and self-worth, and when we don't get it how we expect to, we become sad, depressed, lonely and sick.

When I work with clients on their weight loss journeys, I always start by doing some healing work around who they are losing the weight for. I do this to help them get away from validation-seeking behaviours and any external motivations they may have for participating in the programme.

If you are on a weight loss journey, at some stage you will inevitably ask your partner or someone close to you whether they think you have lost weight. If they don't look excited enough, don't have the right facial expression or just don't care, you might be triggered to give up, especially if you were trying to lose weight for their validation.

This validation-seeking behaviour could be something you need to quit if you want to heal.

You heal for yourself. And yes, healing will have a knock-on effect leading to relationships with friends and family. However, the sole purpose for healing is for your health and happiness, not for others.

Trust me– you may feel virtuous for doing it for others, but the moment they show you an inkling of irritating behaviour, you will quit going towards the healing goal. Your subconscious pattern will be "Screw you then, I'm having the chocolate!"

Sound familiar?

I once had a client called Raquel who was sent to me by her partner who wanted her to lose weight. It was a birthday present from him to her. Raquel was a beautiful, lovely, bubbly, bright young woman, a successful solicitor, and led what seemed to be a vibrant life, full of family and social events.

In our sessions, she would be very focused for a few weeks, then she would have a blip and be back to square one, gaining and losing weight. Before she came to me, she had tried to lose weight by taking shakes, and she'd lose dramatic amounts only to gain it back a few weeks later, at the expense of her health. She had terrible skin issues and her hair was even falling out in parts.

After a few weeks of bipolar dedication, I suggested we do some healing sessions instead of physical training in the gym.

When I give healing, I often see things in images or feelings. I don't like to label myself as a psychic or clairvoyant- but call it deep intuition and divine messaging.

Often it can feel embarrassing for me to voice what I am feeling or seeing, but I do believe I am saying it for their greater good, so I always, say what I see.

I felt that Raquel had not been intimate with her husband for a long time and that there were many issues stemming from this which impacted on her health and weight loss journey. I could see this because of feeling and seeing stale energy in her sacral chakra and then I asked the question

'why' and saw an image of what was happening to create that.
When I allowed her to hear what I was seeing, the tears started to flow and she admitted that her husband would not have sex with her unless she reached a certain weight goal.

The problem was she wanted to lose weight for her husband so he would love her and be intimate with her again, but she felt unloved and angry with him for not accepting her as she was.

Every time she came close to achieving the weight loss goal, she got angry at her husband and ate it all back again.

She hadn't actually worked this out for herself as she was so sad and consumed with her unhappy marriage. I did wonder who her husband was having sex with if it wasn't Raquel, and I know she thought about it too. This was a young, very attractive couple in their 20s who had not had sex for a year and a half. Raquel's weight gain was not the issue, but her husband had used it to sabotage his own path of healing.

Raquel thought she could lose weight through her need for his validation, and he thought he could help her lose weight with the promise of sex when she reached her goal.

However, her healing would never be achieved, and neither would his, until they stopped their validation-seeking behaviours and started being honest with one another about what a sham their marriage was. The thing they actually needed to quit for their healing journey was each other.

I have seen this pattern of behaviour in countless situations– people motivating themselves to do something for the sake of their children, their boss, or their mother or father's approval. It doesn't work.

I had another client called Sarah whose mother was beautifully presented all her life, She forced Sarah to swim at a swimming club every morning before school. In her mother's eyes, this was to make her daughter gain and retain a good figure. Sarah actually excelled at swimming and swam for her county. She also had an incredible swimmer's physique growing up.

But she also resented swimming every day, missing out on social events, missing out on part of her childhood, and eventually quit. Sarah never was one for being pristinely well-groomed like her mother, but was happy with the way she looked. She married, had three children and lived a lovely life.

A similar story to Raquel's played out when Sarah's mother contacted me wanting to buy her daughter access to my weight loss training. It wasn't long before mother and daughter manifested a behaviour similar to what I had witnessed between husband and wife.

In both cases, one party attempted to bribe the other by withholding love. Whilst Sarah continued trying desperately to win her mother's approval, the carrot was being dangled until she got to the weight her mother approved of.

It was a hopeless situation. Both mother and daughter were angry, and neither of them would achieve their goal.

Quit seeking external validation– Do it for you.

Instead of seeking validation, seek practical advice for your healing journey and ditch the rest.

Back to my own spiritual hygiene practice– the way I deal with positive social media comments is to accept a little flattery and the happiness it brings. However, what I love the most is seeing people heal.

If the comments are negative, I put them into two camps.

Is there anything constructive in there?

Are they offering me a way to improve my business, my health or my life?

If the answer is yes, I thank them for their valued lesson that perhaps I would have spent time and money learning.

For instance, if someone says they are disappointed by something I did and I agree that I could have done it better, I learn from that. There is no point in getting upset, I just learn and continue. I know I am doing the best I can, so if they are impatient because I am not doing something better, or quicker, I try and put things in place that could improve my business or my life.

Sometimes, if people don't say things out loud, they may be saying it behind your back. Business or friendships can then be lost, and we wouldn't know why. So, be thankful for people who express their negative views openly, even when they are a bit annoying.

If their criticism is not constructive, like "You're fat, you're ugly" type of comments, then they're trolls, and trolls get no time in my space. They are instantly deleted and blocked.

I don't even let their energy enter my clean and beautiful space because their comments have no meaning to me. They have their issues and by letting them in, I'd be allowing their lack of self-worth in too. Their issues become mine and I already have mine to deal with.

Whether you are on social media or not, whether you are famous or not, you can still adopt this strategy.

The advantage of social media is we can easily block and delete people because we don't necessarily have a relationship with them. With friendships and relationships, it becomes a lot more complicated. Sometimes, when we are on a pathway to healing, we may realise that we need a limited supply of some family and friends' advice, so they don't drain our energy.

When I first started healing as a young child, I didn't have a clue about spiritual hygiene.

However, I knew that although the tap wasn't turning off, my energy was being used and manipulated. At this stage, I realised I needed to learn healing as a proper art, and over a six-month period, I became a Master of Reiki.

This art taught me to ritualise a cleansing process both before and after a healing session, which is important for both the receiver and the healer. It's not just important, its vital.

One of my flaws is that I want to help everyone and everything, and unfortunately this has impacted my health over the years. It's something I feel naturally talented at and drawn to do, but I haven't managed it all well in the past. It's also tricky being self-employed and creating space between the amount of work you take on and earn, versus allowing yourself time off and not earning.

Every time my work affects my health negatively, I make a concerted effort to change my behaviour and structure my life in such a way that I have more help. At one point in my business, I felt like I was an octopus with hundreds of tentacles feeding people. It was a terrible feeling. My desire to help wouldn't stop, but it was literally sucking the life out of me. I also didn't have a good self-love or self-care ritual to compensate for the energy being sucked away. To salvage the situation, I put more barriers in place so that whilst clients still got my help, it was always within clearly defined timeframes. I made more time for self-love and self-care rituals, which resulted in my spiritual hygiene improving, and thus my mental and physical wellbeing were restored.

If you are a healer, a carer or just a generous person, you can probably relate to my story.

We all need to find a balance to ensure our spiritual hygiene is switched on. If we don't, we become ill.

Overgiving can also be a sign of avoidance. Helping everyone but yourself could be a sign that you're running away from yourself and your issues. I have seen this thousands of times in my 26-year career and have been guilty of it myself. In fact, I am a master at overgiving.

Remember, you are the gate keeper. It is your duty to keep people from invading your space. Creating boundaries is imperative to sending out the message that you have a time and a place for them. Initially, creating boundaries can feel stressful because people are used to invading your space, but in the long run, it will become a healthier environment for you and everyone else.

Lack of boundary setting can lead to dishonesty as well. I remember when I first started getting asked out as a young teenager, I had no idea how to say no. I just used to lie, give a wrong phone number, or give the right number but then always tell my household to say I was out. I told many lies because I had no idea how to communicate.

I'm sure we can all relate to this in one way or another. Over the years we become good at some forms of communication, but not so good at others.

If we don't consciously set boundaries to protect us, we can subconsciously set them in our bodies instead. Dr Gabor Mate, MD explores this in his book When the Body Says No: The Cost of Hidden Stress, which uncovers how our inability to say 'no' may result in our body saying 'no' for us through disease. Saying 'no' means setting boundaries.

"What is psychoneuroimmunology? As I learned, it is no less than the science of the interactions of mind and body, the indissoluble unity of emotions and physiology in human development and throughout life in health and illness. That dauntingly complicated word means simply that this discipline studies the ways that the psyche–the mind and its content of emotions—profoundly interacts with the body's nervous system and how both of them, in turn, form an essential link with our immune defences. Innovative research is uncovering just how these links function all the way down to the cellular level."

Improving your spiritual hygiene means making more time for yourself. Making more time for self-care and spending more time in nature leaves less time for time suckers and energy vampires to get in. Like every other skill that is learned, it takes practice. There is more on ways to help your spiritual hygiene in Stages 4 and 5 of **the healed state**.

So I ask the question again– "What do you have to give up that is making you sick?" Is helping people so much and avoiding yourself one of them?

Spiritual hygiene is about being aware of your energetic space. It's not so much your physical construct, but your aura, your chakras, and the energy field that beams and blossoms around you. As we can't see this, it's easy to neglect.

Creating poor boundaries and allowing muck and grime in to mess with your energy without having a process to clear them out can lower your energy and leave you feeling depressed, anxious, and alienated or detached from yourself. You essentially abandon yourself because so many other people are housing themselves in your energy.

In Stages 4 and 5, I will share more on how to regularly clean your energy field and set boundaries for your mental, emotional, physical and spiritual health. Here in Stage 2, we are simply focusing on what you need to quit doing and, in this case, it's giving too much of yourself away.

Being hygienic is a balancing act of allowing some dirt in to enable your body and mind to learn to handle a bit of opposition. Opposition allows growth and development and is integral for healing, but too much dirt can be overwhelming. It's all in the balance.

Over sanitising and creating so many boundaries that no one is allowed in will create a sterile environment for your body where nothing can thrive or be enhanced.

Having no boundaries and no self-care means your body is consumed with stagnant energy. There is no light.

Balance = Homeostasis.

Processing emotions can also be an important part of boundary setting, and allowing time with these emotions can be vital. Whilst we don't want to spend too much time in the negative spectrum because our body ultimately seeks homeostasis, we always need to process.

In the book Mind over Medicine, author Dr Lissa Rankin puts this beautifully:

"Anger protects our boundaries and helps us lessen our attachments to people who treat us poorly. Fear is related to intuition, clarity, instinct and attentiveness. Sadness brings the gift of release, helping us let go of something that isn't working anyway, preparing us for grief."

Ideas on what you might need to quit to allow you to heal

Food

- Sugar
- Caffeine
- Alcohol
- Dairy
- Wheat
- Gluten
- Red meat
- Artificial flavouring
- or anything you may be intolerant to

Behaviour

- Victim mode
- Anger
- Resentment
- Blame
- Jealousy
- Fear of missing out
- Judging others
- Judging yourself
- Being overly critical
- Slander
- Being mean
- Seeing everyone as better than you
- Cold
- Overgiving

People

- Are there people that give you highs and lows that you need to quit?

Habits

- Going to bed late
- Being on your phone in bed
- Excessive screen time
- Not washing daily
- Not being organised
- Not having an exercise routine
- Not having a healthy eating habit
- Snacking on junk food
- Living in a dirty environment
- Not drinking water regularly
- Not allowing creative time
- Not allowing fun play time
- Not allowing spiritual time
- Not being in nature

SPIRITUAL HYGIENE

the healed state

STAGE 3
THE RAW STATE

To be free of something is not the same as getting rid of it. To be free means you are neither grasping nor rejecting it. If you are pushing it away it's still got you

Jamie Catto

1. Who am I — are you ready to receive healing?
2. Your Authentic Self
3. Create a new setting
4. Surrendering and forgiveness
5. Understanding what healing is
6. Process for being ready to heal
7. Meditation
8. Reconnect and listen
9. Essence of you
10. Journaling

Are you ready to receive healing?

In Stage 0 of **the healed state**, we found ourselves in the Apathetic State, understanding how we progressed through the journey of our life to arrive at this stage.

In Stage 1 we were in the Destructive State, thus tuning into what we wanted to heal.

In Stage 2 we were in the Artificial State- asking ourselves what things that made us artificial are we willing to give up in order to be healed.

Now, in Stage 3 we are in the Raw State, asking ourselves if we are willing to surrender to being healed.

Who are you?

As we begin the journey of Stage 3, we need to delve a little deeper than before. We are now going into the raw state where we are unveiling the layers and being completely honest with ourselves about who we are.

I want you to look into the mirror and ask yourself - Who am I?

When you ask yourself who you are, you are asking for you.

We have many different personas - the person we are at work, the person we are in front of our parents, the person we are as a parent, the person we are around our siblings, the person we are around our long term partner, the person we are around a new love interest, the person we are around old friends, the person we are around new friends, the person we are when we meditate, the person we are on camera/social media, the person we are around art, the person we are around spirituality, the person we are when we eat junk food, the person we are when we eat healthily, the person we are on holiday, the person we are at home. We have so many instances of 'Us'.

Of course, all of those people and situations will bring out a certain part of your personality but are you being your authentic self in all of these situations?

The reason why I am asking you this is because the real you needs to be healed, not the you that is being something else, for someone else.
If the pretend you is being healed, the healing will be superficial and the real you will keep knocking on the door, bringing up old baggage again and again.

In understanding if you are being your authentic self, are you overly adjusting who you are around these different sets of people?

What vision of yourself is inspiring to you? (Not inspiring or impressing others.)

Your Authentic Self

We cannot be our authentic self for many reasons. Probably the biggest is being afraid of losing something if we do. Perhaps it's losing relationships/friendships, losing a job, losing money - and fear of offending someone.

If that's your first thought, you definitely are not being true to who you are.

We can also be our inauthentic self when it comes to our life goal, or our life goal changes, or our relationship changes as we grow. Perhaps once it might even have been perfect for us. but as we develop so too can the people or the work we want to be around.

The amazing thing is that if you do decide to be your authentic self you may lose something along the way, but you will attract people who appreciate and honour who you are. This is really living. It's also sending out the message that you are ready to be healed. As the saying goes 'Your vibe attracts your tribe.' This can work either way. If you are being inauthentic you won't attract what you want, and you will wonder why you are attracting people you either don't connect with or like.

Are you open?

Hiding allows no energy in.

Being your authentic self is about ownership, owning who you are and loving the process.

It's also about adoring the journey and not saying, "I will only love myself when I get there", but loving the process - creating a life of doing what you love right now.

Feeling judged is a choice. You don't have to feel that way. We all judge, and we are all prejudiced against things. It's a way of us sussing out who to trust and who to like. It's also a way to help our ego feel superior over someone, but the more we judge others the more we feel judged. The less we judge, the less we feel judged.

Focusing on what we appreciate, and living with an attitude of gratitude, helps us judge less and stops people judging us - or at the very least it stops us caring about anyone judging us.

We all want to be loved, but needing someone's love or an affirmation that you are good enough before you go about your business, means you are not focused on loving yourself - this means you will feel that you don't deserve it unless someone affirms you do. If you don't deserve it, then you won't let the healing in.

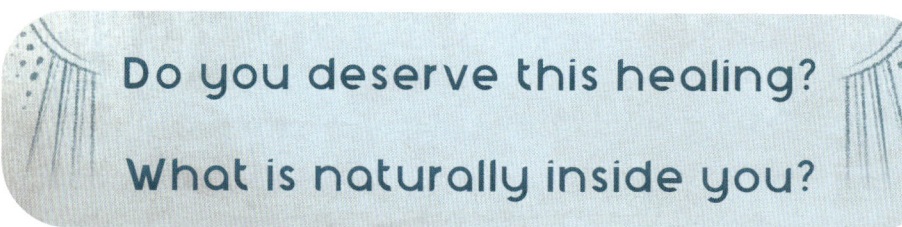

Do you deserve this healing?

What is naturally inside you?

Mantra –
I forgive myself
it's okay to make mistakes.

I have felt this many times throughout my life within business, relationships, creativity and spirituality. When I feel something is changing within me to the negative and I don't like how I feel anymore, I change what's going on around me to reconnect to my authentic self again. This distends from making many mistakes in my life.

Growing up I was brought up as a practicing Catholic, went to convent schools from the age of five through to 16, went to church every weekend so my parents would be happy, and I read the Bible and prayed every night.

However, I didn't enjoy going to church. It seemed like a punishment that I had to endure to clean my soul. I found it very boring, I never listened and I just drifted off into my own dream world.

I loved praying at night though. To me it was like a chat with Jesus. We got to know each other and I felt very protected and loved doing that. So as a young teen I started exploring and researching other spiritualities that focused more on the connection to the spiritual realm than "Church" itself being the religion. I wanted my inner religion that wasn't criticised but was just love.

So I did just that.

My Aunty Odile was into practicing yoga and lent me a yoga VHS tape with 'Jerry Hall'. I really enjoyed it- it made me feel me.

The first time I went to a Buddhist monastery I was with my Granny, at the age of 16. She was at the front sitting on a chair whilst everyone else was sitting cross legged on the floor. My Granny was interrupting them every five minutes because she was deaf. 'Excuse me, dear. Can you speak up? I am hard of hearing,' still cracks me up to this day.

It was the first time I had met Buddhist monks and I marvelled at how young and contented they looked. They looked very different to the nuns and priests I was brought up with- more like earth angels, almost floating as they walked, with not so much as a frown line on their faces. This was just a romantic notion. I am sure they were also very human, but it sat better with who I felt I was and wanted to be.

My Granny, bless her, was a hoot. She also used to sneak me into the field behind her garden and demonstrate how to hug trees. She had read that it was very healing for the body, so she explored it with me and I felt privileged. She definitely did not fit the definition of the open-toed sandal brigade. She loved material things, was always beautifully presented in designer clothes, had perfectly coiffured hair, was dripping in jewels and I liked seeing her flit from the glamorous her to the earth loving her, as it was still her; she wasn't pretending to be anyone else.

As a result of this I was now focusing on how I wanted to feel my most authentic self in spirituality, rather than how I wanted to make others feel better at the sacrifice of myself.

I read my first 'Self Help' book (other than the Bible) in my early teens. It was entitled 'The Road Less Travelled' by M Scott Peck and I then went onto read an array of self-help classics like 'The Celestine Prophecy', 'You can Heal your Life, 'Feel the Fear and Do it Anyway' and 'The Alchemist,' all of which had a profound effect on me throughout the 1980s and into the 90s.

I was never very interested in reading fiction, which was labelled at school as less than favourable. However, give me a self-help book and I could finish it in a day!

We have all shone the light on our inauthentic selves, or the extended best version of ourself, in a new relationship. We start out ruffling our brightest feathers and showing our greatest self, only to eventually show who we truly are, and as a result the relationship can die a death.

In my first long term relationship I had as a teenager I did just that. He was the best looking guy in the group of boys we went round in. He had spiky hair, wore only black and loved punk music.

So I started to morph into him a little before we got together (to impress him), and slowly as we went out with each other, we began to look like twins. He showed me where to shop for my clothes (Mainly Camden, London) taught me how to spike my hair the highest I could- the process was heat the crimpers up, put gel on your hair, backcomb it, use hair spray it, and then crimp it. It would sizzle with smoke every time and stink of burnt hair, but would be rock hard and stay put at about five inches high for several days. Somehow I thought this looked cool, mainly because he thought it looked cool.

Whilst my peers were listening to bands like Bros and 5 Star, I was forced to endure The Sex Pistols and The Anti Nowhere League- whose songs went something like this *"I'm an animal, I'm a living abortion... why am I so ugly"*

Sometimes I would look lovingly at my old colourful clothing whilst staring in the mirror at my porcupine mullet and gothic attire. I even remember my first boyfriend saying that we don't call ourselves gothics. We don't want to label ourselves goths because goths are losers. But we looked just like goths!

It wasn't a terrible relationship and there were some fun and loving moments, but he had a lot of control over me, what I wore, what I did, who I was friends with, when I went out.

At 16 years old I called it quits and I felt utterly liberated. I could wear what I wanted, listen to music that would make my heart sing, be me. I vowed to never be controlled again.

Since that moment there have been many times in my life where I felt that hint of not allowing me to shine through, and if that happens I take a good hard look at myself. This has been in relationships, friendships, creatively and also in my business life.

We can all get extremely passionate about a project and then decide after a few weeks, months, years or decades later, that we want to allow more expansion from our souls to experience a different route. Learning to listen when we need to change is the key.

If you don't know who you are, how are you supposed to take care of yourself? You won't be able to listen to the needs of your body because you aren't even in your body.

The journey of life should be doing things you are most passionate about, not the least.

> *You are allowed to be both a masterpiece and a work in progress, simultaneously.*
> Sophia Bush Hughes

In Stage 2 I asked you what you are willing to give up in order to heal and when you give this up, it allows the real you through rather than the blocked you. This allows you to be your most authentic self.

It is good to remember that you are not 100% yourself if you have done anything to alter yourself or your state.

I remember at university I lived for a few months with a group of people who had their own marijuana plants growing in their cellar. They were heavily into drugs. Every night they would come in off their heads from a night out, trying to have a conversation with me.

It was like talking to aliens in a different language. People who are high on drugs and trying to talk to people who are not on drugs does not work. Don't get me wrong, I loved to party, but alcohol was my only drug of use. However, even with alcohol you can think that being your drunk self lets your inhibitions down, and allows you to be more you- but have you ever tried having an argument with someone who is drunk? You are totally on different wave lengths.

Remember you are using certain foods or drugs to put you into an altered state, not to be who you are.

Every now and then for recreation is fine for some of us, but once you start using these drugs (sugar, caffeine, alcohol, drugs etc) to alter your state because you don't like the natural state you are in, it's time to look at who you are.

Going to university was also a period of self-discovery in identifying who I was and what my needs were. At 19 years old I went to Sheffield Hallam University. I chose the wrong course, the wrong university and the wrong town to live in. I was pretty miserable for the whole duration I was there. I hated the degree I chose, but I felt I had to complete it as an act of martyrdom. However, when I completed it I was lifted out of the dark and knew never to allow that suffocation of my creativity again.

Most people's university days are thought of fondly. My memories are pretty bleak, but again it taught me a lot about allowing my authentic self through. The moment that heavily depressed feeling comes over me where my creativity is being stunted and my spirit feels imprisoned, I know my path needs some tweaking.

And for me this is still a work in progress.

Once a year I usually go on a juice fasting holiday because there is nothing quite like it for getting you into a raw state. It allows me to sit with myself, away from the me with all the different personas, and away from the me that dumbs myself down with external stresses and sometimes desensitising foods.

The fascinating thing about juice fasts, or fasting, is that instead of being in your most dumbed down state, you are actually in your most heightened state. You feel everything, and can get into that heightened state without any external help. You feel more alive with no food than with food itself. Every sense is heightened and it can help you experience life being the real you.

One of the biggest ways people can be their most inauthentic selves is on social media or being in the public eye. The result is often a cacophony of exaggerations, mistruths, or downright lies. Perfect images, perfect marriages, perfect life. In the last year or two many people on social media are highlighting this and displaying their warts, cellulite and all.

It's a balancing act.

In my parents' generation probably the biggest way to be your most inauthentic self-involved wealth or your sexuality, but now with new movements around sexuality it is far easier in my daughter's generation to be who you want.

In the past, ways that I have felt my true self revealing itself are through emotion or illness.

If I am laughing through tears, if I suddenly laugh out loud, if my heart skips a beat or beats very fast, these are all signs to me that I am suddenly around the right people, in the right place, doing the right thing. Or on the contrary, I can get signs, very strong signs, that it is all wrong.

These can be subtle to begin with, but if I don't listen, the universe gets louder, and suddenly I get weaker and feel negativity stronger. Listening and taking time to understand not only the needs of your body, but also the needs of your goals are all there.

You just have to listen.

Sometimes your authentic self can come up when you least expect it. I was a personal trainer for many years and also offered a healing service to my clients. Many of my professional clients just wanted the training, and many of my healing clients just wanted the healing. But I love it when the cross pollination of both happens.

Create a new setting

Giving healing to a cynic is so much fun. They fight with all their might not to believe anything can possibly improve with healing, and give rational explanations for anything and everything they are witnessing, until they can't anymore and then they don't.

Alex, my PT client, was a scientist who ran her own company. She was extremely academic but had suffered with a low level depression for most of her life. She wasn't depressed about anything specific, but just didn't feel happiness within herself. Despite being slim and beautiful, having a gorgeous husband, four amazing children and living in a mansion, she was flatlined about everything. She was also the only person I have ever trained in 25 years who didn't feel lifted after our training sessions. It was like her feel good hormones were permanently switched off.

Quite a few times I mentioned giving her healing to help unravel what was happening with her low mood. She politely declined saying, 'Healing was a load of shit'.

One day her gorgeous little dog got run over, broke his pelvis as well as many other bones, and it was touch and go whether he would survive. He spent several weeks in a special pet hospital being given the best treatment, and he slowly started to mend.

When he came out his prognosis was good for living, but it was likely he could be crippled for life. He still couldn't walk properly and he whimpered in pain.

Following this, I went round to Alex's house and gave her the usual training session. I couldn't ignore the whimpers from the corner of the room and asked Alex if she minded if I gave their dog, Berty, some healing.
'You can,' she replied, 'but I still don't believe it can do anything.'
'That's fine,' I replied. 'You don't need to believe it will happen for it to

happen.' However, I must admit that I was excited to show her what was to come.

As Alex was running on her treadmill, I got to work on Berty.

Animals are amazing to give healing to because they guide you. They don't block you, they don't have preconceived ideas about how you should heal, they are totally connected and totally understand the healing process. When I heal animals they move their bodies around to influence my hand where to go next.

Berty and I had a wonderful session. He was visibly more energised and happier at the end and Alex could see this.

'Hmmm, his whole energy has changed. He seems far perkier. How strange. He was dead to the world an hour ago. I guess he just likes your attention,' she commented.

Alex still wasn't having any of it.

I said goodbye to Berty, who thanked me in the way animals do with their expressions, and cuddles, and left the house.

Later that day Alex noticed how much more sprightly Berty was, but over the forthcoming days she said he was whimpering and limping, and not feeling great again.

I came back a few days later for another PT session with Alex and walked into their front entrance hall. As soon as I came in, Berty leapt in the air, gave me a cuddle, then turned round and nudged my hand to place it on his middle back. Alex saw him do that and was astounded.

'Wow!' she exclaimed. 'He has barely got up for days. I can't believe it'

Again I asked for permission to heal him whilst I trained her and she agreed that something about what I was doing was making him happy, so she suggested I continue.

A cynical scientist would typically argue about the placebo effect. If you are going to tell someone you will make them better through healing, they will often make themselves better.

With animals you cannot argue that case.

We had a similar session with me on the floor being guided by Berty as to where to lay my hands, and me barking orders at Alex as to how to perform her exercises.

Once again Berty was so much happier, moved better and was lifted following the hour of healing.

Alex couldn't ignore it this time, and reluctantly asked me to come back the next day to see if he would get better again. This led to daily healing sessions spanning over several weeks. Each day I would be greeted with a very energetic and happy dog, waggling his tail and waiting for his healing session.

Alex saw how much more quickly Berty was getting better, in his pain, in his movement and in his mood, and one day out of the blue she asked if I could do a healing session with her. How wonderful that her dog showed her the way because of the placebo effect (she couldn't argue that the dog manipulated anything). I don't think she would ever have believed it otherwise.
"Of course!" I said.

I gave Alex weekly healing and training sessions for several years until she moved out of the area. The combination of these helped lift her mood and helped her feel things again. Alex wasn't flatlining anymore. She was actually starting to feel life, and feel in a good mood. She still didn't understand the healing and couldn't rationalise it, but she didn't care anymore. It just made her feel good and that was all she needed to know. She even asked me to give healing sessions to her children when they were sick.

There were certain things in Alex' life she realised needed changing and the healing sessions allowed her to let them be revealed. She wasn't feeling because she wasn't happy with some of her relationships and her work, and her way of coping was to block out any happiness coming to her. It takes a lot of bravery to make changes in your life, but when you do, it can heal you. When you don't, it can make you sick.

This type of scenario happened many times, usually with my professional clients who lived in London. I remember very clearly one client, Sam, whose wife had died of cancer a few years before we met. He was a functioning alcoholic, five stone overweight and on a diet of junk (albeit at Michelin star restaurants), but nevertheless junk for his body. He was on medication for high blood pressure, Type 2 diabetes, anti-depressants and sciatica. Most mornings it took him an hour to crawl out of bed because he was in so much back pain. He had to start on the floor and slowly work his way up the wall. He wasn't living and was barely surviving.

Sam worked in the City as a broker and devoted his life to work, eating and drinking. Since his wife had died, he lost all meaning to his life and was clinging on to the last grains of hope at the end of a bottle.

When we got to work with the training sessions, he responded very quickly. He lost five stone in weight within six months, gave up alcohol and his beloved coffee and came off all meds. He no longer was T2 diabetic, no longer was on pain meds for sciatica, no longer was on anti-depressants and no longer was on beta blockers as his blood pressure was stable. His Doctor was astounded.

This is a very normal reaction to my eating and exercise plan, but I never lose wonder at the mightiness of our body's repair mechanisms. Given a little love, focus and direction, the body can achieve great feats of healing.

However, I wanted to take Sam a little deeper than he had gone before, as despite his Dickensian academic nature, I felt he should be introduced to some ethereal energy.

We started with some yoga. I have found yoga to be fantastic for sciatica (if practiced correctly) so I introduced it as a way of improving and preventing his condition.

Within a month of his first yogic session we were doing headstands in the park. Sam would roar with laughter at this new him, practicing headstands at the age of 60, five stone lighter and pain free. Whereas once he would spend his Saturday afternoons at the Ritz enjoying the finest Champagne, he was now submerged in nature looking at the world from a different angle- upside down! He couldn't believe this new him! He was really good at headstands too!

After a little while of enjoying more new age ways of moving his body I suggested a healing and meditation session to help with the grief of his wife passing away. All the work we had done had been a fantastic success, but as grief doesn't disappear I wanted to connect him to the healing internal process rather than being addicted to exercise as another way to block pain.

The sessions were very emotional, very raw and very healing. Ten years later he is still treating his body as a temple, enjoying the high life with the earth life and allowing the healing process each day.

Alex and Sam were living their lives under a haze of being disconnected to their true selves. Because of their circumstance they were living something else and were unhappy. Allowing healing in means knowing who you are.

Being honest with yourself is about listening. If you don't know your true self you can't listen to its needs.

The more honest you are with yourself, the more honest you are with others.

The more honest you are with others, the deeper your connections and the more intimacy you receive in life. Intimacy allows the release of Oxytocin, which is a feel good hormone. Unlike dopamine, which is your instant gratification fix, Oxytocin gives you lasting feelings of calm and safety.

In short, if you are not living your true self you will create a barrier to the more consistent feelings of love, calmness and safety, and draw in the dopamine short fixes instead, which can turn into addictive patterns and no satisfaction. You can't let the healing process begin unless you start being yourself.

One of my favourite quotes of all time suits this perfectly.

"Our deepest fear is not that we are inadequate. Our deepest fear is that we are powerful beyond measure. It is our light, not our darkness, that most frightens us. We ask ourselves, Who am I to be brilliant, gorgeous, talented, fabulous? Actually, who are you not to be? You are a child of God. Your playing small doesn't serve the world. There's nothing enlightened about shrinking so that other people won't feel insecure around you. We are all meant to shine, as children do." - Marriane Williamson

Raise your consciousness of who you are and who you want to be and everything changes. Start absorbing. Healing is when you stop reacting, when you stop living in a reactive state.

Other regular practices of tuning into your authentic self are journaling and meditation (in this chapter).

So how can you live your true potential? Who are you?

YOUR NOTES

Surrendering and forgiveness

*It takes immense discipline
to be a free spirit*
Gabrielle Roth

As we have seen through my own personal examples as well of those of my clients, surrendering is allowing the healing process to begin.

Surrendering from your old beliefs, about how you saw or see the world, about the way you used to numb yourself (in Stage 2) and about the layers upon layers of protection you have built up over the years to run away from who you are, or what you have been through.

Surrendering is a process, and to go through each stage in this book will take time. You may find yourself unable to perfect some of the stages and they just need to be a work in progress alongside the other stages. Surrendering and forgiveness may be two of those that take a while, even a life time.

Surrendering can leave us feeling vulnerable- and vulnerability can be seen as a weakness, something we have to protect. This then can lead to self-sabotage because our safety net isn't there anymore, and we go back to feeling we need protecting again.

However, as we saw with Sam, he grew stronger and stronger as he became more vulnerable but it took him six months to get there and it is still something he would be working on to this day.

Forgiveness

Anger is always directed towards someone and is poison for us. Because if I eat poison I die, not the person I am angry with

Buddah

I have two incredible stories on forgiveness about two ladies who I interviewed for my Podcast show. (you can listen in full here www.thebodyrescueplan.com/podcast)

One of them, Bev from the US, forgave her drunk stepfather who was drink driving with her in the back seat. Inevitably he crashed the car, leaving her unable to ever walk again. She saw forgiveness as an integral part of her healing journey. She had a lot of pain, trauma and healing to go through in her new physical paraplegic body and the last thing she wanted to add to that was anger and bitterness at her stepfather. Bev has to get on with her life, and feeling good helps her to feel good.

The other lady was Jo Berry from England, who forgave the man who killed her MP father in an IRA attack. They have even become friends. Jo originally sought to understand why something so brutal happened to her father, and wanted to confront the man who robbed her of her growing up with a dad. Ultimately they have both been through a huge process of grief, forgiveness and developing a new positive friendship as a result.

These stories are not fleeting stories of 'I'll try and forgive and move on'. They are genuine heartfelt stories of strength, surrender and courage. Forgiveness is for you, not for them.

As author Brene Brown of the best-selling book, 'The Power of Vulnerability' states:

"To forgive is not just to be altruistic. It is the best form of self-interest. It is also a process that does not exclude hatred and anger. Forgiveness is not forgetting or walking away from accountability or condoning hurtful acts:

it's the process of taking back and healing our lives so we can truly live."

If you want to allow energy in, it is necessary to release blocked energy out.

Forgiveness also stops you playing the victim game. If every story you tell portrays you as the victim, it renders you powerless to allow good energy in as your narrative is always about your suffering. If it's someone else's fault, it means you have no power to change, but they do. Focusing on forgiveness rather than focusing on you being the victim stops you being the victim. It doesn't change what happened, but it changes the outcome of what happens. It doesn't mean you condone the behaviour, it means you release yourself from the chains that being a victim holds on you.

Anger is an emotional prison.

The steps to forgiveness begin with acknowledging the hurt. Sometimes, we don't even know we are angry at someone and that there is any forgiveness work to be done. Other times, it is very obvious, and we can boil up even thinking about them. But what we are usually boiling up about is what 'they have made us become' and we have the power to 'become' someone, or something else, other than the victim.

Accepting you cannot change the past is crucial for forgiveness. You need to learn from the experience and allow the process of forgiveness to begin, all the while understanding that when you forgive you release the control and power the person that you are angry at has over you.

One of my favourite Hawaiian mantras is the 'Hooponono' mantra that goes:

> Please forgive me
> I'm sorry
> Thank you
> I love you.

When I want to forgive, I say this to set the tone for healing. I say these words out loud and feel them coming from the offender. I also say it to them for the hurt they have received. Most offenders were at one time offended. It's a cycle that needs to be untied.

Surrender – forgiveness – receiving pleasure

When we think of surrendering, we visualise a scene in a war film of someone waving a white flag after battle, or putting up their hands after a long fight and saying, 'I give up!'

I see surrendering in a different light. To me, to surrender is to have faith that everything is going to be alright.

It's allowing a flow state within you, an alpha state (as shown in Chapter 4). It is to stop having to control everything you do and just be in the process of allowing. It's being in the process of receiving pleasure and living in a healed state.

I can particularly connect with this when I create - writing, painting, dancing, singing, making music. One can panic about not being able to write a book, or create something beautiful, but you just start and the magic happens through many of the steps below.
Playing, allowing the flow state, being in alpha, moving your body joyously, being in connection- they all help this surrendering state.

I can also relate it to doing something a little more daring and dangerous, like extreme sports. I like to ski, wakeboard, surf, longboard- the list goes on.
People say. "Oh, you like the adrenalin sports, you like the adrenalin high". Actually it's that I can really get into that state of surrender, that flow state, and the feeling of connection it brings. When I wakeboard, I sing the whole time, one; to relax me, two; to give me a rhythm (flow state) and three; to let music and vibration take me to a different space.

They take me inward to my core essence, while also making me very present.

Surrendering also is forgiving

As long as you don't forgive, who and whatever it is will occupy a rent-free space in your mind.
Isabelle Holland

When we don't forgive, we lose our openness and we stop receiving. We somehow think this gives us the power to stop bad things from ever happening to us again. In reality, all we are doing is blocking the good stuff.

Lack of forgiveness leads to anger, and anger switches on your "fight-or-flight" response, which in effect renders you immune to healing.

We can struggle with forgiveness because it feels like you are letting the world know that you are letting this person who hurt you, off the hook, after what they did to you. We are brought up with the notion that people should be punished for their negative actions, but what about the negative action of not forgiving and allowing the ball of anger to sit within you? That is punishment for you- you are punishing all the cells of your body, your skin, your organs, your mind. When we don't forgive, we make ourselves ill physically and mentally.

The root of "forgive" is the Latin word "perdonare", meaning "to give completely, without reservation".

Oh a physical level, according to medical experts the negative effects of lack of forgiveness creates stress in the body and will then create an imbalance in the hormones, particularly elevating cortisol and adrenaline. This causes the sympathetic nervous system to be heightened, leading to high blood pressure and muscle tension.

This can result in even more ill health for the body, including irritable bowel syndrome (IBS), pain, tension, fatigue, anxiety, depression, heart disease, reproductive issues and poor immunity.

In 2021 The British Journal of Psychiatry published statistics showing a strong correlation between lack of forgiveness and mental illness. The researchers studied 134 people who were participating in the South African Truth and Reconciliation Commission who were victims of gross human rights violations. There was a high rate of multiple traumas and abuse.

Out of the 134 people studied, 63% had a mental illness, and the findings showed a higher rate of mental disease among those who chose not to forgive. The conclusion was that lack of forgiveness carried with it an even higher rate of mental illness.

Pain is obviously a process of healing. When you look at how your body behaves on a physical level, you will observe that after an injury, you are in a raw state, you suffer a lot of pain, and you take time to heal. It doesn't happen overnight, and neither does forgiveness. It's an ongoing process.

If you were to put a knife in a physical wound it would not only stop the healing process, but also make the wound worse. So not allowing forgiveness to be part of the healing process is like driving a knife deeper into your mental wound.

Persistently rehearsing painful memories and harbouring grudges will perpetuate negative emotions which can make any physiological issues you are experiencing worse.

This then becomes a commitment to being angry rather than a commitment to being in a healed state.

Releasing anger and creating more forgiveness takes a persistent force of energy going towards a healed state over an angry one.

It's focusing on you rather than them. It's raising your vibration to feel the best you can feel in this life. Forgiveness does not excuse the offender. It releases you from the attachment to them.

Forgiveness does not change the past, but it does enlarge the future.
Paul Boese

I have a wonderful meditation that I created as part of my Manifesting Abundance Course called 'Releasing the Wild Horse.' It's a meditation that releases the chains that control you and that block you, allowing you true freedom.

There are two meditations to listen to for this chapter. One is to release the chains and one is to forgive. You can listen to them here.

Forgiveness and surrendering are things to be practiced daily, which can be difficult. However, they are a lot easier to do because you and you alone are the starting point.

Another study by Amy Owen, PhD, Duke University Medical Center, showed that people with HIV who forgave someone who had caused them pain, showed improvement in their immunity. This study reviewed how CD4 cells (T cells) behaved. These are white blood cells that fight infection and are vital for your immune system.

Owen states:

"*Higher levels of forgiveness would be associated with higher CD4 cell controlled for demographic and behavioural variables as well as viral load. So there is something special going on between forgiveness and CD4 cell counts.*"

Understanding what healing is

Having come this far through the stages, you probably have an idea of what healing means for you.

It could be a symphony of focus, forgiveness, giving something up, allowing something in, surrendering, etc.

When you are preparing your body to receive healing and getting it into the raw state, you can start feeling what this healing might be, so that you want to stay in the raw state for this stage.

In Stage 4, we go through the process of allowing healing in, but for now just get a sense of what it feels like to be healed.

And ask yourself this:

What do joy and happiness feel like in your body?

For me healing is a feeling of surrendering and being taken care of in whatever capacity I need the healing in.

YOUR NOTES

UNDERSTANDING WHAT HEALING IS

Processes of allowing yourself to be ready to be healed

How meditation works for allowing healing

As I mentioned previously, one of my first live meditation experiences was with my Granny at a Buddhist monastery.
My Granny was brought up in the Victorian era, but was very open-minded toward exploring ways of connecting with nature, spirituality and relaxation.

All the Buddhist monks had shaved heads, used no make-up, and wore orange and red robes, but they looked so beautifully serene. Their skin was almost wrinkle free and they were not young.

Of course you could attribute their youthful glow to several things, including wholesome food, stress-free living, no alcohol consumption, a non-attachment to wealth, and non-aggressive behaviour. But a huge part of it would also be the meditative nature in which they live.

I was so inspired by this beautiful little monastery that in my 20's I became a yoga and meditation teacher. I have since used my meditation and mindset techniques to help clients all over the world to allow their bodies to work for them.

Through conscious yoga and meditative breathing you become aware of the connection between mind and body, which has anti-ageing benefits. Yogic breathing has been shown to oxygenate the cells, ridding them of toxins, helping prevent illness, and making skin radiant.

In fact, regular meditation can make you look and feel ten years younger, increase health and longevity and prevent brain-deterioration. Just by focusing on your breathing, you can control your heart rate and allow your body to relax, thus slowing down the ageing process.

Creating stillness in the mind also stops your body from creating joint tensions which can lead to ageing diseases like arthritis. With less tension, your body's clock is set back, allowing your system to detoxify more efficiently, and giving you younger-looking skin.

Meditation practice is rapidly becoming a powerful alternative to the multi-billion dollar anti-ageing industry, with experts and studies revealing that the effects go beyond feeling calm and peaceful for a few minutes. And its FREE!

Meditation works so well because we all have built-up stress, limiting beliefs, greed, lethargy and self- sabotaging patterns of behaviour. If the world's top athletes need meditation to get out of bed in the morning, it may also be helpful to you too!

The process of healing the body starts in the mind.

You may be on a healthy diet and getting restful sleep. However, you are less likely to heal unless your mind can access that part of you that releases stress and promotes happy cells. Meditation as a daily habit takes you to that place.

Meditation allows you to literally step out of time because it taps into the pineal gland of the brain. The function of the pineal gland is to produce hormones that regulate biorhythms, immunity, perception, and ageing.

Meditation lowers blood pressure and oxygen demand, and enhances psychological well-being. Perhaps the most significant determinant of healing with meditation is telemore length (telemores are the end cap of our DNA), which is a very important marker of ageing and longevity. Longer telemores are correlated with less illness and longer lifespan.

The impact of meditation on ageing, particularly the ageing brain, has been a topic of research for many years for Dr. Dharma Singh Khalsa, the Founding President and Medical Director of the Alzheimer's Research and Prevention Foundation in Arizona.

> *"Our research reveals that meditation lowers the stress chemical in the blood called cortisol. Cortisol kills brain cells and leads to cognitive decline. Our research also shows that meditation helps brain blood flow in critical areas of the brain and reverses memory loss."*

Incidentally Cortisol also leads to weight gain, which can be very ageing to the body on the inside and out.

When you also combine meditation with diaphragmatic breathing your oxygen intake will increase, which increases blood flow. There are a billion oxygen molecules in one red blood cell - very important because blood nourishes all of your body system's cells. Adults come with a total number of 100 trillion cells. Each of these cells is an important life form that depends on oxygen and blood to transport nutrients, gases, waste, and hormones.

Keeping our cells healthy slows down the ageing process.

Essentially, meditation is a key way of taking charge of your own health, looks and longevity. The meditative state restores the body's optimum functioning and harmonious nervous system function, benefiting our organs, skin and circulation, because cells receive the healthy nutrients they need.

The amazing thing about meditation is that we can do it anywhere for any amount of time. Whether you do it for five minutes or two hours, it's free, and you can access it whenever you want.

Whilst anyone can meditate, it takes regular practice to learn the process and see its benefits. Practicing meditation is like working a muscle– the more you do it, the stronger your mind becomes at accessing your relaxation mode and the deeper your relaxation becomes.

When you focus on doing something in meditation, it can be easier than just emptying your mind.

There are many meditation practices to choose from- walking meditation, breath work, guided meditation, transcendental meditation, focusing on one object, sound bath meditations and many more. Some are attached to religions and others have no dogma or religion attached to them at all.

It is said 'Prayer is when you speak. Meditation is when you listen'

In this book, I have many wonderful meditations for you to listen to.

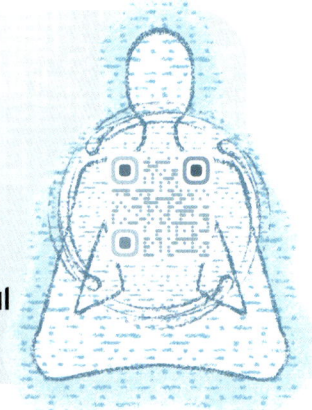

Mindset work is also a really important part of the healing process. When you look at a child's energy, they can have indomitable spirits that light up entire rooms and ooze positivity.

Meditations can help you to be positive, but you also have to make that little bit of effort to wake up each day, focusing on the glass half full than half empty.

If you want to be in truly great shape, feel fantastic, have the energy of an athlete, have incredible will power, look the best you can look, be calm, focused and confident, it all starts with mindset.

If you are changing your routine to alter your body and mind, your mindset may need a shift.

PROCESS FOR BEING READY TO HEAL

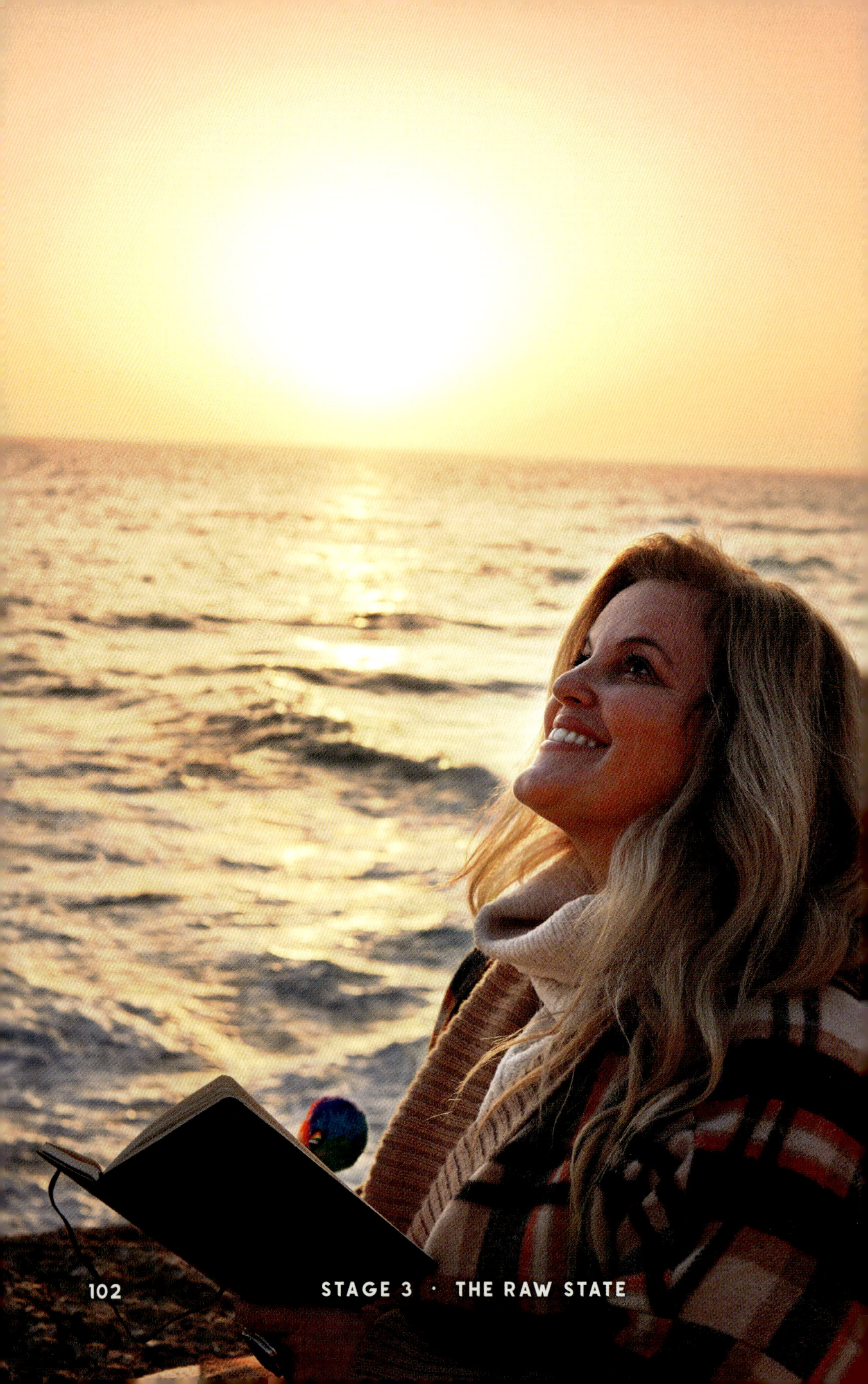

Visualisation and guided imagery

Picturing yourself as a confident, successful and admired person can be a very powerful tool.

If you can believe it, you can achieve it. Your conscious mind accounts for about 10% of your functioning. The other 90% of your mind controls the rest of you!

Our mind can cause physiological changes in our bodies just through our thought. In sports, we see people change their degree of their performance through mind control just by visualising the win.

The UK Javelin champion, Steve Backley, used visualisation whilst he was in plaster from an injury. He regularly practiced throwing the javelin in his mind through guided visuals and when the plaster was removed his muscle had only shrunk slightly, to the great surprise of his doctors.

The body cannot tell the difference between imagined situations and real life. If you think about writing an exam, you can get physical anxiety symptoms weeks before, or if you watch a horror movie your hair may stand on end, your heart may beat faster, or your body can have a sexual response to something you imagine!

This is also how the placebo effect, some forms of hypnosis, meditation and even prayer work. The power of your mind is enormous and can be both positive and detrimental depending on how you choose to use it. The same forces that imprison you, can also empower you.

To demonstrate how this works, I want you to imagine going into your kitchen, and walking towards your chopping board.

You take out a big juicy lemon from your fruit bowl, and place it on your board.

You then take out a sharp knife and cut into the zesty lemon. As you cut into it, you see some of the juice fly out. Then you hold the lemon up to your mouth and squeeze.....'

What did you notice happened when you visualised this? - You should have salivated.

This is your physical response to your visualisation.

When we visualise things, our brains can't distinguish what is real from what is not when it comes to our physical response. This is explains what we experience when we watch a scary movie- our hair stands on end and our heart beats faster. We have a similarly vivid response to reading something emotional- we may cry or get a lump in our throat, even though the story is entirely fictional. The same goes for something that makes us laugh, or even a sexual response to something mentally arousing!!!

The point is that our bodies respond to our thoughts, and so when you visualise your body as healthier and happier, and when you say your positive mantra, your body will respond by getting healthier. In the same respect if you feel negative about your body and don't believe you can ever get the body you want, then you never will.

In her book *Mind Over Medicine*, Dr Lissa Rankin explains how powerful the placebo effect is with just the control of the mind. She explains how patients who participate in double-blinded clinical trials as part of the control group can also can also experience the negative side effects of the drug being trialled even though they were given the placebo drug (sugar pill). This is known as the nocebo effect. Around 25% of people who take the placebo will experience symptoms like fatigue, vomiting, muscle weakness, colds, ringing in the ears, change in memory and taste, and many more symptoms which cannot be explained by the sugar pill, but are consistent with the effects of the drug being trialled which they were warned could cause those side effects.

Patients with split personalities have also demonstrated the power of the mind to alter the body. There are documented cases where some personas of a split personality were found to have allergies which other personas didn't. There was also a case where one persona of a split personality had Type 2 diabetes, along with corroborating blood glucose levels, while other personas did not show diabetic symptoms.

Throughout **the healed state**, you will listen to many meditations that help change your mindset and beliefs on how to heal your body.

Reconnect to the core essence of you

When I was a child, I was taught that we all had a soul, and that when we died the soul would live on.

I was also taught that every time I lied or committed a sin, my soul would darken, and that to lighten it again I would have to do something extra good, not just obey the Ten Commandments.

When I talk about your core or essence, I'm referring to your soul, but I want to get away from guilt and shame and judgment.

My belief is that everyone's essence is pure, and nothing can change this. The problem we have is that the layers of toxicity that we build up as a protective mechanism become so overwhelming for us that we become totally disconnected from our essence. When you see that everyone has this core beauty, but have built-up protective but suffocating walls to cope with what life has thrown at them, it becomes easier to empathise with who they have become.

The more you allow your light to shine through, the more you can teach others.

My Client, Aby, had self-sabotage issues with food. In our first session, I asked her questions about what she instinctively felt she wanted to heal. She replied, "Overeating, getting to a point with a diet and then giving up, wanting to be a size 12 when I am a size 18".

Incidentally, the bouncing back and forth with weight always interests me. I have found with some of my weight loss healing clients that when they get to the weight they want, they tend to relapse to old eating habits and regain the weight they lost, because they are triggered by a trauma they experienced at that exact weight. So I always help such clients explore what traumatic incident they may have experienced at a particular weight that made them feel vulnerable, leading to destructive self-soothing habits like overeating.

Aby said she felt vulnerable when she was younger and slimmer. She didn't like the attention, and she lost female friends because of the male attention she attracted.

Deeper work, however, revealed that Aby's issues were rooted in her experience of having a very strict father in her youth. He would become a tyrant at dinner time and would force-feed her and her siblings to the point where Aby felt so sick that she would often make herself vomit later when no one was looking. Aby also spent many years defending her younger siblings from her father's anger. Unsurprisingly, her university years were spent in a drink, drug and self-abuse frenzy.

Yet here she was speaking to me in her middle age, confused about why she self-sabotages with food.

The second part of the session, the healing part, was taking her to find her core essence. I told her it was safe, she was not in a vulnerable state, and that anything that would come out would be healing. I told her to allow the tears if they came, or whatever reaction she had.

When people tune into their core essence it can be seen in so many different ways.

For Aby, at her core and in her essence, she was a baby. And when she realised this, she cried throughout the session. She expressed to me that the sadness came because that was the last time she felt this beautiful part of her, but here she was at 50 years old feeling it again.

What was fascinating about her journey was that her weight gain and struggles with self- sabotage with food began after the birth of her first child; and the last time she felt that deep connection to her self was her own birth. So the birthing was a trigger for her. The biggest message for Aby was that the moment she started shining brightly from within, she could understand the need for her father's brightest energy to also shine through.

Just like Aby, her father had built-up a lifetime of blocks which resulted in his own negative emotion. Everyone in his life would be a chain reaction of more negativity around him. With Aby's new found energy, that could start to change.

How do you tune into the essence of you?

For some, it's harder than for others. Some may see glimmers of their essence, only for it to disappear. The easiest way for me to show you the essence of you is to take you on a soul journey through meditation.

This is guided and very easy to follow.

So what I want you to do is listen to the first essence meditation here.

If you can't answer all the questions below then try again with the meditation.

Please do this step - it will only take 10 minutes of your time. Do it when you are ready. This is deep soul cleansing work.

Then answer the following questions.

- How did you feel through this meditation?
- Who or what is the core essence of you?
- When no one is looking, when it's just you floating through the air- who is that?

ESSENCE OF YOU

Tune into the essence of you each day

- What is the essence of you?
- Have you ever thought of this?
- Who exactly are you?
- Apart from what you look like, your clothes, your house, your friends, your pets, what is the essence of you?
- If you were buzzing around like fairy dust with no shell, what colour are you?
- What vibration are you?
- What tone/note are you?
- What do you smell like?
- And what does that core essence live off to thrive?
- What makes that core essence happy?
- Is that where you want to be?
- Now look at all the building blocks that make you who you are- the blood, bones, cells, muscle fibres, skin, and all your organs. Picture them all growing on top of that core essence.
- How good does that feel to be fresh- feeling that core essence shining through your organs and skin, like you are an earth bound angel, being new for the first time?
- How does this feel?
- Who are you?
- And what feeds you?
- What do you smell like?
- What makes your soul sing?
- Where does this body want to go?

You can keep revisiting your core essence regularly for self-healing

STAGE 3 · THE RAW STATE

Journalling and Listening

Unravelling the essence of you can mean working through many layers. One of the issues I see people struggle with when it comes to healing is blocking themselves with layers of protection. I have also done this myself. It takes a lot of work to not do this, especially if it's a habit we built up as a child.

In fact, many overweight clients I have worked with in the past have built up layers of fat as a form of protection, or built up tumours, or disease, or disfigurement or pain as layers of defence.

Perhaps you know you do this, or maybe you don't. Perhaps your eyes are now being opened.

If you are willing to give up what makes you sick (Stage 2), are you also willing to give up the layers of protection?

Some clients have overeaten, overeat or consume toxic foods, drugs or alcohol to numb themselves or make themselves forget. It could also be a way of not facing themselves or what happened to them in the past. Worse still, self-sabotage could be their way of punishing themselves for past mistakes. They won't forgive, so they try and forget.

So ask yourself now:

> **What am I protecting by holding on to this issue?**

Sometimes I journal with angels. Journalling is a very simple way to release, and break down barriers and blocks. You can say anything you like, and you can ask your inner wisdom or guides to help you.

When I was going through a difficult time, I asked what I call 'Angelic Questions'.

Angelic questions
"I feel you around me and I'm sorry I sometimes block you. Why do I block you?"

The answer was:
"*To release the block is to release the power. Love is the most powerful thing in the universe. It is more powerful than money, more powerful than wars, and more powerful than hate. Release the power you are trying to hold on to and let the biggest power in.*"

LOVE.

Love will empower you more than anything. More than gifts, physical and material things. Love, when you fully absorb it, means you are the brightest shining star and when you have the highest energy, nothing can consume or overwhelm you because of the immense positive energy you carry within."

Me
"How do I stop self-sabotaging?"

Answer:
"*Tune in to love every day, every morning. Tune in to angels, to God, to music, to dance, to light, to feeling light.*

The moment God energy leaves you, stop what you are doing and play back to when you were feeling it. God energy, angel energy, is with you every second of every day. Keep tuning in. If you find yourself going into ego energy, old energy, or unbelieving energy, keep bringing it back to joy.

Bring back joy to chores, love to tidy because it creates more joy for you and your family."

Me
"How can I achieve the life of my dreams without guilt?"

Answer:
"*Guilt comes from a lack of energy. Angels are not here to make you feel guilty, and neither is God. God wants you to enjoy all the riches in life to the fullest with love and happiness. The more joy you have, the more joy*

we have. The more joy you, your friends and family feel, the more they can share this love with others.

Money is love. It's everywhere, its within you.

You will get your beautiful house on the cliff top over the sea, but you have to feel it and ask for it. Absorb its energy and it will easily come to you.

No one is jealous of the brightest shining star, when there is an abundant energy.

Match your energy to what you want to feel in your heart and soul. Your blueprint is for your core, What is it?"

Me
"It's a huge, powerful, abundant, flowing, beautiful energy that has no pain and is always there,"

Answer:
"Yes! It is! Keep tuning into that. Imagine that house, that animal sanctuary, that endless healthy energy.

It's here! Absorb it!"

With asking so many questions to ponder, you are probably already keeping a journal.

If it feels right for you, go and buy a lovely notebook you connect with, put it in a special place, with a special pen and make it a practice to write each day. Write your emotions, release and then allow in words what you need to feed you.

Do you feel ready now to receive healing?

the healed state

STAGE 4
THE HEALING STATE

Nature repairs everything
Baron de Montesquieu

1. Routine
2. Allowing yourself pleasure
3. Living in colour
4. Mindfulness
5. Flow state
6. Nature
7. Microbiome
8. Water
9. Ceremony
10. Smudge
11. Vibration- your words.
12. Sound healing
13. Triggers

How are you feeling?

Have you been through all the stages so far?

Observing who you are, tuning into what you want to heal, quitting what makes you sick (or at least being aware of what makes you sick), understanding if you are ready to be healed?

That's a lot and this process can take time, so do allow time.

Sometimes we have to get worse before we get better, "The breakdown, before the breakthrough". Not all healing is going to feel heavenly. Some parts can feel rough, but that's growth and sometimes we go through pain in order to achieve growth.

I remember when my daughter, Angelique, was learning to walk as a toddler she would bump into things, fall, and sometimes hurt herself.

As a healer and a Mum, I felt compelled to take the pain away so whenever she bumped or fell, I would rush to give her healing. However, I soon realised this was not helpful.

The pain I wanted to take away was important because it was instructing her neuromuscular pathways to switch on and control her leg muscles so she could manoeuvre around the furniture. In essence, me taking that pain away was stunting her ability to walk and blocking her muscular growth because the pain was a vital part of that process.

A similar thing happens when we take drugs to numb our physical or emotional pain. We don't develop the skill and resilience needed to deal with pain and as a consequence we eventually don't feel anything. We just create more blocks to more pain.

Stage 3 was about being in that raw state so that you are ready to receive, even if you have to breakdown before you breakthrough.

Now, finally we are in the Healing State! Stage 4.

There are two Stages in the 'healing state'. Stage 4 is more about creating an environment around you that always heals you, and Stage 5 is more about creating healing within your body. So 4 is external and 5 is internal.

Routine

When I met with Lucy, my first business mentor, back in 2002, one of the first exercises she got me to do to enhance my business was to clean out my study.

I am naturally a messy person, a typical creative who can have an explosion of mess going on around them and still be in my element for creation. In some ways it's a superpower. I am great in a crisis! In other ways, it's a problem because it slows down my progress towards wherever healing may be needed in my life.

My office was in a summer house at the end of our garden (it was a glorified shed) and at the time I met my mentor I couldn't even get through the door. Prior to having to break the door down, I had spent a month making it the most beautiful office ever, I made cushions, seat covers, curtains and blinds, and had wallpapered it to match. It looked fabulous! But after several months, I couldn't keep up with my paperwork and it mounted so high that my office frightened me, and I stopped going in there. Over time, because I rarely used it, the office turned into an oasis for wildlife in the area, rather than a productive work environment for me!

The problem was I had zero routine.

So, under Lucy's instructions, I got to work on my study. After making my way through the cobwebs, spiders and mice, I spent a week throwing stuff out and reorganising my work life. It was at a time when most paperwork could be digital, and I didn't need piles of paperwork anyway. It was liberating.

For some of us routine, is normal, enjoyable even. For others, it feels like we are being strangled. But if we don't have some order, it's very difficult to harvest healing and expansion in all areas of our lives.

Routine for a creative can feel dull and boring. You feel like someone has sucked the life out of you. It's also exhausting as you are accustomed to using the right side of your brain and suddenly your left side is being exposed and burnt out. But, if there is no order in your life, there won't be room for the fun creative stuff. So order and routine are essential for having excitement and balance.

Having a routine means that you regularly do certain things at specific times so that the foundations of your healing can provide the support needed for deeper work to flourish.

In Stages 0 - 3, you did the groundwork for healing. Liken it to a decorator going in a room and doing the prep work. They have to initially clear the room, clean the walls, sand certain areas, place masking tape where the paint should not go, cover the floors with cloth to stop the paint from staining it, etc. In fact, the prep work can often take longer than the painting itself. And in a few years, this new paint will need general maintenance which will again require prep work in addition to the odd touch up and a repaint. It is important to have a routine for maintaining the groundwork you did in Stages 0 - 3.

Getting a cleaner is one of the best investments I ever made towards keeping my office and my life in order. And even when I cut my budget for other things, I always make sure I have enough set aside for regular cleaning services because doing so helps me maintain my groundwork.

Without my cleaner I fall apart, so she is essential. It also stops pointless rows between my husband and I (he is tidy and the state of my study drove him mad) and it means we can live a more balanced and harmonious life. Now I won't ever get to the stage where I have to break a door down to get in a room again.

To understand where your routine needs tweaking is to understand where you need balance.

Where are you out of control in your life?

Where do you exhaust yourself?
What is neglected?

You can establish routines in many areas of your life. The problem is we are so busy that if we do not set routines, something will always get neglected. This can then lead to lack of self-love and self-care along with feelings of guilt and disconnect.

Here are some areas in your life you may need a routine...

- Your bills
- Your cupboards
- Your fridge
- Your food shopping
- Your clothes shopping
- Your children's activities
- Your office
- Your money- spend and income
- Your self-care
- Your learning (books / courses)
- Your boundaries
- Your spirituality
- Your Fitness
- Your friendships
- Your dating life
- Your intimacy
- Your time with yourself
- Your pets
- Your cooking
- Your cleaning
- Your holidays or time off

What else needs a routine?

One thing that has been a revelation for me is expanding the time to organise. This means I can allow for a lot more fun in my life. I always have pockets of time for spontaneous pleasure, which I could previously never find the time for because I was always chasing my tail.

Books I have found useful for organising are:
Marie Kondos: 'The Life Changing Magic of Tidying up'
Gay Hendricks: 'The Big Leap'

There are also professional services to help you organise your home more efficiently, should you need it.

Allowing yourself pleasure

When we are more routined it becomes easier to let pleasure in and have spontaneous moments of fun. Whilst your healing started at Stage 0, it is in moments of happiness or pleasure that you will experience its liberating effects. The closer you are to healing, the more self-love and self-worth you have, and the easier it is to allow, feel and enjoy pleasure.

In Stage 2, we learnt about dopamine and that artificial highs lead to a comedown and potentially, a dependency or an addiction. Allowing pleasure means allowing good energy in, without the drawback of addictiveness.

Feeling pleasure also evokes bigger emotions like love, connection, hope and intimacy. All these sensations make us feel 'safe,' which in turn allows the hypothalamus of the brain to stop triggering the stress response. When we are safe, we can heal.

If you Google 'How to allow more pleasure', the first 15 pages relate to sex and then on page 15 it brings up theme parks.

How interesting that Google can't differentiate between enjoying the pleasures of life and separating it from sex and theme parks.

Pleasure is our God given right as a human.

> What does pleasure mean to you?
>
> What areas of your life do you want more pleasure?
>
> What areas of your body do you want more pleasure?

On my signature programme, 'The Body Rescue Plan', we have helped people quit addictive patterns with food and lose weight over the course of 12 weeks. Participants then transition to 'The Body Rescue Maintenance Plan' for life where one of the rules is that they get one to two days a week to have all the toxic foods they want purely for 'pleasure' and not out of need. For instance, prior to starting my plan, many people's days were a drug frenzy.

- They needed caffeine to wake up
- They needed sugar to pick them up throughout the day
- They needed sugar for stress
- They needed a glass of wine to help them come down from their wired brain at night

It's drugs, drugs, drugs.

So what I teach on Maintenance (after you are not addicted to them anymore) is how to have those drugs purely for pleasure and not because you depend on them to wake you up, chill you out, or get you to sleep.

When you live life drugged up, you have no real pleasure.

And absorbing pleasure is not about seeking pleasure and desperately needing to find it. It's about soaking it up like a sponge and being open to it whilst not having an unhealthy attachment to it.

It is about waking up your senses and doing a dance with them every day in the pleasure boat.

How can you allow more pleasure in?

Allowing more pleasure means your feel good hormones come alive.

The first thing I do to allow myself more pleasure is to create time for it. Pleasure is all about stimulating your senses, so I make sure that I do a series of things daily, weekly, monthly and even yearly that fulfil those sensual connections.

For me, the daily things are rituals that allow an opening for my senses.

Your senses are Sight, Sound, Smell, Taste, Touch and 6th Sense

- **Walking in nature** (Sight, Sound, Smell, Touch)
- **Meditation** (Sound, 6th Sense)
- **Swimming in open water** (Sight, Sound, Smell, Taste, Touch)
- **Playing music** (Sound, 6th Sense)
- **Lying in the sun** (Touch, Smell)
- **Lying under the moon & stars** (Sight, Sound, Smell, 6th Sense)
- **Hugging my loved ones** (Sight, Sound, Smell, Touch)
- **Eating delicious healthy food** (Sight, Smell, Taste, Touch)
- **Walking bare foot** (Sight, Sound, Smell, Touch, 6th Sense)
- **Listening to music** (Sound, 6th Sense)
- **Reading and learning** (Sight, 6th Sense)
- **Something creative** (Sight, Sound, Smell, Touch, 6th Sense)

Pleasure is about connection.

My weekly, monthly and yearly sensual rituals are also extensive and include intimacy, singing, holidays, exercise, fun activities with Angelique, dance, romantic nights out or weekends away, meet ups with friends, concerts, festivals, art classes, etc…

We are all different and we all need to think about what we are lacking, and what we need more of to create a healing environment for the body.

For instance, I naturally smile and laugh a lot. It's instinctive. It's not something I have to control or work on, it just happens. With some clients I have to instruct them to create more laughter in their lives. When I have treated very sick clients, and they are constantly in pain and fear about their condition, I really encourage them to create pockets of pleasure in their lives every day. If you struggle with fear and negative thoughts it will be difficult to switch them off and lift the gears to positivity. It takes conscious effort to make a shift and laughter is a great way to create an opening for healing.

Laughing hysterically releases the feel-good hormone called endorphins. Even the anticipation of laughter can relax you.

Peter Derks, a Professor of Psychology at the College of William and Mary has studied the effects of laughter on the brain.

"About four tenths of a second after we hear the punch line of a joke but before we laugh, a wave of electricity sweeps through the cortex,"

Derks found that the entire cerebral cortex in the brain is used, both right and left hemisphere, when you laugh.

Laughter has so many physical and mental benefits. It increases blood flow; stimulates your vital organs like the heart, lungs, and muscles; activates and relieves your stress response; improves your immune system; relieves pain; improves your mood and helps you connect with people.

Laughter also comes with a feeling of release that allows a surge of good energy in, much like an orgasm.

Contrary to what Google thinks, pleasure is not just about sex. However, we certainly want to receive pleasure through this healing modality and if you are not receiving pleasure sexually (and want to), tuning into your senses can be a very good start.

I am not a sex therapist, but I have helped many people who have had barriers to sex. I have had clients who have had very low libidos because they have a very poor nutrient diet with high stress. Once this was balanced through my Body Rescue Plan, they found they wanted sex a lot more (and enjoyed it).

Poor nutrient diets and high stress mess with your hormones, which can greatly affect your libido. Other issues could be a history of abuse– sexual, mental or physical– which often affects the ability to want to feel. Again, I have found that when clients eat better, they can then peel back the layers of protection, start loving themselves and allow that love in.

Desensitising yourself is a very common form of protection, and can be related to poor sexual health. Sex is a connection with someone else, but it can also be a connection to ourselves. It allows us to receive the pleasure without guilt, without taboo, and it's a very good way to lift our souls and create a healing energy within us.

Studies also show that a healthy sexual relationship can improve the health of your body. According to Dr Lissa Rankin in 'Mind Over Medicine';

"Those with healthy sex lives live longer, have a lower risk of heart disease and stroke. Have less breast cancer, Bolster their immune system. Sleep better, appear more youthful, enjoy improved fitness, have enhanced fertility, get relief from chronic pain, experience fewer migraines. Suffer from less depression, and enjoy an improved quality of life. **Sex isn't just fun, it's good for you!** *"*

Is receiving sexual pleasure part of your routine?

Receiving pleasure does not have to be overwhelming and instructional. It is a natural part of your life. Once your senses have been lit up, they will guide you, making it easier for you to receive pleasure all day, every day, and find pleasure in everything you do, even the boring stuff. When you can see the beauty and happiness in everything that you do, your body welcomes pleasure and negates pain.

One way to tune into the pleasures of life is to go without for a while.

If you have ever done a juice fast, or restricted something in your life, you'll know that when you have it again it becomes a very sensual moment. The first time I started eating solid food again after having carried out a week's juice fast, I spent ten minutes sucking on a slice of melon.

It felt heavenly just to have that texture in my mouth.

Remember, quick, artificial highs, highs that are not for the greater good of everyone, highs that make you feel low after, will oversaturate your senses and make you lifeless and ill.

YOUR NOTES

A little exercise

Heightening your senses is a combination of eliminating things that desensitise you (as in Stage 2), and making a conscious effort to boost your senses.

Exercise 1

First of all, just being aware of what you have in your life on a regular basis that you use those senses for..

Exercise 2

Then making a conscious effort to use those senses on a daily basis (you will find this becomes second nature eventually) This also puts you in the present which is where we receive pleasure, and pleasure is where we are present!

Touch

Start touching everything around you with more conscious awareness.

- Touching the food you eat or prepare
- Feeling your household objects with your fingertips.
- Feeling the earth beneath your feet.
- Feeling water on your skin
- Feeling the wind on your skin and hair
- Feeling nature upon your finger tips
- Feeling your skin
- Feeling your partner's skin
- Feeling your pet's fur or skin

What else?

Sight

What colours radiate out of...

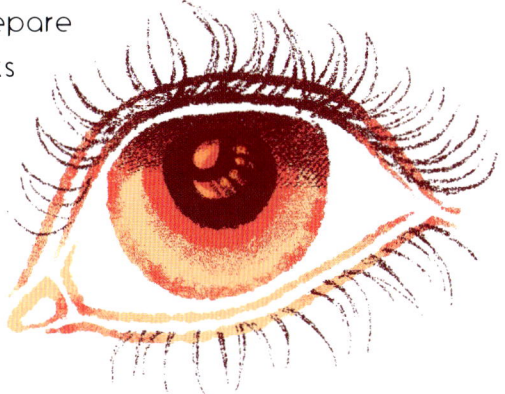

- The food you eat or prepare
- Your house hold objects
- The earth
- Water
- The wind
- Nature
- Skin
- Your partner's skin
- Your pets

What else?

Smell

Start smelling everything around you with more conscious awareness.

- Smelling the food you eat or prepare
- Smelling your household objects
- Smelling the earth
- Smelling water
- Smelling the wind
- Smelling nature
- Smelling your skin
- Smelling your partner's skin
- Smelling your pets

What else?

Taste

What tastes do you feel from...?

- The food you prepare
- The air
- The water

What else ?

ALLOWING YOURSELF PLEASURE

Sound

What sounds radiate out of...?

- The food you eat or prepare
- Your house hold objects
- The earth
- Water
- The wind
- Nature
- Skin
- Your partner's skin
- Your pets
- Music
- Speech
- Traffic

What else?

6th Sense

You can heighten your 6th sense with quite a few methods...

- Heightening the rest of your senses as above
- Meditating
- Engaging in healing
- Doing my chakra clearing meditation (The third eye is your intuition chakra)
- Being creative
- Being in nature
- Tuning into what does God smell like - ever thought of that?
- Being in the Flow state (as below)

Exercise 3

Listen to my meditation for heightening all your senses - here.

Allowing yourself pleasure can be extended to all areas of your life. Absorbing pleasure in relationships, your physical body, creativity, spirituality, sexually, with money, and in your surrounding environment. These will help negate the biggest killers which are loneliness, anger, stress, fear and trauma.

Many studies show us that happier people are healthier people, and being more aware of your senses makes you happier. Being happier negates stress. Anxiety causes a multitude of diseases from heart disease, immune dysfunctions, cancer to the common cold.

And remember, even challenges can be pleasurable because they allow growth and expansion. They give you wisdom, and wisdom is pleasure.

YOUR NOTES

STAGE 4 · THE HEALING STATE

Living in Colour

Mere colour, unspoiled by meaning, and unallied with definite form, can speak to the soul in a thousand different ways.

Oscar Wilde

When we feel our senses heightening, colour can help lift our mood. It can also affect how we express emotion and behave. Colour can awaken us, stimulate us, agitate us and help us rest. It can even help us heal.

Within ancient cultures such as Egyptian, Greek, Chinese and Indian; colour temples were used for healing. In the ancient Greek city of Heliopolis - City of the Sun - red or blue cloth was hung over the windows in the temple, with the sunlight shining through the cloth to treat human ailments.

The practice of chromotherapy (healing with colour) was used and is even still practiced today. In fact, Pythagoras applied colour light therapeutically in 500 BC.

We know that certain colours can brighten up our day and also have the capability to dampen our spirits. Picture walking through a gloomily lit street where the buildings are dark, and there are grey clouds overhead. We feel heavy. When walking through a street with blue skies, and bright sunshine lighting up the buildings, we feel lighter, brighter, even euphoric in comparison.

I recently went to a wedding in Scotland and had been away from home for three weeks. I felt tired from travelling and not in the mood for going at all. So I went out and bought myself a bright orange dress, and my spirits and energy were instantly lifted. It was astonishing to me that the change in my mood altered so much as soon as I put the dress on. I don't even normally wear orange.

I also remember when I was at university we had a new lecturer in for a term, and I expressed to him that I was feeling particularly low in my mood and lacked inspiration. He instructed me to paint three boards that would surround my desk, one bright blue, one bright red and one bright yellow (the primary colours). At 19 years old I thought he was barking mad, but I was also intrigued, so I found three pieces of old cardboard and painted them in these bright colours.

When I placed these boards around myself my mood was instantly lifted. Those boards stayed around my desk for the entire year and they really did work in keeping me happier and more motivated.

In the 1980s psychologists found that painting prison cells with a bright pink hue calmed aggressive inmates. The colour became known as "Drunk Tank Pink", and other football coaches began painting their locker rooms the same colour in the hope of creating the same atmosphere.

Colour therapy is not just a wacky idea for painting walls and cloth. It is also used in orthodox medicine now!

In 1902, Niels Finson received the Nobel Prize in Medicine for treating lupus vulgaris (skin TB) and smallpox, with red light therapy. Progressively, light therapy is still being used to this day to treat skin conditions, wounds, pain and injuries.

Researchers have shown that 40 Hz light therapy improves memory and nerve function and it can even help Alzheimer's patients.

Colours serve as a nutritional purpose too! As well as looking beautiful on your plate, eating a rainbow of fruit and vegetables will enable your body to receive a good variety of important vitamins and minerals to help you heal. Even your good bacteria like colour, the more varied in colour your plant food is, the more varied your microbiome is (More on this later).

Mindfulness

We can feel the need to be constantly stimulated by foods, drink, work, people, social media, or fun. We can search for that high wherever we go, and if we can't get an instant high through food, or people, we then try and buy things to make us happier. If these don't make us happy, we can then find ourselves on Facebook, Twitter or YouTube. We find ourselves always plugged in, always stimulated.

The problem with this instant high, this need to be charged up, is that we stop appreciating the beauty around us. We then only desire big things, the sparkliest thing, the strongest tasting food, the high sugar or salt. We lose our taste buds for food, and we lose our taste buds for life.

Mindfulness has been a buzz word over the last few years, and is very much connected with heightening your senses. It is about being in the present tense rather than worrying about the past or future. When you heighten your senses, you are far more in the present tense, but you can take it one stage further in observing how you feel in the moment, and listening to and observing the people around you.

Essentially, being mindful just means appreciating, showing gratitude, feeling the moment, not living in the past or future but being present. Of course, this is nothing new. Many religions have been practising this through prayer and meditation for centuries, but it has led to a new word, "Mindfulness" because of the rising decay in our society from being ever present.

When we look at allowing pleasure with heightening our senses, this is a practice of mindfulness.

We can also add to this a practice of non-judgment to our observations. And further still we can notice how our body feels in a mental body scan, and listen to how our emotions sit in a mind scan.

We can also observe when we don't feel great, when we feel addicted, craving, negative, etc, but rather than reacting to it we can heighten our awareness, to allow the emotions to flow through and back out. Remember, your body wants to go back to a state of homeostasis, and, given half a chance, it will. So these moments of sitting still and just being with ourselves, rather than reacting or running away from ourselves, are vital for the healing process.

Why is mindfulness so good for healing?

Studies reveal mindfulness lowers blood pressure, improves your heart, decreases cognitive decline, improves immune response, reduces ageing cells and reduces psychological pain.

Several studies show that mindfulness meditations raise T-cell activity in cancer patients and improve various bio markers.

Another study showed people who practiced mindfulness had increased levels of interleukin-8 in their nasal passage, which results in an increase in immunity.

Mindfulness can also reduce cell ageing.

In fact, there are so many studies into mindfulness and anti-ageing that I could write a whole book on that subject alone.

So, this shows us is that if you want to heal your body and mind, you would be daft not to allow it into your everyday routine. Not only is it highly beneficial, it's very simple, does not take up much time and it's free.

Ideas on mindfulness are:

- A body scan
- A mind scan
- Sitting and chanting
- Sitting and observing one thing, like a flame from a candle or fire, or a ripple on the water.
- Saying a mantra over and over
- Doing breath work and observing your breathing (Stage 5)
- Observing nature and being present of how it feels within and around you
- Hugging a tree and observing it in all your senses

Being mindful is being grateful, being in the attitude of gratitude so you don't have FOMO (Fear Of Missing Out).

One of the reasons I get clients to do a detox is to appreciate what they put in their mouth, to relish every mouthful.

I tell them to go into a supermarket and think how lucky they are to have access to the incredible gifts that are offered to them.

Someone, somewhere, grew that for you, picked that for you, packaged it for you, sold it to you and then what about the vegetable or fruit itself? It is packed full of hundreds of vitamins, minerals and nutrients that can fight cancer, heal your gut and give you energy - not high energy, real energy, that can cleanse your blood and increase your focus.

Do you ever just stop and think — 'WOW! How amazing is that?'

So the next time you think you are somehow missing out because you can't have these foods for a few weeks or a few months, the next time you feel sorry for yourself because it's not fair, the next time you feel deprived, give yourself a metaphorical slap around the face and say, 'I AM MISSING OUT RIGHT NOW!'

I am missing out on feeling good energy.
I am missing out on a good night sleep.
I am missing out on being happy.
I am missing out on good health.
I am missing out on feeling attractive.
I am missing out on having good skin.
I am missing out on being able to wear the clothes I love- I am missing out on all my senses working...

Remember, each thing you are learning in **the healed state** does not have to mount up to having to practice a hundred different things daily. Most of them cross pollinate with each other.

The Flow State

Being in a flow state is one of the most pleasurable emotions you can experience. All your senses come alive.

I heard the term 'flow state' a few years ago, but have been experiencing it for a lifetime. It is always curious to me when something has 'coined a phrase', and suddenly we are more aware of it. By naming something, you can tune into it more.

Being in a flow state is allowing. It is being in a state of downloading rather than thinking, it's being able to perform without conscious awareness, it is weaving through obstacles with little or no fear, just flowing. There is a symbiosis between your body and mind, and your senses are heightened.

You may have experienced flow states many times in your life, or you may never have done.

The flow state is the antithesis of stress. When you are stressed, blood vessels travelling to the digestive system, hands and feet contract, whilst in contrast the blood vessels travelling to the heart, brain and larger muscles open. Your pupils dilate, your breathing increases, your heart rate races, your muscles become tense. Cortisol is raised which suppresses your immunity so that your possible sustained injuries have less inflammation.

Your stomach acids increases, reproduction and sexual function are shut down to make way for the more important impending threat (you don't want to get horny whilst fleeing a lion). In stress your body is just focusing on being sharp, fast and strong to keep you protected, whilst your digestion, libido, reproduction, sleep and immunity all effectively become switched off.

However, allowing the flow state is the opposite of stress.

To give you some examples of what a flow state looks like:

I can achieve a flow state whilst painting a picture or creating. I might start with a bit of fear, or anxiety when I look at the blank canvas or white computer screen, but I then start writing or painting and suddenly I am in the process of receiving, of downloading and I am able to transfer that to the whiteness, without stress or consciously focusing.

I also feel this flow state when meditating and just being – sitting with mindfulness.

But actually flow state usually happens when I am also doing something extremely challenging. It creates a relaxed state so that I am able to perform something potentially dangerous or difficult, with ease. This is not the same as being calm in a crisis, as this usually comes with post-traumatic stress.

If I really thought about each move I make when I ski, surf or wakeboard, I would feel like a beginner, and be consumed with fear. The flow state allows the fear to be released and the movements to work in harmony together.

When you are totally focused solely on one task and immersed in your passion, you may find yourself in a flow state. The beauty of being in a flow state is that the mind's usual distractive chatter diminishes, and the usual stress that absorbs you can fade away. Being in a flow state is like being in a natural high.

It is also wonderful to watch other people in their flow states:

Imagine when you watch a musician, a conductor, a singer, a sports person, an artist.. you can see them being transported into another world, you can see their eyes wander elsewhere and you can see their bodies creating something incredible without any worry or fear. It can be utterly thrilling to watch.

Fear will be the number one emotion that will block the healing process for you, so allowing the flow state - no matter how worried you are - will take you out of fear and exude the release of positive endorphins. The flow state releases a feeling of ecstasy and clarity.

I remember the first time I watched my husband play football when we first met. Football really wasn't my thing, having been brought up with brothers and battling every Saturday morning over whether I would get to watch cartoons on the television over them watching football. This always turned me off, because my brothers always won. The whoops, the cheers, the chanting from the crowds exasperated the struggle, and for me it was just a big fat negative. I hated football.

However, I was excited to be at a live event and watching my new boyfriend play on the pitch. I enjoyed seeing Robbie run about, being part of a team, calling to his team mates and being in a union of achievers. It was also funny hearing people in the crowd chant his name *"Robbie Wood, Robbie Wood, Robbie, Robbie Wood. He's got long hair, but we don't care, Robbie, Robbie Wood."*

When he got the ball I noticed his whole energy change. His eyes changed, his body changed, the heightening of his senses was palpable. He was like a dancer weaving through the crowd of players, he knew where everyone was around him even though he was running at a great speed. He wasn't distracted by the crowd or the players and his body and mind were working in a beautiful symbiosis - he was in the flow state.

It was utterly thrilling for me to see, and definitely raised the bar for my attraction to him. Not because I want the kudos of being a footballer's wife, but because watching someone in a flow state is a huge turn on.

Have you ever observed someone in the flow state?

How did it make you feel?

We can also observe animals in a flow state. When they hunt, you can see total focus. Their eyes change, their energy changes and they are not distracted by anything.

The flow state usually presents itself during something a little challenging, something that requires focus. Imagine if once Robbie got the ball he was consumed with the thought that, 'Oh no, the crowd are watching me, the sponsors are watching me, the agent is watching me, my new girlfriend is watching me. I am going to mess up. I can't do this.' He would not be in the flow state. The flow state allows you to jump out of fear altogether, but still makes the right decisions for your safety. The flow state helps you concentrate without stress, keeping you very relaxed and very focused.

When I do anything creative I get into the flow state - writing, playing music, dancing, singing, painting. Other pastimes can get me into the flow state, such as swimming in the sea, meditation, Tai chi, Qigong.

I would say I spent 90% of my childhood in a flow state that was constantly being knocked out of me by my educators, and now I am spending 90% of my time trying to get it back again. But even in the flow state it requires movement to not be stagnant.

If I am writing or painting and fully submerged in the flow state, I have to have reminders to get up from my desk or my easel and move my body, have a glass of water, or get some fresh air. Even in a flow state we can create a hostile environment because it's so utterly enjoyable you can forget to do anything else. The best way for me to keep moving is to have my dogs by my side. They want to be let outside approximately every 20 minutes, and that is perfect timing for me to move. I used to find it annoying having to get up all the time for them, but now I see it as a blessing.

We can learn a lot from animals in the way they move gracefully, the way they exert themselves, the way they groom themselves - and the amount they rest. They really are living the life of dreams. Happy with their lot - enjoying affection- relaxing in the sun, chasing, playing and being forever loyal.

Living in a healed state requires movement, not stagnant energy.

If you look at water and how it behaves when it moves, it becomes full of life. It creates new areas, it breeds new life, it exudes negative ions into the atmosphere which are very positive for us. Water travels, gathers momentum, and is the feeder of all life. Conversely, when it doesn't move, it can become stagnant, poisonous, and lifeless.

Healing energy requires movement. Movement leads to a creative state, and a creative state leads to a healing state - the flow state.

Our bodies are designed to move, as are all life forms - even plants.

This also includes those suffering with disabilities. I've worked with many disabled people over the years whilst doing charity work, but also one of my first jobs was in an old people's home when I was 15. My cousin and I got jobs by mentioning that we went to Lourdes every year. It was a very well paid job for our age and we were very excited to save up and spend the money travelling around Europe.

I was actually far too young to cope with what was thrown at me. On my first day I had to take a blind man's glass eyeballs out and help him clean them. I helped another chap with his catheter and read 'Anne of Green Gables' to a motionless lady on an inflated mattress. I felt so heartbroken for her as she was in the final stages of MS, and looked totally bored with me reading in a monotonous way. In her bedroom were photos of the old her, being active, getting married, going on hikes, running on the beach. It was gut wrenching. Actually, all I wanted to do was heal her. I had no idea how to protect myself at that stage, I just wanted her to feel better.

This lady didn't look older than 50 and I felt so sad for her. One thing I had to do throughout the day was move her to prevent her getting bed sores.

Paralysed people cannot survive lying still. They have to be moved to prevent this stagnant energy. This is something I also felt at school - sitting still was creating stagnant energy in me too.

Even though it was just one day in my life, it has remained with me and ever since then I wanted to know how to heal properly.

The biggest time in my life where I felt the flow state was my first time presenting on the shopping channel QVC. It was 2015 and I was selling my first book 'The Body Rescue Plan'. This was a very exciting period, as my book was already a great success, every national newspaper had written pages about it and the lady I was presenting with on QVC, Catherine Huntley, had lost 3.5 stone following 'The Body Rescue Plan'.

Selling live on air is not easy. I only had ten minutes to explain what the book was about, allow Catherine to speak and ask questions, present some of the recipes and try and remember key things I should say whilst also remembering the things I was not allowed to say. (The legal team sit you down before hand to remind you of all the jargon you cannot present live for fear of litigation).

You then have to look good, sound good and sell without sounding like you are selling. If no one buys your product, QVC make you buy the stock back. Prior to this you have to buy all the stock out right, so in some cases brands can go bankrupt.

I was nervous before I went on air, but as soon as the lights went on and the camera lights went green, all time slowed down. I literally felt as if everyone was speaking really slowly. I noticed every part of Catherines face, every hair on her head and I could even hear my heartbeat. My senses were so heightened I felt like I was in heaven. I had zero fear, and was utterly submerged into the flow state. It was bliss. We sold out of all stock.

Your brain activity in the flow state is often at Alpha level. Alpha waves are the sweet spot for accessing your subconscious without stress.

There are five brain waves functioning in your brain.

- **Gamma brain waves** are the fastest waves your brain releases and are activated when you are highly alert or very focused. They measure above 35 Hz.
- **Beta** - Being awake and alert. They measure 12 to 38 Hz range.
- **Alpha** - Day dreaming and drifting off, meditation and Flow state. They measure between 8 and 12 Hz.
- **Theta** - The First stages of sleep or in a meditative, deeply relaxed state. They measure 3 to 8 Hz range
- **Delta** - Deep sleep. 0.5 to 4 Hz range.

We want alpha waves throughout the day to allow for an awake relaxing cycle. If we do not allow for this, we become sick.

How can you create more flow state in your life?

Remember, in this Stage we are looking at creating a routine of activities that allow our bodies to feel healing every day without effort. It is difficult just pushing negative emotions, pain, fear out of your body, so filling up your day with positive conditions around you helps the internal releases flow more easily.

The benefit of achieving flow state is allowing the ability to concentrate and focus with clarity and less fear. It's being in a mindful state that allows pure pleasure in.

There is no fear in flow state, so heightened healing can ignite.

Charge with Nature

As children we wouldn't dare go through a day without constant pleasure, we are in the flow state constantly! Pleasure in playing, in creating, in eating, in laughing, in dancing, in listening to music- we feel it all.

My childhood was always spent outside, climbing trees, cycling with the wind in my hair, creating camps outside, and even just the simple pleasures of jumping in puddles in the rain seemed very stimulating.

All of nature can heal you - we can co-create with nature.

The moment we stop being connected to each other, to ourselves and to nature, we lose our ability to heal.

When I give healing to others it is important for them to understand they are actually part of the healing process themselves, not just at the healed state period but all the way through the stages. Whether you have a healer or not, you have the ability to heal yourself.

We can actively seek healing, or we can actively seek harm. Or we can choose to be ignorant to both.

When we actively seek healing we are in a place of being in a healing state. We are allowing good stuff to happen to us whilst activating that switch that says 'Yes! I allow the good in'.

This can be as simple as going for a walk in the woods, observing wild animals and plants, being amongst beautiful ancient trees, and feeling their spirit and wisdom around you. If you can't feel that, at the very least you can know that you breathe out carbon dioxide for them to inhale and they breathe out oxygen for you to inhale. We literally cannot live without each other. We live in a symbiosis- which means we are equally healing together.

When you walk amongst nature, know you are being healed, breathe in the power around you.

You may have noticed with this process of healing that there is a cross pollination of many of the positive and empowering methods I am suggesting.

Nature lights up every sense. Whether we are conscious of it or not, it will be highly stimulating for everything we feel.

- **Smell** - The aromatic sense of the plants, wind, animals. Even water and sunshine have different smells to them, the warmer or colder the climate is.
- **Sight** - The incredible bright colours that nature offers us. We are literally looking at the best artists work in the world when we observe nature with our eyes. Even if we are looking at just greenery, the variation of greens are astounding.
- **Touch** - How often do we pick a leaf, or play with grass, or stroke petals, or run our hands past hedges? We love to feel nature in our finger tips.

- **Sound** - The sound of nature is so pleasurable to our ears that even meditation music is replicated from nature. The sound of wind in the trees, water running through a stream or waves crashing and lapping. The sound of whales or dolphins in their wild habitat, or the sound of birds tweeting in the trees. When we become very heightened, we can even be stimulated by the sound of a leaf falling to the ground.
- **6th Sense** - Being in nature gives us such a sense of wonder that we can connect to the higher spirit realm, the creator, or the spirits of trees. Feeling a sense of awe and wonder have also been linked to lowering inflammatory compounds in the body.

Being in nature, enhances all of your senses, is a mindfulness practice, you can achieve the flow state and you can exercise within it. I'm not giving you a list of a thousand things to do to get healed, you can create it all in one.

One of the simplest ways to go out and seek forces that heal, rather than forces that harm, is to be in nature. The more you are in it, the more you are healed.

Using nature for healing is also termed as ecotherapy.

STAGE 4 · THE HEALING STATE

Light up your senses

When we feel the earth beneath our feet,
When we touch the sky with our eyes,
When we caress the skin of our babies,
When we smell the love of the Devine.

When we soak up sounds that hum the earth
When we dance through fragranced fields
When we embrace peace in silent tones
When we taste the honey of being healed

When we relish the flavour of the sun
When we see the floral tones
When we smell the animal instincts
We have found our healed home.

a poem by Christianne Wolff

Did you notice that this poem raised your senses? Words can light you up too.

The term 'Forest Bathing' originated from Japan in the 1980s as a physiological and psychological exercise called shinrin-yoku "forest bathing" or "taking in the forest atmosphere."

The idea was to allow people to reconnect to the countryside and help the never ending screen time we all endure have an antidote.

Researcher and forest bathing expert, Yoshifumi Miyazaki, of Chiba University in Japan concluded that people who walked 40 minutes a day in cedar forests had lower levels of cortisol, the stress hormone. Cortisol can exasperate many diseases in our body, so reducing it has the potential to help heal your body.

Professor, Dr Qing Li, a researcher at Nippon Medical School in Tokyo, discovered that trees and plants release phytoncides, which are aromatic compounds we naturally inhale.

This has a similar effect to aromatherapy and is extremely therapeutic for our bodies. So much so that Li's rescarch showed whether you walk in the day or stay in forests overnight, the changes in your blood showed great improvements for healing.

These improvements showed better immunity and a lowering of blood pressure. This is because phytoncides increase NK cells, which support the immune system. NK cells can also help infections, autoimmune diseases, diabetes, heart disease and inflammatory issues. If you walk daily, you can increase your NK cells by 50% and this can sustain at this level for a month, even if you just walk in nature for two consecutive days.

Another study published in the Journal of Environmental Health Perspective in 2016, showed that women who lived in greener areas had a 12% lower risk of death from all causes, compared to those living around less vegetation.

Being in fresh clean air is also a big factor for restoring health away from pollution. Other studies show being in nature also helps depression, anxiety and attention disorders. Walking by moving water can also help alleviate depression and anxiety due to the negative ions released in the air.

There have been many studies that reach the conclusion that being in nature is profoundly healing for our mind, body and soul - of course we already knew this.

It's not just being outside either. Having a little nature indoors too - indoor plants, using aromatherapy oils, crystals, using plants as medicine - all help us to connect with nature. In a study by Li, he concluded that indoor plants release phytoncides too.

Studies have also shown that even views of nature are also deeply healing for the mind and body. A room with a view can improve attention and reduce stress. One study showed that patients who saw tree lined views whilst recovering in hospital from abdominal surgery, were released faster than those who did not have the same view, despite having had the same surgery.

On top of this, you can even get heightened healing from nature that isn't even around you, such as a photo or video or from the TV.

And it is not just during the daytime that we can connect with nature. We can even connect with nature at night too. Have you ever laid under the moon and stars at night? If you have, you'll probably have noticed how wonderfully relaxed you felt.

Moon bathing has been practiced all over the world because it is recognised as having healing benefits of resting and relaxing under the gaze of the twinkling lights above.

Ayurveda is an ancient Indian healing practice, where moon bathing is believed to have a cooling effect, helping balance pitta and dosah to create harmony. This then helps reduce inflammation, the root of most diseases.

CHARGE WITH NATURE

If you think of sunbathing as a kind of charging energy, we are like a plant soaking up the sun's rays and producing energy within. Moon bathing is the cooling down bit, the balancing, the reduction of fire and anger and is believed in Ayurvedic medicine to help diseases like hypertension, migraines and skin issues. It is also treated to help fertility and help soothe menstrual and menopausal symptoms.

Interestingly, because the moon reflects light off the sun, it can also boost Vitamin D levels and gives us nitric oxide, which can reduce blood pressure.

If it is too cold to venture outside, you can leave a bowl of water out at night so it is charged by the moon and add it to your bath, cooking, indoor plants or even cleanse your crystals within it.

We can also go about setting intentions at the start of the new moon's journey- more on that a little later.

For every symptom there will be a plant that can heal us in nature.

Ways to spend more time in nature:

- Sit under a tree and have your lunch
- Hug a tree
- Go for a walk
- Get a dog - you will have to walk every day!
- Go cycling
- Swim in nature
- Join a walking, cycling, or wild swimming club
- Exercise outside - boot camps, buggy workouts, jogging, to name a few
- Meditate outside
- Sunbathe
- Moon bathe and star gaze

This tree is 1770 years old, and has immense energy to be around

CHARGE WITH NATURE

151

Microbiome

Another reason why nature is just so good for us is because we share the same microbiome!

Microbiome is the home of a community of microorganisms such as fungi, bacteria and viruses which live in many environments around us, including water, soil and the air.

These microbes also live within us, mainly within our skin, vagina and gastrointestinal tract.

Our body is home to trillions of these microbial cells.

We ingest about a million microbes in every gram of food. and what we eat directly impacts whether our gut microbiome thrives, survives or dies.

Your healthy microbiome within your gut controls the storage of fat and helps with breaking down toxins and absorbing nutrients. They also replenish the gut lining, skin and replace damage and dying cells.

They also fight the bad bacteria. Junk food, alcohol, high fatty foods, sugar, antibiotics, anti-bacterial solution, stress, lack of sleep and illness can all detrimentally affect the health of our microbiome.

Interestingly, some of your good bacteria are affected by poor sleep because they have their own time for working, some when you are asleep and some when you are awake, and run on a regular clockwork. So people who do shift work, people with insomnia or those who travel a lot and get jet lag could be affected with the health of their microbiome.

To help replace good bacteria and improve your microbiome you can take probiotics in tablet form. These are particularly useful after taking antibiotics which can kill both your good and bad bacteria.

You can also consume probiotic foods which can help improve digestion, reduce depression, improve skin and promote heart health. These foods contain live bacteria that stay live when we eat them.

Good forms of pro-biotic foods are...

- Kefir
- Kombucha
- Sauerkraut
- Live yogurt
- Tempeh
- Kimchi
- Miso
- Pickles

Equally, foods high in fibre (most plant based foods), particularly foods high in polyphenol compounds, help to boost the health, diversity and vitality of your microbiome.

Polyphenols and high fibre are food for your good bacteria. These are known as prebiotic foods. The more varied your diet is in these foods, the more varied the good bacteria, because different good bacteria like different polyphenols foods. The more varied your good bacteria, the healthier your gut.

The good news is that chocolate, or rather the cacao found within it, is high in polyphenols. However, you would want to find a sugar free version because processed sugar is not good for your good bacteria. In fact, it can make other parasites like candida thrive in your colon and vagina which lower your good microbiome.

Coffee and red wine are also high in polyphenols, but because of their other toxic ingredients, it is better to have berries and home-made chocolate instead.

Sugar free chocolate is very quick and easy to make!

Scan here and you can see me making some. It takes you five minutes to make and tastes delicious.

A very simple way of ensuring you feed your good bacteria daily, is by having plants (vegetables, fruit, herbs, beans, nuts) and one food high in polyphenols at each sitting.

The best foods for polyphenols are:

- Raw cacao powder
- Pomegranate
- Berries
- Flaxseed
- Almonds
- Olives
- Beans
- Spinach
- Red onion
- Herbs

Other foods that have polyphenols in them are:

Fruit

- Pears
- Apples
- Peaches
- Plums
- Nectarines
- Apricots
- Grapes
- Cherries
- Lemons
- Grapefruits
- Oranges

Vegetables

- Asparagus
- Artichokes
- Shallots
- Garlic
- Broccoli
- Carrots
- Red lettuce

Legumes

- Tofu
- Tempeh

Nuts & Seeds

- Pecans
- Chestnuts
- Walnuts
- Chia seeds
- Hazelnuts

Carbs

- Oats
- Wheat
- Rye

Here are some gorgeous recipes from The Body Rescue Plan Books that are high in both polyphenols and fibre.

MICROBIOME

STAGE 4 · THE HEALING STATE

Breakfast

Apple Sauce & Chia Breakfast Bowl

Prep time: 15 minutes
Cook time: 20 minutes
Soak time: overnight
Serves 2

Ingredients

For the Apple Sauce
3 large apples, peeled and diced
¾ cup organic apple juice
2 tbsp. chia seeds
1 tsp. cinnamon
1 tsp. vanilla extract

For the Chia Bowl Oats
½ cup rolled oats
1¼ cups unsweetened almond milk
2 tbsp. chia seeds
1 tsp. vanilla extract
1 tsp. cinnamon

Preparation Method

• For the apple sauce – add all the apple sauce ingredients into a medium sauce pan and bring to a low boil. Stir regularly to combine all ingredients. Once boiling, reduce the heat to medium-low and cover the sauce pan, letting it simmer for approximately 20 minutes.

• Continue to stir to avoid sticking. When the apples are soft, remove from the heat and mash. Allow to cool and then store in the fridge in an airtight container.

• To prepare the chia bowl oats, combine all ingredients in a small bowl and stir to combine.

• Once mixed well, place in the fridge overnight.

• The next morning, layer the oats with the apple sauce and continue to do so until your bowl or serving cup is full.

Nice to Know: The apple sauce can be stored in the fridge in an airtight container for up to one week.

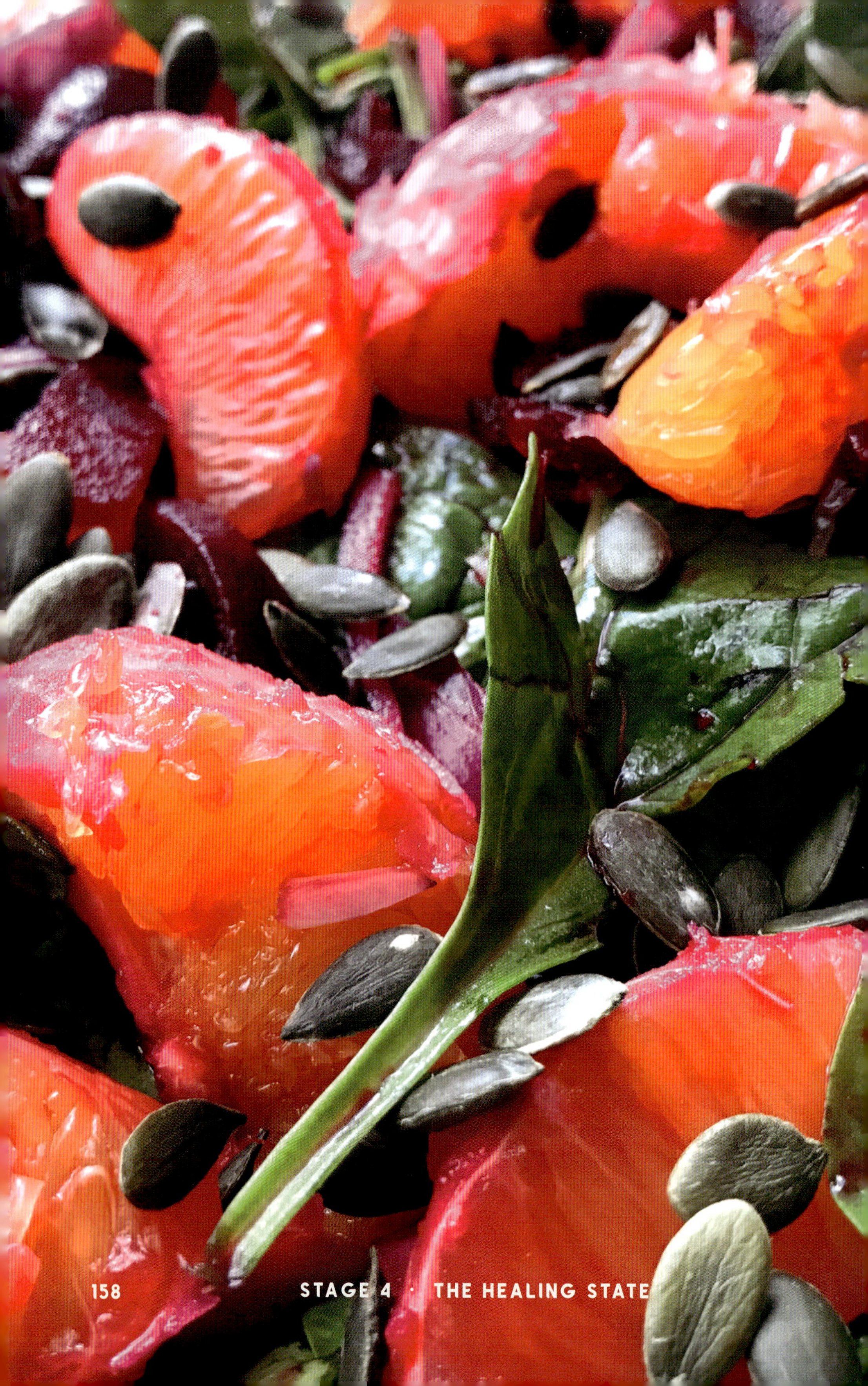

Lunch

Beetroot Salad

Prep time: 10 minutes
Cook time: 15 minutes
Total time: 25 minutes
Serves 4

Ingredients

2 large beetroots, golden or red
½ red onion, sliced or chopped
6 cups baby arugula or spinach leaves
2 oranges, peeled and sectioned with seeds removed
2 tbsp. orange juice
¼ cup raw and unsalted pumpkin seeds (optional)

Preparation Method

• Peel the beetroots, trim the ends and cut in two halves. Slice each portion into four or eight slices. Place into a saucepan and cover with water.

• Bring to the boil and then reduce the heat to medium-low and cook until tender, approximately 15 minutes. Cover the saucepan with a tight-fitting lid.

• While the beetroots are cooking, place the onion into a saucepan and cook while stirring continuously on medium heat. Add water to prevent the onion from sticking and cook until lightly browned, approximately three to five minutes. Place into a medium bowl once cooked.

• When the beetroots are done, drain and rinse under cool water and place them in the bowl with the onions. Add the arugula or spinach leaves, oranges and orange juice. Mix well and sprinkle pumpkin seeds to garnish.

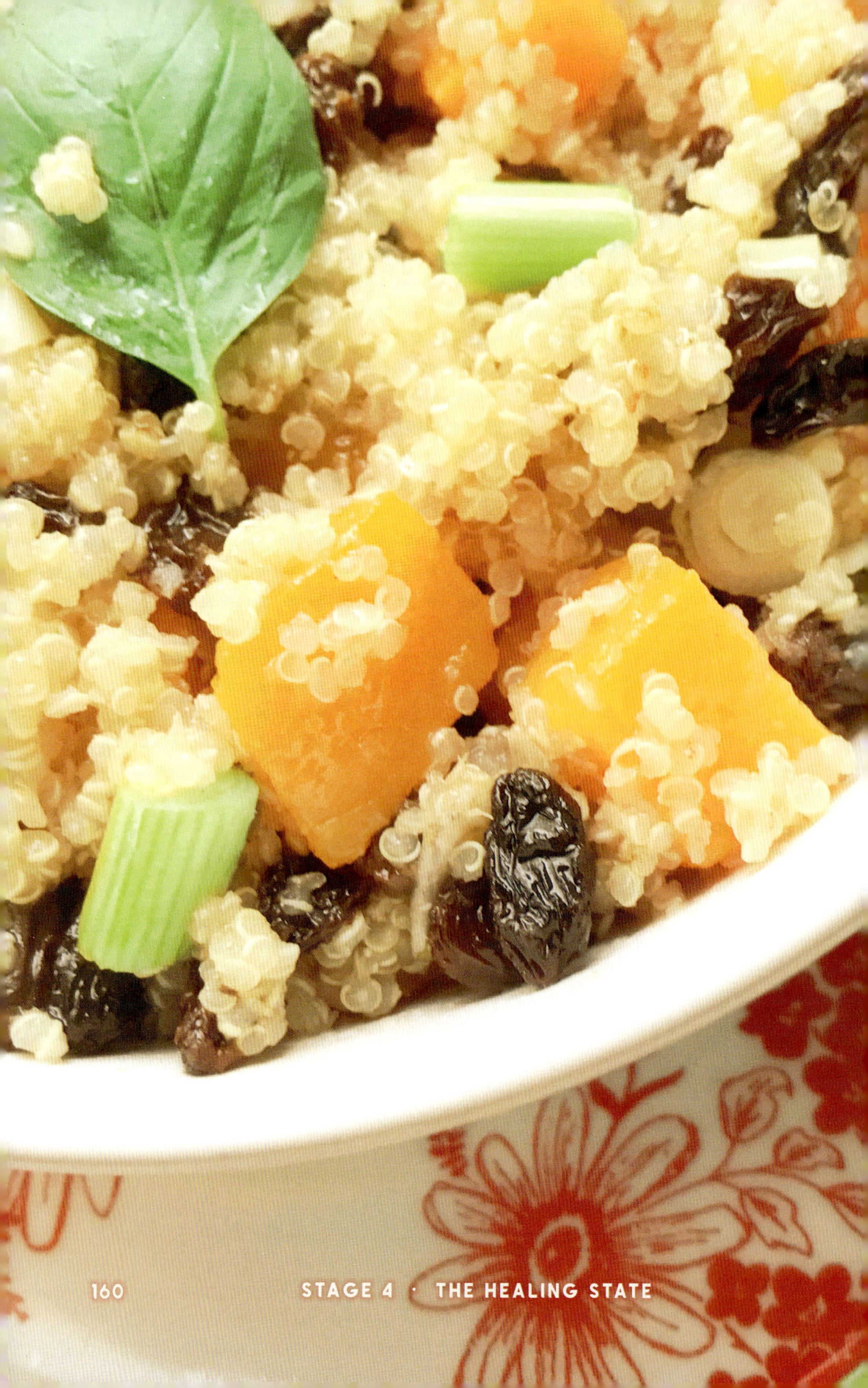

Supper

Quinoa Butternut Squash Salad

Prep time: 15 minutes
Cook time: 35 minutes
Total time: 50 minutes
Serves 4

Ingredients

1 cup of quinoa, cooked
1 butternut squash, diced
1 cup pomegranate seeds
⅓ cup of raisins
2 tsp. fresh parsley
2 spring onions, greens only, chopped
½ cup olive oil
2 tbsp. lemon juice
Lemon zest
Salt and pepper to taste

Method

- Preheat oven to 200 degrees and line a baking sheet with tin foil.

- Cut the squash in half lengthwise and scoop out the seeds. Cut the squash in half again lengthwise. Continue to cut the squash until it is in ½ inch slices, making it small enough and easier to roast. Spread the squash evenly on the baking sheet and drizzle with some olive oil and salt. Roast in the oven for 35 minutes, or until tender.

- For the dressing – combine the remaining ¼ cup of olive oil, lemon juice, lemon zest, parsley and spring onions. Season with salt and pepper to taste.

- Remove the squash from the oven and let cool. Meanwhile, mix the quinoa, pomegranate seeds, raisins and top with the dressing. Season with salt and pepper to taste.

STAGE 4 · THE HEALING STATE

Pudding

Crispy Quinoa Cakes

Prep time: 15 minutes
Cook time: 35 minutes
Total time: 50 minutes
Makes 15 cakes

Ingredients

4 tbsps of coconut oil
1 ½ tbps almond butter
4 ½ tbps maple syrup
2oz / 55g / ⅓ cup raw cacao powder
1 ½oz / 45g popped quinoa
Small cake cases

Method

- Put the popped quinoa into a mixing bowl and set aside.

- Place all the other ingredients in a saucepan and heat gently for a few minutes, while stirring, until the ingredients melt and combine to form a smooth mixture.

- Pour the melted mixture over the popped quinoa and stir until thoroughly combined.

- Spoon the mixture into small cake cases and place them in the freezer for around fifteen minutes or the fridge for about half an hour.

- You can buy your quinoa ready popped or pop your own in a heavy bottomed pan over a medium heat. Cover with a lid and shake regularly to prevent sticking.

Microbiome also lives within your home and within your pets. Going to other people's homes and being around plants and pets gives your body a good variety to choose from.

The more diverse your microbiome, the better the balance. We get this balance through a varied diet and being around different plants, people and pets.

Having a diverse microbiome also helps with your immunity, blood sugar levels and appetite.

Exercise can also improve your gut microbiome. Exercising outside is even better!

The microbiome in soil is closely related to the microbiome in your gut. Even just allowing your hands to submerge into the soil has been proven to be healing for the body.

The Human Microbiome project was a huge study funded by the National Institute of Health from 2007 to 2016 and was instrumental in making a connection between the soil microbiome and the gut microbiome. The HMP discovered that the soil and the gut contains similar amounts of active microorganisms. The health of our gut is not only about the fibre we eat, but the soil that plants containing the fibre were grown in.

Amazingly, there is also a connection between the human and ocean microbiome sharing 73% microbes. Half of the Earth's oxygen is produced by the microbiome of the ocean.

The Second Brain

In recent years our gut has also been referred to as the second brain, and there is a direct relationship between the health of your gut and the balance of your mental health.

In fact 95 per cent of the body's serotonin is found in the bowels. Serotonin is your feel good hormone, and if you are low in it, so too will be your mood.

Surprisingly, studies have also found a lack of serotonin produced by the gut can lead to post- menopausal osteoporosis. Further studies are being carried out relating to the relationship with other diseases.

Our low moods can also be felt within our gut area. Butterflies, nervous tummy, not letting go (constipation) and anxiety eating are all related to our gut health. The vagus nerve, which is the largest nerve in the body and connected to the gut, can be stimulated to help heal depression and anxiety (and many other issues). In fact, scientists are using electrical stimulation of the vagus nerve as a treatment for depression as it can mimic the gut to brain signals. But we can also stimulate the vagus nerve ourselves. More on that in Stage 5!

Microbiome expert and author Dr Alan Desmond states:

> *"We've got more little bugs in our large bowel than there are stars in the Milky Way or trees on planet Earth.*
>
> *The bugs that we carry in our gut microbiome are actually very primitive and they're the ancestors of the earth. The very first inhabitants are these little microscopic organisms.*
>
> *They're biologically and metabolically active. They're producing hormones and vitamins, minerals and proteins. Biologically active substances directly influence our health just like any symbiosis.*
>
> *Their health depends on our health, and our health depends on their health."*

What is fascinating beyond this is that when we die, the gut microbiome continue to live off our body, working their way through the organs into the soil that our body resides in, into the plants that live in the soil and into another being again.

We are the earth and stars, and the earth and stars are us.

I have experienced many gut issues during my life and, not surprisingly, as a consequence I have also had depression and attention disorders.

As a young child I had an onslaught of bladder and kidney infections, so was given regular antibiotics. I resisted taking them a lot of the time because they tasted so awful as medicine, but the problem was that if I didn't take them the infections would often spread to my kidneys, which was extraordinarily painful. Whilst I am grateful for the antibiotics stopping me from dying of an infection, they had shocking effects on my body and can still play havoc with me now, if I am not careful.

My daughter also has similar issues, but there is a wonderful herbal tincture she takes called Uva Ursi that literally works within about an hour of her taking it. I found this tincture in my 20s and it's been lifesaving for me too. I very rarely have to give her or myself antibiotics, and I am very grateful that in nature we have so many plants as an antidote to our health issues.

I noticed my gut issues beginning at around the age of 12 years old. I would go days on end being constipated, once even for two weeks, and I always had headaches. I found concentrating at school impossible, and would often do something naughty just to get sent out of class so I could 'breathe'. I was also extremely sensitive to certain foods and would get hyper after many, and then crash and become depressed. I was also always tired.

At 16 years old I went on a journey of self-discovery. I was fortunate to have an older sister who is now a naturopath doctor. She recommended I start on a course of colonics.

Following that I gave up sugar for seven years.

This was 1988, a time when there was very little alternatives to sugar, and very little information out there, so I had to do the majority of research myself. I hadn't heard the phrase microbiome in 1988, but did take acidophiles (a probiotic) to help restore my rejected colon.

Interestingly, when I spoke with my GP about colonics and probiotics in 1988, she was absolutely appalled, thought it was dangerous and totally unnecessary. Frustratingly, she had no interest that it actually saved my life. I was no longer depressed, ill, no longer had hideous highs and lows, no longer suffered with constipation or even poor immunity.

In 2022, 34 years later, I was prescribed my first lot of probiotics and enzymes by my doctor (in Portugal). I was so emotional that finally an orthodox doctor was tuning into a more holistic way of healing (ie treating the cause), rather than prescribing a drug to treat the symptom.
We spoke for a whole hour and I am elated that the new generation of doctors are not so blind sighted.

At 16 years old I understood that processed sugar was not good for me and plenty of fruit and veg were. I listened to my body's needs and stopped getting constipated, depressed and could actually start concentrating. Or if I was depressed it was for an actual reason rather than just feeling empty and sad over nothing. This was an absolute revelation to me, because as a teenager I felt very out of it for a lot of the time. In fact, parents of many of my friends presumed I was on drugs, which was never the case. The mental and physical transformation within me was so dramatic that I decided to make a career out of it. I wanted to help as many people as I could, get healthy, get off meds without their side effects and really start living!

I've had thousands of clients come off a multitude of medications as a result of following 'The Body Rescue Plan'. When I first wrote it in 2014 I had no idea of the impact it would have on people's lives. I originally wrote the plan to help people quit sugar and get rid of their food addictions, and as a result help them lose weight.

I certainly didn't anticipate the number of diseases my plan would help, and how many people would contact me each day to say they no longer have symptoms of their said disease and have come off medication. This is absolutely incredible.

As there are no processed sugars or addictive foods in 'The Body Rescue Plan' and there is a very good process with mindset work to stop you being addicted. It focuses so much on lowering cortisol and the result is you have a body that is far lower in inflammation.

Stress and inflammation are the main causes and contributors to most disease. So it never stops fascinating me how people who think they are old and it's part of the ageing process, suddenly feel young again.

I will mention more about this in Stage 5 but for now I'll focus on my experience with depression as it's so linked to microbiome and gut health, and it's something I have personally also suffered greatly from.

Lowering or quitting processed foods, exercising, being in nature, and lowering your stress all gives you a thriving microbiome, which in turn makes you feel mentally and physically well and helps you stay that way.

Lynne East was a client who followed 'The Body Rescue Plan' to help heal her depression.

"The last time I felt this good was before my accident 17 years ago," she wrote. *"Being left with chronic pain and a disability isn't fun, especially when it isn't your fault. I changed overnight, and as the years went by I found I was losing more and more of the old me. I was in a deep place of depression and even asked my surgeon to remove my leg in the hope it would stop the pain. I couldn't look after my children properly and I couldn't even look after myself.*

Then, in 2012 I started my training to become a counsellor. I knew this was the time for me to start my healing journey. Fast forward to January 2019 and I no longer wanted to be controlled by my disability, I was going to gain back that control and I was going to do whatever it took to be better, physically, mentally, and spiritually.

Working with trauma survivors I knew that over time the brain can form new neurological pathways and can heal itself from the physical pain and memories by forming new ones.

Since I started the new eating plan, giving up all that sugary rubbish, I am blown away at how well I feel, how much stronger I am, how much more energy I have, I can concentrate and focus on what my clients are telling me, I feel more present in the room with them.

Christianne, you have changed my life (tearing up now) and I can't thank you enough, I just so wished I had known about you many years ago."

Louisa-Jayne Viccars is another lady who changed her life around following The Body Rescue Plan.

"I've had depression for so many years and had a few very dark days, but when I joined your sugar free challenge by the end of the five days there had been such a big change. It had such a massive effect on me that my family noticed I was less grizzly bear and more cuddly bear.

I used to binge on grab bags and suffered with my weight, I had T2 diabetes, high cholesterol, depression and anxiety. I'm the corner stone of the family, I support everyone else and if I am sinking I can't do that.

In 12 weeks on TBRP I came off anti-depressants, am not on any diabetic medication anymore and I've lowered my cholesterol.

My medication for my depression and anxiety is getting on my bike now. I am a happier person a more confident person, you are almost crazy not to do it, it's very empowering.

Invest in yourself, ooh I'm getting all emotional now."

I have thousands more examples of clients I have worked with over the last 26 years who have reversed so many conditions, and I do believe a major part of it is improving their microbiome - even though 26 years ago I didn't even know that myself initially.

You can actually get the diversity of your microbiome tested by a nutritionist or a medical expert. One of my clients, who does not eat fruit because she is worried about the sugar within it, had hers tested and found out she was lacking in the microbiome living off fruit fibre.

Faecal Transplant

As well as being able to get your microbiome tested you can also get a faecal transplant from a healthy (alive) donor, known as Faecal Microbiota transplantation or FMT for short.

This is a relatively new procedure in Western civilisation that actually originated in Chinese medicine more than 1700 years ago.

FMT is usually done by screening the healthy donor's faeces and their gut. After that the faeces are extracted, treated with a saline solution and fed into a tube, which goes into the patient's rectum and into their colon. Yes, you can now sell your own poop!

Whilst it sounds disgusting, actually it just amounts to the ill patient being fed good bacteria through their rectum; seemingly a far more favourable solution than 1700 years ago when the Chinese fed the faeces through the mouth, without being able to test it for any bad bacteria.

It was first reported in the English language in 1958 to treat pseudomembranous, but in more recent years has been used to treat recurrent Clostridium Difficile (CDI). CDI is a common stomach bacterial infection and is treated with antibiotics. Interestingly around 20% of the people who get CDI have an adverse reaction to the antibiotics prescribed for it- which disrupts the gut microbiome and can then be a serious cause of concern, even fatal.

Using faecal transplants is a very successful way to treat CDI from those who don't react well to the antibiotics, with the overall success rate in a 2014 trial being 90%.

However, now new discoveries have now been found on how FMT can improve or heal many other conditions.

A 2016 review showed faecal transplants may effectively treat:

- Diabetes
- Fibromyalgia
- Obesity
- Hay fever
- Asthma
- Eczema
- Liver disease
- Depression
- Chronic fatigue
- Allergies

What I have not read in this review is whether people with any of the above conditions would initially try to improve their own microbiome themselves. This would be interesting to know as I have witnessed all of these issues disappear with some clients when they take control of their own gut health. Sometimes one does need help though, especially for those with a history of high antibiotic intake.

Interestingly, researchers of FMT are also observing that obese people who have a faecal transplant can lose weight if the faecal donors were naturally slim. Something in the donated healthy micro-biome either boosted the obese person's metabolism, stopped the obese person eating so many calories, or stopped cravings of junk food. This is still being investigated, with research in its infancy, but is fascinating nevertheless.

So, as a conclusion to observing and improving your microbiome, when we go out and seek forces that heal rather than forces that harm, in this healing state ask yourself...

Do I surround myself with good microbiome?

Do I eat foods that absorb good microbiome?

Do I eat foods that feed my microbiome?

What will I do to increase the good microbiome?

Water

When we talk about receiving pleasure, most of us would agree that floating, soaking or having water in and around us is about as good as it gets. I have a slight obsession with water and always have, especially out in nature. I have also always drunk copious amounts of water, perhaps because of my earlier encounters with bladder infections, but water and I have had a long love affair that will never end. In fact it was the main reason why I moved to Portugal. Diving through the waves of the Atlantic Ocean completes me, and I don't feel right without it.

My religious upbringing also taught me water is seen as holy, and we went to Lourdes every year on pilgrimages where the water is said to cure and heal. Perhaps that concept somehow stayed within my psyche, but I do see water as sacred and even alive.

Water is actually part of most religions as being Holy.

- In Sanskrit 'Narayan' is the name of the God "as the one who moves in the infinite waters and is water"
- In Judaism, 'Mikvah' water is used for ridding impurity.
- The Ancient Egyptians and The Ancient Greeks practiced bathing rituals to help them heal
- The Native Americans meditated in sweat lodges as a way of cleansing the body and mind.

Water flows and is symbolic for us, allowing more fluidity in our lives, never becoming stagnant and ever changing, but still staying pure.

Negative Ions

Being around water can give us a great feeling of awe and wonder. We have already learnt how this can change us, boost our feel good hormones and make us feel naturally charged. But also, being around moving water releases 'negative ions' which has many benefits for our body and mind.

Negative ions are molecules in the air that have been charged with electricity. They are released by moving water like the sea, streams, rivers, waterfalls but are also in the ultraviolet rays from the sun, in the air after a lightning storm, and are produced in plants.

Research shows that being around negative ions can reduce symptoms of depression, improve cognitive performance and can promote antimicrobial activity.

The reason negative ions have this positive effect can be the chemical reactions that ions have with your bodily tissues.

Scientific research shows that people who were around negative ions for several hours a day have reduced chronic depression and that people with seasonal affective disorder (SAD) who were around negative ions for only 30 minutes daily, helped their SAD.

The research (which stems over 100 years) showed that negative ions could also help those with poor sleep patterns, reduce stress, balance mood, boost immunity and aid with killing the growth of harmful bacteria, viruses, and mould.

The best way to receive negative ions is to get outside and sit or walk by natural water sources, like water falls, beaches, river banks, streams, or run out in the rain. However, water fountains work too and they can even be found inside buildings.

The other thing you can do is buy an indoor or outdoor fountain or get an ioniser which releases negative ions into your room.

We already know that the sea releases microbiome around it and now you have learnt it releases negative ions too. With the wonder and awe of the sea's majestic power, is it any wonder we are all so drawn to it?

Are you around moving water or negative ions daily? If not, how can you change that?

The ocean induces us into a hypnotic state and we are all magnetised towards it. It wakes up all our senses, the sound mimics the sound of the womb, holding us and comforting us, the colours light up our energy, the vastness feels expansive and energising, the smell is fresh and clean and the feel of the silky water gliding and sliding around you feels refreshing and healing in every part of you.

Watching the sea also induces a state of mindfulness, which has been proven to have benefits that reduce stress, anxiety, and depression, but can also help sleep quality, reduce pain and help mental clarity.

An English census published in the journal 'Health Place,' showed that those who live in and around the sea had reported improved physical and mental health when compared to those who do not. From my own perspective, I know that since moving near the sea my mood has been a lot more balanced. I used to have to do intensive cardiovascular workouts every day to ensure my mood was happy. Now I get the same results walking on the cliff tops or sitting on the beach.

Cold water therapy

Cold water therapy means immersing your body in cold water that is less than 15° for a therapeutic effect. You can do this yourself in an ice bath, a cold shower or having an outdoor swim for a few minutes to receive this therapy.

Or you can go ice swimming in 5°C. Dutch extreme athlete and author, Wim Hof - otherwise known as 'The Ice-man', has gained popularity

WATER

with his combination of cold therapy, breathing techniques and mind exercises.

> Cold water reduces swelling and inflammation which then helps reduce soreness and tightness in muscles. It can also lower blood pressure and cholesterol, boost immunity, improve circulation, improve skin conditions, boost energy levels, improve metabolic function, improve wellbeing and boost immunity, helping to lower the risk of infection.

Dr Barnish who is a cold water enthusiast explains...

"*Top laboratories around the world are discovering being cold for a short period, using water or not, seems to extend your life expectancy. Being exposed to uncomfortably low temperatures, the key word being uncomfortably, seems to activate the longevity genes engaging our survival response, a key player in making sure our DNA is repaired before new cells are made.*"

If you want to try cold water therapy make sure you gradually build up your tolerance and keep it brief. Try cold showers to begin with to see how your body feels. If you are trying open water swimming there are many organised groups now, so you feel safer being supervised.

If you have never tried cold water therapy before, surprisingly afterwards you feel warm and energised.

I personally don't enjoy cold showers and much prefer diving into the ocean, but we have to do whatever is practical for us. I will dive through the waves throughout the year in Portugal, but in the winter months will keep it to a minimum of just a few minutes. I always dive my head under as for me that is the most healing part. I feel all my worries have been washed away and I have been given a new fresh head. Diving through the waves feels like the water is caressing my body, I feel very much in union. It's hardly surprising as around 70% of the worlds surface is made up of water, and around 70% of our bodies are made up of water too.

If we lose over 50% of the water in our body, we die.

As humans we are mainly water and so is the Earth.

If cold water really is not your thing, don't fret as there are also benefits to floating in warm water too.

Floating allows the feeling of weightlessness in mind, body and soul. Research also shows that floating in warm waters lowers cortisol levels, lowers pain and reduces stress in the body. You can achieve floating within your own bath by filling it up with warm water, Epsom salts and a little aromatherapy oils. Create an ambient setting by turning off the lights, lighting candles and playing soothing music. Allow everything to be released and relaxed.

You can also experience this in floatation tanks and sensory deprivation centres that are listed worldwide.

Drink Water

Drinking water is essential for our body's health. I can't tell you how many clients I have come across who don't like drinking water and have tea and coffee as their main drink - or diet sodas. The problem is that caffeine is a diuretic for the body, which means that drinking it will not only not hydrate you, it will actually dehydrate you, so you need even more water after having it. Diet sodas are full of artificial sweeteners that play havoc on your body and most other drinks are full of sugar.

We have been programmed by advertisers to not like water. This is not normal programming for any human being or animal on Earth. Imagine giving your pet caffeine or Diet Coke. If you wouldn't do it to them, why would you do it to yourself?

Whilst you may think of water as a tasteless substance that just adds fluid to your body, it is actually full of minerals.

The choice for most people is tap or bottled spring water.

Your average tap water contains calcium, chlorine, copper, fluoride, iron, magnesium, manganese potassium, molybdenum, iodide, sodium and sulphur.

Minerals help you maintain a regular heartbeat and blood pressure, flush waste out of your body, aid digestion, regulate your body temperature, help cognitive function, improve skin, transport oxygen, create saliva, increase strength, prevent constipation, help you absorb nutrients, aid your immunity, lubricate your joints and support the health of your organs rejecting bad bacteria from your body.

Aim to drink around 2.5 to 3 litres a day. If your mouth is dry you are already dehydrated, so drink little and often throughout the day.

Spring water can offer more health benefits as it is denser in minerals. In fact, two litres can provide up to 15% of your daily calcium requirement, and 33% of your magnesium intake. Carry a steel bottle of water with you at all times, and sip throughout the day.

Do you drink enough water?

Drinking water also helps negate junk food cravings and aids weight loss. If your body is dehydrated, your metabolism is lowered! Drink that water.

Water Memory

Water has memory. It carries nourishment throughout our body by transporting energy, so therefore absorbs what it hears and sees.

Japanese researcher and author, Masaru Emoto, studied the effects that energy had on water in his book "The Hidden Messages in Water". He showed studies where he played music, wrote words, and prayed to water while it was freezing.

The crystal shapes would change depending on the energy which was influencing its shape. Positive energy resulted in beautiful shapes and negative energy resulted in ugly crystal shapes.

This then posed the question- if we are made up of so much water and so is our world, and all the food we eat, how do positive and negative energies affect the water within and around us?

Emoto said, *"Water is the blueprint for our reality and that emotional energies and vibrations could change its physical structure."*

He tested this theory in many ways. One of which was by putting cooked rice in two containers. On the first container he wrote "thank you" and on the other container, he wrote "you fool".

Emoto then told his students to say the words out loud every time they passed the rice. After 30 days the rice that the students said 'thank you' to showed little change but the rice labelled "you fool" was full of mould.

So, if angry words are making these changes in water and food, what are they doing to us? Remember we are made up of up to 70% water.

Conversely, if positive words make something thrive and survive we can then make those changes within ourselves through intention setting. If water is made to reach every cell in our body, we can talk to water to transfer energy with messages too, and even reach our DNA.

You can try this yourself. It is so simple and easy to do. See if your intention setting changes you internally.

You can do this in a few ways:

- Drinking a glass of water and setting your intention as you hold the glass, then allowing it to travel through your body and reach the places you want it to hit, with that positive energy. What message do you want to transport?

- Writing an intention or prayer under a glass of water before you drink it.

- Writing an intention or prayer under the glass of water you set under the full moon for a double charge and use that water for cooking.

- Bathing in water or swimming and visualising the negativity being washed away. I find putting my head under water is important for releasing the stress from my brain.

- Having a healing nectar meditation shower. Visualise the water being a healing nectar and visualise all the areas in your body that need this nectar.

Or do my Water meditation and scan this QR code - be at one with the water in you, and the fish and the plants here.

Ceremony

Many of the healing modalities I am suggesting in Stage 4 you could either do as part of your everyday routine, or make a ceremonial occasion for them to ground them in their importance.

Ceremony is an essential part of most religions and spiritual practices, but you don't have to be religious or spiritual to create ceremonies. They are just a firm way to connect to your self-care, boundary setting and core essence.

However, mind, body and soul health are intimately connected and heal well together.

Ceremonies may sound like an extravagance, as we generally associate them with ball gowns and trophies, but when we create something ceremonial we are marking life's essential moments. They can reflect our intentions and can motivate and stimulate what we want to achieve, or what we have achieved. They can also be a good marker for our healing journey and a way to remember to heal.

Ceremony is an ancient part of us. Our ancestors performed fertility dances around the fire more than 10,000 years ago.

You can create a sacred place within your home or countryside and perform various rituals to signify to your mind, body and soul to unite and help each other on your healing journey.

You can even create your own altar, or corner of a room, that reminds you to connect to yourself and your higher self each day. Your ceremony could be a daily or even several times a day event, or weekly, or monthly, whatever suits you best. But making it a regular performance means you are sending a message to your subconscious self that you are important and so is your healing.

This is a very personal journey and each person will differ according to whichever ritual or ceremony feels right for them. Perhaps none of these connect to you, and this is also fine.

Being in water and around nature is my nature spirit. It's where I feel most connected, but I also have an 'altar' of sorts where I have a big gong, some beautiful crystals, some incense, and many native American instruments.

My altar is a place I connect with on a regular basis, but I also like to go to cacao ceremonies once a month, around the new moon. These are becoming more popular in the Western World but were part of the Mayan and Ancient Aztec civilisations as long ago as 1500BC.

Cacao ceremonies last for around two hours, and allow a moment for intention setting and healing. Their purpose is to open the heart through the use of cacao and often include other modalities like meditation, sound baths and breath work.

Ceremonies not only help us heal, they remind us that we are busy creatures. They are useful to ground us back to the earth and connect us with our core essence of who we are and what we need.

I even create opening and closing ceremonies on my online groups. The opening ceremony creates 'the why' and the intention for the journey, and the closing ceremony creates gratitude for the past journey and the expectation for the future.

Smudging

Incense, or smoke, can play a huge role in many spiritual ceremonies, including those of the indigenous Americans. They use certain herbs to bless people or purify places. This can be called smudging, and dried bound sage is a common herb to use for this practice of cleansing and clearing.

I have a sage smudge stick and some palo santo wood by my bed and at my 'altar.' I burn the sage for cleansing and the palo santo wood for intention setting and healing. Palo Santo is Spanish and means 'Holy

SMUDGING 183

Wood'. It smells divine. It is also great if you are on the move as a small piece of Palo Santo wood lasts a long time, I keep mine in a little box of matches for travelling.

Again, scent is a personal preference and there are other herbs you could use too.

Burning scents for healing quickly takes you to a place of inner tranquillity. So, if you are stressed and out of sorts, or you are very busy, the ceremony of burning to create a healing aroma will act as a quick reminder to heal you.

Other herbs that are used for smudging are:

- **Cedar** for grounding
- **Rosemary** for purification
- **Rose** for love
- **Lavender** for peace and rest
- **Frankincense** for prayers
- **Eucalyptus** for refreshing and energising

You can buy these bound, or make them yourself, wrapping the whole dried herbs tightly bound in string and leave for two weeks until you burn them.

The best practice to use your smudge sticks is after a room has been cleaned. To energetically cleanse your home, light the end of your smudge stick and go into each room wafting the smoke in a circular, clockwise motion. Once you finish using it, just simply run the burning end under a tap until the next time. You can also use the smudge stick around you. When I go to the cacao ceremonies, we get smudged when we enter the room.

If you don't like smoke, you could also use essential oils in a diffuser for the same effect.

Herbal Teas

The use of herbal teas can also create rituals for healing.

Herbal teas have many medicinal properties and come in delicious flavours and varieties. They can help with cravings, restore your energy, help with indigestion and more.

Whatever you choose, make sure they come from a good source. You can make them from fresh herbs, dried herbs or buy herbal teas ready-made. Herbal teas need to be brewed for five to ten minutes to get the full healing properties.

- **Peppermint tea** - Relieves symptoms of abdominal gas and bloating and is good for nausea. Peppermint tea can also be made using fresh herbs from the garden, and it's one of the easiest herbs to grow.

- **Ginger tea** - Drinking ginger tea both stimulates and soothes the digestive system, and helps with nausea. It is anti-inflammatory so can help sore joints too. You can make your own ginger tea by cutting a small slice of ginger and allowing it to brew.

- **Rooibos tea** - This tea is high in Vitamin C and other minerals, and is grown in South Africa. It has many antioxidant properties and is anti-ageing.

- **Milk thistle & dandelion tea** - Milk thistle or dandelion teas are gentle liver cleansers; they can also help our digestion.

- **Rose-Hip tea** - From the fruit of the rose plant, this herbal tea is one of the best plant sources of Vitamin C, which helps the adrenals and immune system.

- **Chamomile tea** - Chamomile comes from a flower and helps the body relax. Many prefer to have this tea before they go to bed to help induce sleep and combat insomnia. It also can help soothe indigestion.

- **Nettle tea** - Nettle tea is made with the leaves of stinging nettles. It can help anaemia, high blood pressure, rheumatism, arthritis, coughs and colds, and helps cleanse the bladder.

- **Lavender tea** - This has many healing properties. It can help lift your spirits, and also soothes the digestion and induces sleep.

- **Echinacea** - This is a powerful herb that contains active substances that enhance the activity of the immune system, relieve pain, reduce inflammation and have antioxidant effects.

- **Rosemary tea** - Rosemary can help your muscles to relax and it aids digestion. Rosemary tea also relieves coughs and mild asthma symptoms.

- **Cardamom tea** - Cardamom is an evergreen plant that's grown mainly in India and Guatemala. Cardamom tea helps treat indigestion, prevents stomach pain, and relieves flatulence. It can also help with coughs.

- **Hot water & Lemon** - I also like to have hot water and lemon. This alkalises the body and feels fantastic on your digestion, especially at the start of the day.

Do you need to create a regular practice of focusing on you?

How will you do this?

YOUR NOTES

STAGE 4 · THE HEALING STATE

Vibration and Sound healing

Each celestial body, in fact each and every atom, produces a particular sound on account of its movement, its rhythm or vibration.
All these sounds and vibrations form a universal harmony in which each element, while having its own function and character, contributes to the whole.
There is geometry in the humming of the strings. There is music in the spacing of the spheres.

Pythagoras

Not only was Pythagoras the greatest mathematician and philosopher of his time, but he was an exceptional musician too. Pythagoras was also the first person to prescribe music for medicinal needs and he called this practice 'Musical Medicine.' He would sing and play music to heal animals and humans alike, from mental to physical conditions.

Vibrations are everywhere. Depending on our hearing we can be acutely aware of them or not at all. Even the Earth has a hum.

How we speak, who we speak to and what we listen to can alter our own moods. We know this already as listening to a sweet melody can relax us, listening to hard rock can excite and invigorate us, listening to dance music can make us move. We are all different in our tonal choices, but what we all have in common is that vibrations literally move us internally.

In 2005 I broke my leg whilst in Egypt. I had just arrived at the hotel and was about to teach a yoga holiday. That was until I tripped over a room divider and boom! My whole leg snapped off. If you have ever broken a bone you know the intense pain you feel. This was three bones and was totally unexpected as I was not doing anything dangerous, I was just walking! The shock of what happened and the surging pain made me scream my head off. Upon my third intense scream I realised the screams themselves were affecting my body's ability to heal. They were sending their own shock waves to my body to panic and I could not breathe properly.

So I calmed myself down, took some deep breaths and gave myself healing. I noticed that the sound of my breaths away from the screaming fits made me feel far better. I even managed to get my bones to slot back into place so the pain was not so acute. Apparently, at that point I should have fainted, and maybe I would have done had I continued to scream and wail.

A few years later when I became pregnant with my daughter Angelique, I learnt the methods of hypnobirthing, which signalled to use breathing techniques and primal tones to induce the body into a more calm and healing state, whilst enduring extreme labour pains.
Whilst other pregnant ladies in my ward were screaming in pain at their pending babies' births, I was focusing on my breaths and gentle omming sounds. Their screams were actually irritating me far more than my own labour pains!

However, sometimes a good scream does help us get rid of pent up tension. Screaming also activates the limbic system in the brain, which then activates adrenaline and cortisol, Adrenaline then triggers blood vessels to contract, which in turn makes us feel less pain.

This is a fight-or-flight response in case you are in danger and need to run with an injury.

However, my screaming for the third time was actually stressing me out, and I then felt the urge to allow the healing to happen as there were no lions to run from.

It is said that the vibrations from screaming can cause an avalanche. What then are these sounds doing to us and the people around us?

Omming, chanting, praying, singing, the tones and words that are expelled from our mouth every day can create healing or harm within our body.

I love a good chant and sing and chant or omm every day.

One of my favourite songs to sing is "I am the light. I am, I am". You can hear me sing this to the food I dish up on my retreats. Remember, water absorbs frequencies and so do plants, which in turn affects what you eat and drink.

We are all made up of vibration, and we can all be in either harmonious or opposing frequencies to each other.

What we say and how we chose our words affects not only others, but ourselves too. If plants are affected with words like 'I love you' and ' You fool,' as we saw with the example of the Japanese researcher, Massau, then saying those words to yourself must also have a negative effect or positive affect.

You can heal or harm with your words. It's your choice.

Gracious words are a honeycomb, sweet to the soul and healing to the bones

Proverbs 16:24

Sound Baths

The deep resonant tones we can create in our voices, we can absorb in musical instruments too, and they can have a healing effect!

Sound baths is a fairly new term to describe an ancient tradition of sound therapy.

I purchased my first crystal singing bowl over 20 years ago and have never played it to anyone who has not benefitted from its vibrational hums. I now have a collection of gongs, Tibetan singing bowls, native American flutes, drums and more to add to the healing sounds.

Not everyone is blessed with being able to sit still and meditate, so I have found that sound therapy or baths are such a great way of getting into a healing state very quickly and easily. It's actually impossible not to.

The vibrations of the instruments are designed to have a direct impact on the vibrations in you. They shake you up into a frenzy of beautiful tones and then you have a feeling of settling down, but settling into a new, calmer you than before.

Sound baths can help you relax, lower your blood pressure, heart rate and allow your body to heal.

One study performed in 2020 showed that all 105 participants who participated in a 40-minute sound bath reduced their negative mood and increased their positive mood based on a PANAS rating scale. They also reduced their heart rate.

Another study showed that 60 people who were waiting for surgery, listened to a sound bath and lowered their anxiety.

Whilst whale music and bird song is not for everyone, I have found sound bath tones are universally accepted as therapeutic. And unlike just playing music on your phone, the vibrations for live sound baths are deeply healing as they go right through you.

Most sounds we allow around us are very much our choice, so when I posed the statement 'Go out and seek forces that heal rather than harm' at the start of this stage, we can also choose those sounds that heal or harm.

As well as music we can choose the people we surround ourselves with and the tones of messages they reflect to us.

We can choose to use our own throat vibrations in a way to heal us as well. How you speak also reflects on how your nervous system is.

We can all connect to a certain sound, and this a very personal choice.

For instance ADHD sufferers can be soothed and balanced by 'Drum and Base' beats. Others are soothed by classical music, and some by really subtle sounds like white noise or sounds in nature.

Even more subtle sounds are the ones that evoke ASMR- autonomous sensory meridian response. ASMR is a tingly feeling some people get when hearing soft sounds like whispering. There are plenty of ASMR videos and sounds on the internet. See if they invoke relaxation in you.

Triggers

If you fight something you give it more energy. Be sure what you are fighting for is for you, or don't fight at all

Stage 4 has been about seeking forces that heal rather than harm around you- creating a positive external atmosphere so you can feel healing every day with little effort in many cases.

However, make note that at some point on your healing journey you will get triggered. No matter how hard you try to create a harmonious environment, life happens and triggers can set you backwards.

So, if you now create an understanding of what those potential trigger points may be, this will be very helpful. Once they pop up, if you are aware they are going to happen, you can create some contingency plans to help you not to react in a harmful, self-sabotaging way.

> On your healing journey what potential trigger points may come up for you?

> How did you use to act when these triggers came up?

> How will you react instead?

Examples of triggers can be:
- Arguing with your partner
- Money worries
- Boredom
- Not sleeping properly
- Not being organised
- Getting stressed at work

What else?

When we structure our day to be around nature, healing sounds, good food and people, the environment can hold us when the shit hits the fan. To be healed is to understand not only your triggers, but other people's triggers too. When others are triggered, we feel a connection to them. That connection either goes in support of them or against them.

For instance, consider the behaviour of Will Smith at the Oscars. We all felt something when he slapped Chris Rock for suggesting his wife looked like GI Jane. We felt we wanted to protect Chris or we wanted to protect Will.

This stems from our triggers. We are literally triggered by a trigger.

Will himself had been triggered. This should have been the greatest night of an actor's career and yet he massively self-sabotaged. When he reached the pinnacle, he blew it which could be stemmed from a trigger of a lack of worthiness.

We can be far more comfortable dealing with what we know than diving into the abyss of what we don't. Even in Will Smith's case, if that means winning an Oscar, being recognised for his life's work, having more respect and earning more money than ever before, he still sunk that ship.

If we feel worthy or we don't feel comfortable, we self-sabotage.

We will always be triggered, but it's the way we react in any given situation rather than the trigger itself which is important. It's cementing ourselves in our core belief that these are our boundaries, this is who we are, these are our needs and going back to our core selves of what we need to heal.

When we seek forces that heal over forces that harm, we will be less seduced by triggers in our life. However, when we are seduced by them, our inner core value will override the desire to self-sabotage. If you are triggered and you do self-sabotage, it doesn't mean you can't, it means you won't.

So if you won't, go back to Stage 3 of asking yourself if you are ready for healing.

And if you will.. continue to Stage 5

the healed state

STAGE 5
THE HEIGHTENED HEALING STATE

*We don't stop playing because we grow old,
we grow old because we stop playing*

E Bernard Shaw

Physical
1. Breath
2. Vagus Nerve Exercise — yoga
3. Sleep
4. Nutrients

Mental
5. How to rewire your brain
6. Motivation versus routine

Emotional
7. Trapped emotion
8. Placebo and Nocebo
9. Playfulness, Joy and happiness

Spiritual
10. Heightened Flow State
11. Goddess energy

Physical

Breath

Welcome to Stage 5 !

By now you should have ...

- Understood your back story
- Tuned into what you want to heal
- Asked what you are willing to give up that makes you sick
- Asked if you are ready for healing
- Started to create an environment of healing around you

Now we focus on the internal healing within our body. We do this in four ways:

- Physical
- Mental
- Emotional
- Spiritual

So let's start with the physical and your breath.

Take a long, slow, deep breath in. Relax your shoulders as you do this. Feel your ribcage flare out, charging your body with good energy. Now exhale, release and let go.

Repeat five times.

How do you feel?

I'm starting this stage with the breath because it is seemingly a simple thing to focus on to help heal you, and it has very positive results to your health. As mammals we all breathe (if we did not, we would die within a few minutes) and we all perform breathing subconsciously.

However, when we place conscious effort on changing how we breathe, we can lower our blood pressure and pulse, improve our posture, boost our immunity, reduce stress, improve our digestion, reduce mood disorders, reduce insomnia, improve lung conditions, and even increase our life span.

When we don't breathe properly, we exacerbate all those issues until they can turn into disease and even shorten your life.

Whilst we have no control over our other organs, they function for us - autonomically, with breathing we have the choice to allow it to work automatically, or we control the breath consciously. In turn we can then control the cardiovascular system, digestion and other systems within our body.

Every day we take around 23,000 breaths but we all breathe in different ways. This is influenced by stress, exercise, pain, disease, diet, mood and posture. The average healthy adult only uses around 70% of their lung capacity.

'Breath Work' is becoming more popularised, but it is something I have been teaching clients for over 25 years, as breath work is intrinsic within yoga and meditation.

In fact, whenever I have met with one-to-one clients in the past, one of the first things I observe is how they breathe. This is because fixing a body that does not breathe efficiently - with breath work- can dramatically improve someone's life, and very quickly too.

When I was a young teen I read about Buddhist monks who could breathe just twice a minute and how beneficial that was to their health, and therefore rapid breathing meant poor health. As adults we breathe on average 15 breaths a minute at rest. Your heart rate influences how many more breaths you take, so when excited, stressed, ill or exercising it would be higher.

At 12 years old I became fascinated with how breath can alter your mind and body state.

When I was bored and agitated in class I used to see how long I could hold my breath for. I would create all sorts of different techniques for increasing my lung capacity, and what I found worked best was allowing flexibility in my ribcage. I would create a lifted and rounded shape in my torso, take three very long inhales and exhales to expand my diaphragm and stretch my ribs and lungs, and then hold my breath. The longest I held it for was over three minutes. Not only did this help my boredom, it also relaxed me. I would then practice breathing slowly and deeply like the Buddhist monks did, and see whether that made me feel calmer. It did! I didn't learn any techniques from others. I made it up as I went along.

My passion with teaching breathing techniques began when I had my first panic attack at university in the early 90s. I had no clue what a panic attack was, and was convinced I was having a heart attack. I called out the Dr who described it as an anxiety attack and suggested I breathed into a paper bag if it happened again.

My research into breathing for healing extended from there and I have created many breathing techniques taken from Tibetan monk's, yoga that is thousands of years old, to ones I have created myself to the present day.

I even took my breath work into the sea!

> Free divers can hold their breath for up to ten minutes. The world record is held by Alex Segura Vendrell of Spain, who held his breath for an incredible 24 minutes and three seconds while floating in a pool in Barcelona.

Whilst this does not mean we all have to go out and see how long we can hold our breath for, it goes to show that with conscious effort we can train our lungs and breath to improve.

Breath work, in the first instance, is showing your body how to increase its lung capacity. When we get stressed and our fight or flight response is ignited, our cortisol and adrenalin are raised, our pulse and blood pressure have increased and our nervous system is stressed out. As a result we breathe shallow and fast. This is because our heart needs a little extra help in maintaining its fast beat, and our whole body is craving more oxygen to cope with the increasingly stressful environment.

The fight or flight response is essential when running away from a lion, but in our everyday life it's mostly invalid. Therefore we need a way of controlling, nurturing and maintaining its volatile nature so we don't get sick as a consequence. And breath work can do just that.

Not only does breath work help increase lung capacity and therefore alleviate or eradicate diseases and issues attributed by stress, a greater lung capacity can also mean a longer life span too.

The 1980s Framingham Study considered whether a larger lung capacity attributed to a longer life span. After 20 years of research following 5200 subjects, the conclusion was that the greatest indicator of longevity is not diet, exercise or genetics - as previously thought (although still very important). It is in fact lung capacity! WOW! What is exciting about that is we can increase our lung capacity with breath work, exercise and meditation and very easily too.

Another study from Michigan State University shows that your cortisol levels (the stress hormone) will lower in as little as 10 deep conscious breaths- I told you this was quick!

How exciting! Our bodies can heal so quickly given half a chance.

If we want our body and mind to relax and our cortisol levels to lower, deep breathing is integral. We literally need to use the deeper parts of our lungs to induce a more relaxed state. Shallow breathing not only suspends the flight or fight response, but it also creates a lot of tension in the neck and shoulders and prevents the ribcage and back from mobilising correctly, which then affects your posture, creating back issues and digestive issues.

Do you know where your lungs sit?

When I ask clients this question it's very telling, as I feel half the reason people can't get a good inhale is that they don't actually know where the depths of their lungs are. They point to their chest bone and say 'here?' Yes, your lungs are found in the chest on the right and left side, but at the front they start from just above the collarbone and extend to about the sixth rib down. Your lungs extend all the way down the back to the ribcage and finish at around the tenth rib (you have 12 ribs either side). Feeling that breath in the front and back of the rib cage is important!

Is that further than you thought?

For most people it is, so when I ask people to inhale their first deep breath with me, I put my hands on their front at rib 6 (around where the diaphragm is) and on the back at rib 10 (almost the bottom of the ribcage). I then ask them to breathe into my hands. You can try this yourself.

I have found that most people breathe a lot higher, and when I ask them to take a deep breath they automatically breathe into their upper chest and lift their shoulders to help them, rather than breathing into the ribcage and diaphragm.

The clothes we wear don't help either. Tight bras, sports tops, Spanx underwear, tight jeans and compression tops are disastrous for our breath. Everything gets pushed upwards instead of allowing the breath outward. When you get home take your bra off, take your tight clothing off, put comfortable Pj's on and breathe!

Then there is our posture. This is a Catch 22 situation. Breathing affects our posture, and posture affects our breathing.

Sitting on a chair is not a natural stance for our human body, and yet we spend most of the day seated, hunched or slumped over our desk, car or sofa. Then being seated at our desk, whilst being stressed at work, but not having enough room to breathe correctly, worsens the situation. Further still, eating at our desk when we are stressed and not in a good posture, exacerbates everything. We spend the majority of our life doing this and then wonder why we don't feel great.

In 1910 Katharina Schroth developed her scoliosis treatment through breath work.

Scoliosis is where your spine creates an 'S' shape, and in many cases can be so severe that spinal surgery is needed. Schroth created specific breathing techniques to help scoliosis which she named "rotational breathing". Katharina was herself a scoliosis sufferer and developed these treatments through improving her own breathing and moving techniques.

In 1921 she opened her own studio in Germany and became a pioneer in postural work which is still being executed today. Breathing is an integral part of her corrective postural techniques, both in the rib cage and lumbar spinal region and she saw vast improvements in her client's postures within just a three to six month period.

So why is breath work so important for healing?

- Breathing supports the autonomic nervous system.
- The autonomic nervous system is made up of the parasympathetic nervous system and the sympathetic nervous system.

Parasympathetic stimulates relaxation and offers us the feel good hormones like oxytocin and serotonin. It also aids our digestion and feel good responses in sex and mood.

Parasympathetic particularly responds well to deep breaths because the nerves of this system extend into the depths of the lungs, so the more deeply the lungs are used the more relaxed we feel and the better our digestion.

The sympathetic nervous system is the opposite – when we take short breaths our upper nerves of the lungs are stimulated and our body thinks we are in trouble, so gets ready for fight, flight or freeze. We become more alert for a shorter space of time because our blood flow is directed to our brain. However, this is at the cost of our bladder, digestion and genitals, which means if we keep ourselves in this suspended state our digestion, sex life and health will be harmed. You can get into this state in seconds, yet it can take up to an hour to calm down from it.

Throughout the day we need to train ourselves to be more in the parasympathetic state (relaxed) with conscious effort on our breath, if we want to heal our bodies effectively. Initially this does take some focus, but eventually you will find you do this naturally, particularly if you notice when you are breathing more quickly.

One of the first signs of quicker and more shallow breathing is if you suddenly feel tension in your neck and shoulders. You will also know if you are in the sympathetic (stressed) response if your heart rate increases, your palms are sweaty and you are feeling unusually alert.

To improve how we breathe we can also increase our lung capacity with exercise and yoga. A combination of aerobic, anaerobic, and deep stretches allows us to use our lungs in different ways, improving flexibility, strength and depth in the lung. To achieve this, going on a weekly bike ride or jog, or sprinting up a hill would give you both anaerobic and aerobic exercise. Doing a yoga class allows you to decrease cortisol and increase the parasympathetic response, and meditating also helps. Breath work is also beneficial, which we will cover shortly.

However, improvement is not just about allowing the depths of the lungs to work, it's also making sure you use your nostrils over your mouth.

Our noses are essential in breathing for preventing foreign substances entering the air waves, but breathing through your nostrils does so much more than that.

Nitric oxide plays a key role in the differences between mouth breathing and nose breathing. According to Lundberg (2008)
"Nitric oxide gas from the nose and sinuses is inhaled with every breath, and reaches the lungs in a more diluted form to enhance pulmonary oxygen uptake via local vasodilatation. Nitric oxide may be regarded as an 'Aerocrine' hormone that is produced in the nose and sinuses and transported to a distal site of action with every inhalation."

Nitric oxide is extremely significant in helping the cardiovascular, immune and endocrine system.

In other words, nose breathing will boost your health significantly over mouth breathing.

Breathing through the mouth can decrease your health. Your cells will not get as much oxygen as through nasal breathing, which could then lead to fatigue and other health issues.

James Nestor author of 'Breath: The new science of a lost art' - explains:

"The reason why this is so important is because when you breathe through the nose, you are forcing air through all of these very intricate structures. And as that air is forced through these structures, it's heated up, it's humidified, it's pressurised, and it's filtered, So, that air, when it gets to your lungs, can be so much more easily uploaded into your bloodstream.
We can extract about 20 per cent more oxygen breathing through our noses than we can equivalent breaths through our mouths."

> Studies have also shown that breathing through the nose improves your athletic performance and endurance, and helps people with lung issues, allergies, hay fever and asthma.
>
> Studies have also shown mouth breathing can lead to disease and can cause junk food cravings, thus leading to weight gain.

If you breathe through your mouth, and your nose passages are clear- this is a habit you have created that you can easily break. Creating new habits and reminders to close your mouth are important for your health.

However nose breathing is not just for when you are awake, but also for when you are asleep.

Many of us tend to breathe through our mouths when we are asleep without consciously being aware of it. If you feel tired and irritable upon awakening, have a dry mouth, are hoarse and have bad breath, this may be the reason why. You mouth breathe in your sleep. Mouth breathing can also lead to snoring, and snoring can lead to sleep apnoea.

To correct mouth breathing in your sleep it can be as simple as correcting the posture you use in bed. Changing your pillow can also help.

You may also have a congested nose at night due to allergies.

If you want to help mouth breathing because of congested nostrils, there are many over the counter nasal solutions you can take. You can also use air filters, and having a clean room and clean bedding also aids mouth breathing.

If you are opening your mouth in your sleep and do not have a congested nasal passage, the other option is taping the mouth.

Dr E Ravinder Reddy, Senior Pulmonologist, Kamineni Hospitals, Hyderabad says *"Nasal breathing is the right way of respiration – awake or while asleep. Mouth taping certainly reduces snoring and reduces micro-awakening, while promoting quality of sleep and improving cognitive function."*

You can buy mouth tapes online and at pharmacies. James Nestor suggests just using a tiny amount of surgical tape, perhaps the size of a postage stamp, on your lips that can easily come off, if need be. He says that you may hate this initially but after two weeks you get used to it. After two years he would not be without it because he notices such a difference in how he feels when he wakes up.

I will show you some breathing techniques to help.

Simply scan the QR codes on the next page to watch and learn each technique.

Breath work is not just about calming your nerves, boosting your health or influencing greater athletic powers. It is also a great source of allowing you to focus and be present. This is particularly useful within mindfulness but also in taking away pain, both physical and mental.

Wim Hoff created great feats of endurance in his middle age beating 26 world records, which he powers down to the ancient breathing technique known as Tummo. Famous for his iced baths, Hoff used his breathing technique to set the world record for being in an ice bath for 1 hour and 52 minutes without suffering from hypothermia or frost bite.

Scientists were baffled at his feats, and in 2011 researchers from Radboud University Medical Centre began to do some tests on his resilience to disease using his breathing techniques. They injected him with E.coli and observed Wim doing a round of Tummo breathing- he had no reaction and willed the infection off with breath work.

The last thing I want to mention about breathing is how the influence of food that you eat can affect your breath.

Anything you find hard to digest will create tightness in your chest and diaphragm, making it harder to take a deep breath. Remember, shallow breathing leads to the sympathetic nervous response, creating a fight or flight reaction, ie stress.

What you eat can also create acid reflux, which is where stomach acid gets regurgitated from the stomach into the oesophagus. This burning causes shortness of breath.

But it is not just what you eat, it is also the amount you eat at one sitting, how much you drink with your food, if you are eating whilst stressed, if you are eating whilst slumped, (creating acid reflux and indigestion) and how often you chew!

We want to aim for 33 chews, sitting up straight, away from stress and screens, having water before or after, but not during, and eating foods that are not going to cause us indigestion (more on nutrition later).

Are you aware of how you breathe?

Are you aware of how many breaths you take per minute?

Try my breathing technique to aid digestion

Try my alternate nostril breathing technique

Try my breathing technique to increase your lung capacity

In short breathing well will heal you!

The Vagus Nerve

Breath work, mindfulness, meditation, sound healing, chanting, practicing yoga, flow state, being in nature, cold water, feeding microbiome (pretty much everything we discussed in Stage 4) all make you feel more relaxed, all release pain, all release stress, all create that blissed out state thats helps you heal.

The main reason?

Because they are all activating the vagus nerve!

This is very exciting news because you can actually stimulate the vagus nerve whenever you wish to avoid the fight, flight or freeze response and induce calm. Stimulating the vagus nerve has incredible healing benefits for the body, so lets get into it! I mean, its just mind blowing!

Vagus means "traveller" in Greek and The vagus nerve is the largest nerve in the body, travelling from the brainstem through to the thorax and abdomen.

The vagus nerve takes readings from most of your organs and passes that information to your brain and vice versa. It pays particular attention to your cardiovascular and digestive system and the sex organs.

Want better sex, better digestion, better mood, better metabolism, slimmer body?

Then stimulate the vagus nerve!

The Autonomic Nervous System (ANS) ie: heart rate, blood pressure, digestion, sweating, breathing, sexual arousal, even orgasms are all controlled by the vagus nerve.

The Sympathetic Nervous System, the Parasympathetic Nervous System and the Enteric Nervous System are all part of the ANS and as explained in the breath chapter, you can control your fight or flight response with breath work. Why? Because deep breathing stimulates your vagus nerve, and your vagus nerve comes into place when your body feels safe again.

Remember, your Parasympathetic Nervous System calms the body down, allowing the autonomous systems, like the digestion, heart etc to work properly again.

We can have more control over all these systems that we think of as automatically working for us, than we think – via the vagus nerve.

This is incredibly exciting!

AND it can be as simple as rubbing your ear lobe or gargling to stimulate the vagus nerve for just a few minutes a day!

> The vagus nerve keeps us healthy, it controls rest and repair, and teaches us we can self-regulate.

We have an intrinsic heart rate of about 100 beats per minute. The vagus nerve, through the Parasympathetic Nervous System allows that heart rate to rest in the average person at 60-80 bpm. When we get stressed, the vagus drops out and our heart rate goes to the intrinsic 100 bpm, but then the Sympathetic Nervous System boosts it higher to around 120 bpm (so we see a lion and we need a surge of energy to fight, flight or freeze).

The moment our body thinks we are safe, our Sympathetic Nervous System switches back to allowing the vagus nerve to do its duties, such as digesting our food, reproduction, repair. (The lion has gone, we are alright, and we can work as a whole again).

So when we get stressed our reproductive system, our heart and our digestion can slow down. This can be why IBS and digestive disorders are attributed to stress, and why some couples cannot conceive even though nothing abnormal can be detected within them.

Nikki, a client of mine, had been trying for get pregnant for five years. Within two months of working on her stress levels and increasing the vagus activity, she conceived. Couples can also suddenly conceive the moment they stop trying, or when they have decided to have IVF and relax about lovemaking.

I have had countless clients rid their IBS issues when they manage their stress levels.

When we think of our long term health and repair, the word 'safe' is really important here because our vagus nerve responds to calming the body only in safety.

Your health, your sleep, your digestion will be affected if you do not feel safe. Within milliseconds of stress, the vagus nerve drops out – yes, milliseconds! Then cortisol goes through the blood stream within a few minutes after that.

How many times a day do you get stressed?

How many times a day do you self-soothe not only as a response to stress, but to manage your energy?

As the vagus nerve is so closely linked to your gut health (and remember good gut health means better mood) it can transmit signals to the brain, via stimulation, resulting in a reduced depressive state.

Remember when I said that improved gut microbiome means a happier mood? Recent research shows that the gut microbiome can actually activate the vagus nerve, which in turn helps us change our mood. And its clever! The vagus nerve can tell the difference between good and bad bacteria, and will listen to signals to help induce a relaxed state, if needed via what the microbiome tells it. So having a good flourishing microbiome has a knock on effect on calming stress in your body by talking to the vagus nerve.

And there is more! As the vagus nerve wants to induce you into a chilled out state, and keep your body happy in homeostasis, when positively stimulated it will improve your sex life too! If it is under stimulated (untoned), or if you are constantly in the sympathetic nervous state (fight or flight), your genitals are not going to get a look in! But, if the vagus nerve is toned up, your juices and blood will flow! In fact studies have shown that people with spinal cord injuries are able to achieve sexual pleasure due to activating the vagus nerve.

An active vagus nerve also gives you that feeling of satiation (feeling full) and will stop you having cravings.

Here is the interesting part, because the vagus nerve is in the back of your tongue and goes down your throat into your stomach, we can get confused when stressed and want to stimulate this area because subconsciously we know it will help us feel calmer - hence we can then do that with food (emotional eating). Obviously this has a detrimental effect if the foods we are having are spiking our blood sugars and causing us other harm (if they are junk foods) or we are over eating in general. There is a way to combat this- with some vagal toning! More on that in a sec, but just the act of gargling will suffice.

The good news is we can stimulate our vagus nerve with certain food too.

For example, studies show that Omega-3 fatty acids can increase heart rate variability (more on this to follow) and thus stimulate vagal tone for a stronger vagus nerve.

Omega-3 are already healthy for you as they promote brain health, improve risk factors for heart disease, fight autoimmune disorders, help you lose weight and more.

Research from a 2011 study shows how Omega-3, particularly in fish, can change heart rate variability (which affects vagal tone)

"From the sub analyses of heart rate variability it was suggested that a high fish consumption was associated with an enhanced vagal activity and parasympathetic predominance. Thus, this population-based study seemed to

confirm that Omega-3 supplementation can modulate cardiac autonomic function in a favourable way."

You can find Omega-3 in:

- Walnuts • Flax seeds • Chia seeds • Spinach • Brussels sprouts
- Soya beans • Fish and seafood

Other studies show that high-choline foods can also help the vagus nerve. Choline is a precursor to acetylcholine, and acetylcholine is the primary neurotransmitter of the Parasympathetic Nervous System, which then helps the vagus nerve go about its duties.

Choline is found in:

- Kidney beans • Sunflower seeds • Sweet potatoes • Quinoa
- Eggs • Fish • Chicken • Organ meat • Beef

Sodium (salt) is also important in helping the vagus nerve. Obviously too much is detrimental for us, but sodium is actually a vital electrolyte used for water balance, nerve impulses and muscle contraction and we can't live without it.

And remember your microbiome! Interestingly, studies also have shown an increase in heart rate variability (a marker of how well responded the vagus nerve is) comes with a high fibre diet because feeding microbiome is essential for good vagal tone.

Foods that are not of benefit to the vagus nerve and can cause it to be weak are your typical junk foods, sugar, caffeine and alcohol, and also particularly trans fats. A literature review found that trans fat consumption was connected to a decreased vagal tone.

Trans fats are found in:

- Cakes • Biscuits • Frozen Pizza • Chips • Crisps • Fried chicken
- Doughnuts • Margarine

Here are some awesome recipes that are high in Choline, Omega-3 and high prebiotic Fibre, taken from The Body Rescue Plan books.

Eat your vagus clean!

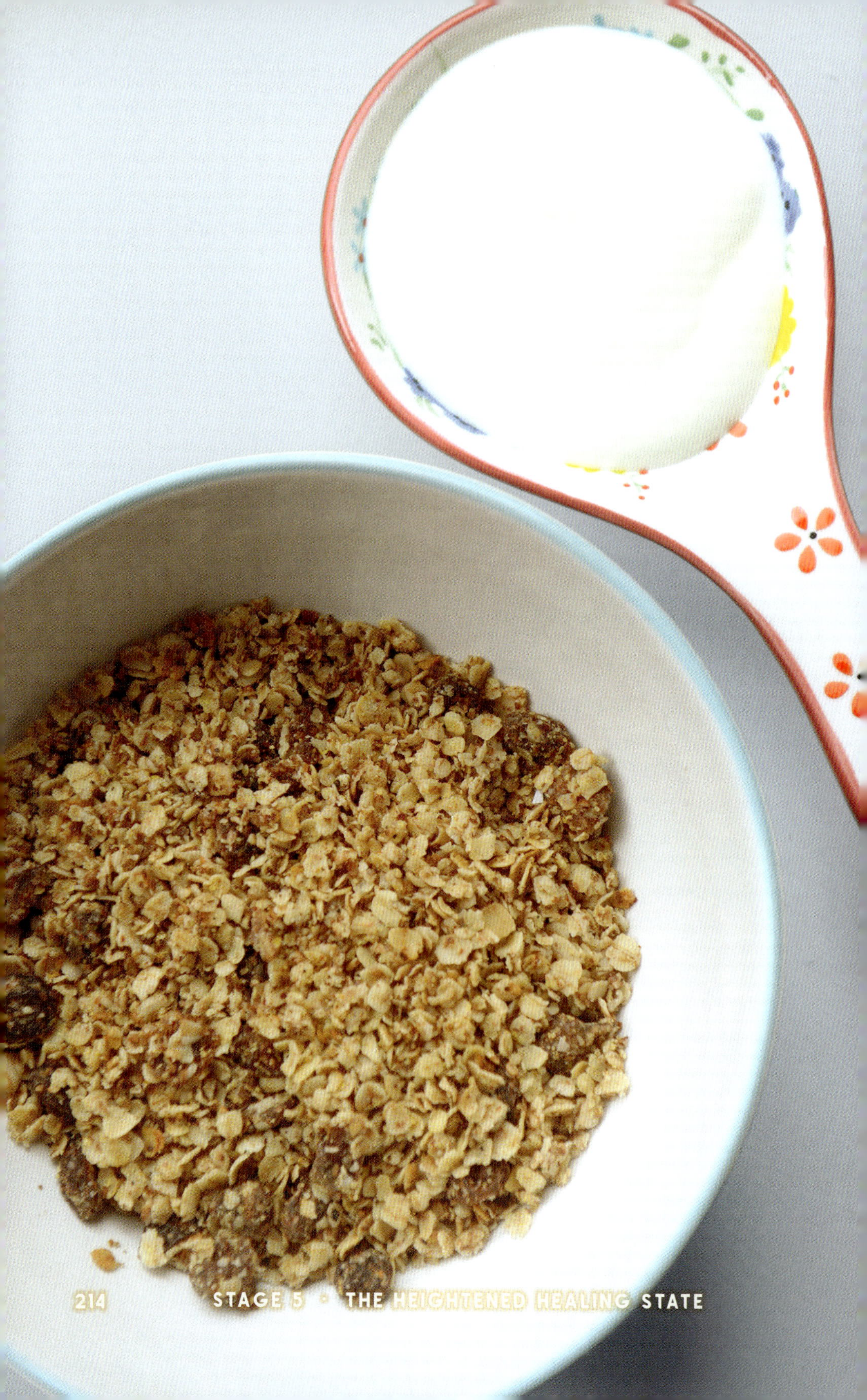

Breakfast

Homemade Muesli

Ingredients

For the muesli:
4 ½ oz / 128g / 1 ½ cups oats
3 ½ oz / 90g / ½ cup chopped dates
3 ½ oz / 90g / ½ cup chopped walnuts and pecans
1 ½ oz / 40g / ⅓ cup milled flax seeds
1 ½ oz / 40g / ⅓ cup sunflower seeds
2 ½ oz / 75g / ⅓ cup raisins
2 tbsp coconut oil

To serve:
Plain yogurt or fromage frais

Preparation Method

- Melt the coconut oil in a wok or frying pan.

- Place all the ingredients into the pan and cook, stirring continually, for six minutes.

- Store your muesli in an airtight container.

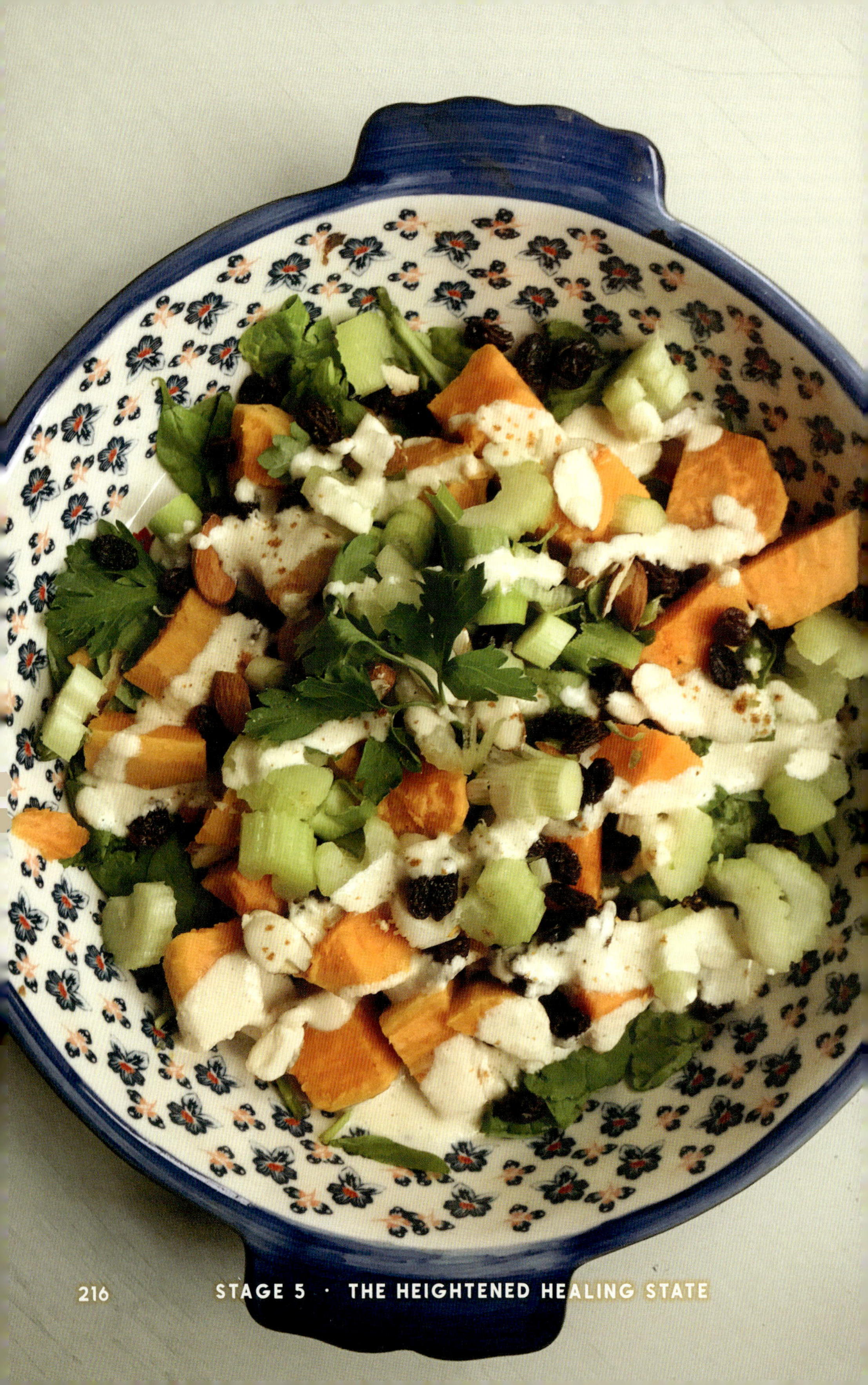

Lunch

Sweet Potato Curry Salad

Ingredients

For the salad:

6 cups sweet potatoes, peeled & cut into 1-inch pieces
2 cups spinach, chopped
½ cup raisins
½ cup almonds, sliced
2 celery sticks, sliced
3 spring onions, sliced

For the dressing:

½ cup water
½ cup raw cashews
¼ cup freshly squeezed orange juice
1 tbsp curry powder
1 garlic clove, sliced
1 tsp orange zest

Preparation Method

- For the dressing, zest the orange and set it aside.
- Place the water, cashews, orange juice, curry powder and garlic into a blender. Set it aside for 15 minutes or so, until the cashews soften and then blend.
- Stir the orange zest into the dressing with a fork gently.
- For the salad, place the sweet potatoes into a soup pan and cover with water. Over high heat, bring to the boil, uncovered. Once boiling, reduce the heat to medium-high and cook the potatoes until tender, approximately 10 to 15 minutes. Drain and rinse the potatoes under cold water and set aside.
- Once the potatoes have drained, place them into a large bowl with the spinach, raisins, almonds, celery and spring onions and pour the dressing onto the salad.

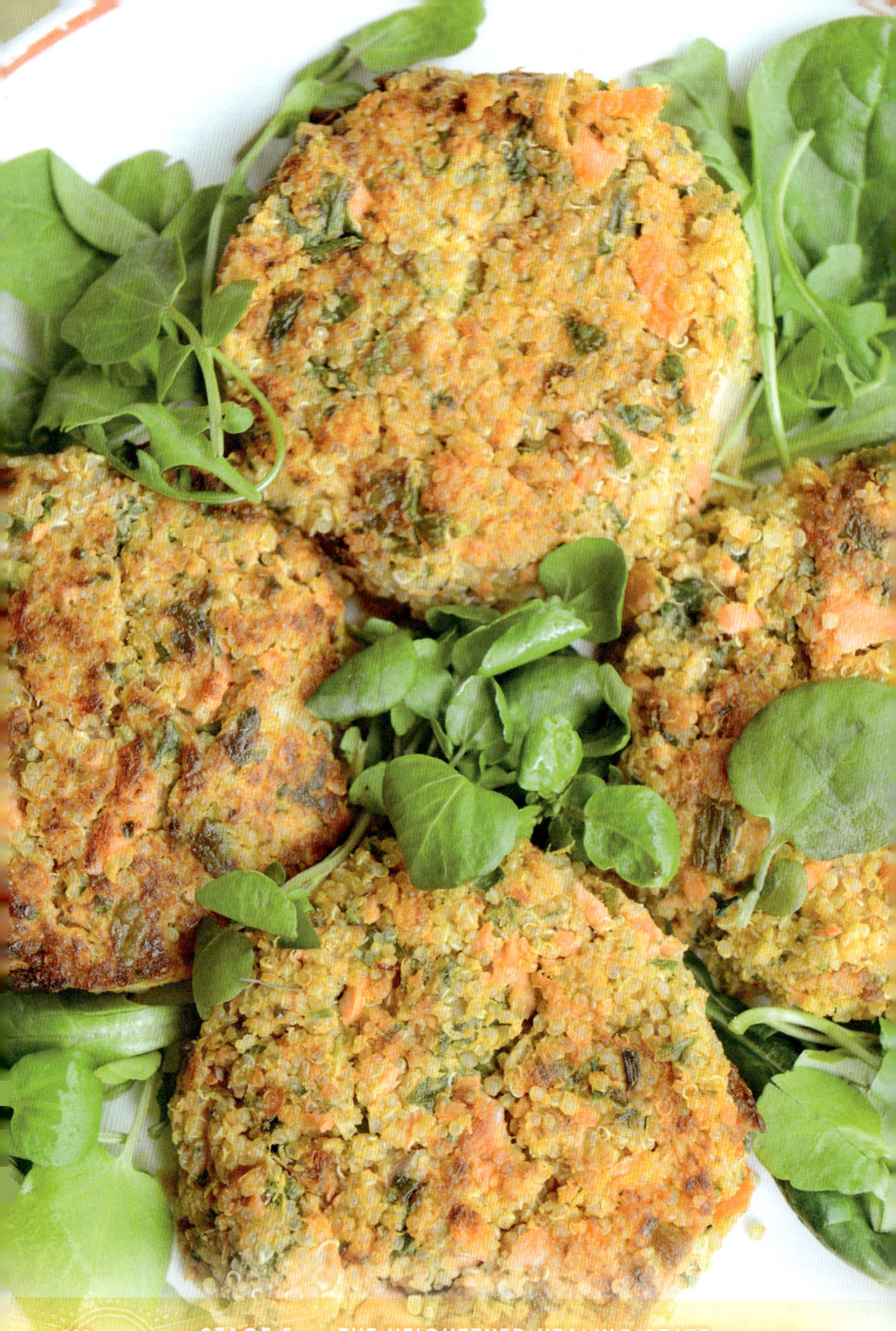

Supper

Fishcakes with Sweet Potato

Ingredients

1 large sweet potato
8oz / 225g / 1 cup quinoa
1 large tin (418g) wild red salmon
1 tsp chilli flakes
1 handful fresh parsley, chopped
1 handful coriander, chopped
1 handful chives, chopped

3 spring onions, chopped
Zest of 1 lemon
1 egg
2 tbsp coconut oil

Preparation Method

- Preheat the oven to 180°C / 350°F / gas mark 4 and bake sweet potato for 45 minutes.

- Cook quinoa in boiling water for 10 minutes.

- Combine salmon, chilli, parsley, coriander, pepper, chives, lemon and spring onions in a bowl, mix in the cooked quinoa.

- Once the sweet potato is cooked, remove skin and add to the mixture.

- Crack an egg into the mixture and combine thoroughly.

- Shape mixture into eight palm-sized patties.

- Add oil to a pan and cook for three to five minutes each side.

- Serve with salad.

STAGE 5 · THE HEIGHTENED HEALING STATE

Pudding

Body Rescue Lemon Drizzle Cake

Ingredients

For the cake:
1 medium sized sweet potato
1 ½ cups ground almonds
½ tsp Baking powder
1 cups Coconut oil
3 Eggs
1 cup Coconut sugar
3 Lemons zested

For the drizzle:
3 Lemons Juiced
½ cup Maple syrup

Preparation Method

- Peel and boil the sweet potatoes for 10 minutes or so until they are cooked.
- Preheat the oven to 180°C / 350°F / gas mark 4, meanwhile in a bowl beat the eggs.
- Whisk in the coconut oil and coconut sugar to the eggs.
- Add the ground almonds and baking powder.
- Mash in the sweet potatoes and lemon zest and combine.
- Grease a cake tin and pour in the mixture.
- Place the tin in the preheated oven and cook for 50 minutes.
- Meanwhile make the drizzle by melting the three juiced lemons and maple syrup together on a low heat in a sauce plan.
- Take the cake out of the oven and pierce a few times with a knife on the top and pour the drizzle mixture all over the cake.

Weight loss and The Vagus Nerve

Vagus nerve stimulation decreases your appetite and therefore helps with weight loss, too. Some studies showed stimulation resulted in slower eating or eating 18% less than usual, leading to weight loss. This is probably because the vagus nerve is linked to neurobiological systems associated with hunger and satiety.

The vagus nerve also has anti-inflammatory capabilities, and when stimulated helps to heal conditions such as digestive disorders, epilepsy, diabetes, and rheumatoid arthritis.

The possibilities seem endless for vagal stimulation. As the vagus nerve is a main channel of communication between the brain and the body, it can therefore be used as a therapy for healing many chronic physical and mental conditions.

Dr Stephen Porges, a scientist and Professor of Psychiatry at the University of Carolina, has studied the vagus nerve for 30 years. He found that many of his patients who suffered various disorders like digestive problems, heart rate problems, erectile dysfunction and diabetes actually had nothing wrong with their organs; i.e. their stomach, heart and genitals. Instead they suffered from a lack of vagal tone. Or in other words the communication between the vagus and those organs was affected through chronic stress. This either kept switching the vagus off, or it ran on suspended animation.

Poor vagal activity is also related to poor memory because your frontal lobe deals with focus and attention and is connected to the vagus nerve. Therefore, a lack of good tone can cause brain fog.

So what can we do to stimulate the vagus nerve?

The great news is that stimulating the vagus nerve is very simple. The key to improving its function is to stimulate it every day to increase its 'tone' and give it more 'bounce back'. So rather than staying in 'fight or flight' all day, you will probably get stressed at some point but spring back quickly. And when you get stressed you don't react so extremely, so the bounce back is even quicker and more restored.

You can also stimulate the vagus nerve through:

- Meditation
- Chanting and humming
- Singing
- Sound baths
- Gargling
- Ear massage
- Cold water
- Breath practices
- Vagus nerve stimulating headphones
- Walking
- Exercise
- Yoga
- Laughing
- ASMR
- Electrical stimulation (like a TENS machine)

Stimulating the vagus nerve can be done externally and internally. As the vagus starts in the brain and reaches around into the ears and face and then down through the throat, we can stimulate points on our face with our hands, particularly the ears! We can also stimulate the nerve by splashing the face with cold water and we can stimulate the vagus nerve in our mouth and throat by gargling or making chanting noises like omming and humming. Even singing can help! Soft induced tones are better as high pitched screams are more associated with stress which can switch off the vagus.

Breath and The Vagus Nerve

As already mentioned in the breath chapter, breathing deeply switches on the Parasympathetic Nervous System, and as you have learnt here this is because it stimulates the vagus nerve.

In one study 47 healthy college students were divided into four groups and asked to slow their breathing at different rates. All the groups improved their heart rate variability (a sign of improved vagal tone - more on this soon), with the greatest improvement in the group taking 5.5 breaths per minute. This is very interesting as many religious practices like praying, doing the rosary, mantra chanting and meditating, naturally get the body breathing at around 5.5 breaths per minute.

A quick note about breathing. If your vagal tone is poor, breath work can initially be difficult to perform. You may want to focus on other ways to stimulate your vagus in conjunction with breathing, so that breathing deeply becomes easier over time.

Yoga and The Vagus Nerve

Yoga has the ability to stimulate the vagus nerve through breath work and meditation, but also deep stretching and twisting through the postures. A randomised, controlled trial found that those who practiced yoga had a higher heart rate variability, better vagal tone, and a quicker recovery from stress than those who did not practice yoga.

Laughter and The Vagus Nerve

Smiling stimulates muscles in the ears, that will in effect stimulate the vagus nerve. Even fake smiling! Studies show that laughter increases heart rate variability and reduces anxiety.

Electrical devices and The Vagus Nerve

Scientifically, vagal tone is taken so seriously that electrical devices are now used in medical practice to help heal all manner of diseases, from mental to physical. These devices can be implanted or placed externally. Also on the market are TENS machine style devices that you can clip to the ear for a few minutes a day to activate the vagus nerve. Speak to your medical advisor before embarking down this road in case of any contraindications.

Ways of knowing if you have a poor vagal tone

If you are wondering how strong your vagal tone is, you can have it tested by a doctor who may test your gag reflex as a way of seeing the strength of your vagus nerve, (incidentally, regular choking or gagging on food and drink can be a sign of poor vagal tone) or you can test it yourself.

According to Stanley Rosenberg, author of 'Healing Power of the Vagus Nerve', look down the back of your throat via a mirror, or get a partner to do it for you, and look for the dangly bit at the back (You may need to press your tongue down to see it). The dangly bit is called the uvula and what you are looking for is symmetry. If it's moving more towards one side than the other, this is a sign of a dysfunction of the pharyngeal branch of the vagus nerve. If you do see a dysfunction try any of the techniques above for stimulating the vagus nerve and look at your uvula again afterwards to see if there is any improvement.

In any case whether your vagus nerve is dysfunctional or not, spending ten minutes a day omming, gargling, singing, or doing breath work could significantly change your life. It takes very little effort, and will teach your Parasympathetic Nervous System you are safe and are fine with being taken out of the sympathetic nervous state. Ten minutes twice a day is all it needs, or also as and when you need to reduce a stressed state.

Intriguingly the humming bird (that hums at around 50 HZ for the majority of the day) is the smallest bird in the world with a heart rate of 1200 beats per minute. Humming, as we now know, has a healing effect on the body via the vagus nerve and could be the reason why this tiny creature lives between two and three times longer than other birds who are bigger but have fewer heart beats per minute. (According to science your heart rate per minute depicts your life span; a human heart beats at around 70 bpm).

Trauma in any form, whether physical or mental needs management and healing. Vagal tone work can help you heal. If you are fleeing your pain rather than managing it you will constantly be in a stressed state, so your vagus nerve begins to become redundant. This has a huge knock on effect on the rest of your body.

Start by as little as rubbing your ear a few times a day and taking some deep breaths!

We need a dance between the Sympathetic and Parasympathetic Nervous System. We need the fight-or-flight or freeze response in emergencies, but we need to be able to get back to parasympathetic quickly. So doing things throughout the day to keep switching on the parasympathetic helps.

I have a massage machine by my desk as my trapezius has sustained whiplash a number of times (from my wakeboarding escapades). I naturally stiffen up, especially when typing.

So the moment I feel the tension mounting, I reach for the device and stop typing. I take a few deep breaths, relax my shoulders and then massage for a few minutes.

I also make sure I stand up every 20 minutes or so, I let the dogs out, I go to the loo, do a few stretches, get a drink (in fact, drinking a lot throughout the day forces you then to get up to go to the loo), roll my shoulders, and listen to some soothing music. It all gives you that good bounce back to a chilled state. Incidentally, research shows that a stiff neck can actually induce poor vagal tone, so take care of that neck!

We also just naturally stimulate our vagus nerve without even knowing it.

- I learnt from a young age that diving into the cold sea deeply wipes my stress away, just like a total refresh.
- When I get irritated I can let out a sigh with a little humming sound.
- When we get stressed we can massage our forehead or temples instinctively, or we can splash cold water on our face.
- We can also become orally fixated when trying to relax or focus. My husband often laughs at me when my tongue starts hanging out of my mouth in a moment of focus.
- We can sing, whistle or hum to ignite good energy
- We can make groaning sounds to relieve pain or induce stimulation in love making.

We actually stimulate our vagus nerve all day with what we now know are scientifically proven ways to do that. Our instincts have known this for a long time. Ancient spiritual practices dating back thousands of years have included chanting, omming, doing breath work, yoga and meditation. Instinct and intuition are quick. Science is slow, but it got there eventually – it took a few thousand years though!

In what way do you think you naturally nurture your vagus nerve without previously knowing about it?

Interestingly, the measure of your health, even the prediction of your death, can be concluded by how quickly your bounce back rate is from the sympathetic to parasympathetic state and you can measure this through a heart rate variability bio feed back monitor. Or tune in each day to how you feel and be aware of your breaths as these are also a good marker.

HRV

Heart Rate Variability (HRV) is the variation in the time interval between heart beats and is measured by the variation in the beat to beat interval. So it is not counting the amount of beats you have per minute, but using a device showing you the time between each beat and how varying they are to each other.

For instance, if your heart rate is 60 beats per minute at rest, each beat would NOT be one second, but perhaps some may be two seconds and some maybe half a second, etc. It is how variable they are that is the key to your health, so the greater the variability the more ready your body is for bringing itself back from stress.

Your pulse is also a good marker for your health. Healthy humans should have a pulse rate of around 50-70 bpm.

HRV is a predictor of health, can predict mortality, predict how quickly you recover from disease and can even predict colic in babies.

> A study undertaken in October 2021 showed that HRV could predict the outcome of patients who had Covid 19. The Study showed that those who suffered with long Covid had an underlying vagal nerve function. Low HRV predicts ICU admission within the first week after hospitalisation from Covid.

High HRV = more youthful, higher resilience, healthier, longer life.

To improve your HRV do the vagal tone exercises and keep stress low.

On average values below 50 milliseconds are seen as unhealthy, 50–100 milli seconds could show some ill health, and above 100 milli seconds are considered healthy.

If you have no inkling to even move your body to help heal you, you can improve your HRV just by thinking grateful thoughts! Another study showed that 70 patients who were engaged in gratitude journalling showed an increase in HRV compared to the control group who did not.

Gratitude brings you back from flight or fight.

Our heart beat patterns reflect our emotions, and our emotions reflect our heart beat patterns. Telling the body we are safe will ensure consistency in healing these patterns, thus raising our HRV, thus strengthening our Parasympathetic Nervous System, thus strengthening our vagus nerve, thus making us live a longer, healthier, happier life.

Exercise and Yoga for healing

In Stage 5 we are exploring ways within us to induce healing. So far we have looked at breath work and stimulating the vagus nerve.

We all know that exercise plays an important role in healing the body. We have already explored within **the healed state** that exercise helps your microbiome, helps with stress, keeps your resting heart rate lower, and helps stimulate your vagus nerve.

The main thing I want to emphasise is just to move your body in whatever form feels good. It does not have to be in the gym, on a bike ride, at a dance class, playing tennis or going for a swim. Whilst all these activities are amazing for our body and our mind, if it doesn't motivate you and is not 'you,' find something that is.

Your body needs to move. It yearns and cries for movement, and if you are able to move it, you should bless your body by activating its limbs every day.

Exercise helps you:

- Manage your stress
- Lower depression
- Lower anxiety
- Lower risk of heart disease
- Lower risk of T2 diabetes
- Improve your sleep
- Mobilise joints
- Lower your risk of Alzheimers
- Boost your mood
- Aids weight loss
- Prevent injury
- Prevent stiffness
- Reduce emotional eating

> Research shows that if we are physically active we have a 35% less chance of death when compared to those who are inactive. If you do not exercise for more than an hour a week you have a 52% chance of dying earlier than those who are active, and you are twice as likely to die of heart disease, or 29% more likely to die from cancer if you do not exercise.

If you start exercising right now and do 150 minutes a week of moderate activities like walking and gardening, or 75 minutes of vigorous exercise like cycling or running, you reduce your likelihood of premature death by 40%!

However 150 minutes a week only amounts to about 20 minutes a day. Forty minutes a day has been shown to be better than 20, and 90 minutes even better than 40 in terms of your longevity.

Resting is also extremely beneficial for the body. The issue we have in our current western climate is how much sitting we do day to day. Being on our devices, watching TV, sitting at our desks working, and driving, all may contribute to a shorter life span. Excess sitting (six hours or more) can shorten our lives by up to 40% regardless of whether we go to the gym in the evening. The answer? Get up regularly, move, walk around, get a glass of water, do some breath work outside. Or get a stand up desk! Or better still, a treadmill under your stand up desk!

Heart health

Whilst heart disease may not play a part in your life now, it is the leading cause of death worldwide. So looking after your heart at any stage in your life is vital. The more moderately active you are, the lower your chance of developing heart disease.

Exercise induces the production of nitric oxide, which promotes a healthy lining of your blood vessels. Did you know that cholesterol can only enter the linings of your artery walls if there is damage to them? So by exercising regularly you are keeping the cholesterol at bay because of a prettier blood vessel lining, which means far less likelihood of a heart attack. (Things which cause damage to the lining of your artery walls can also be high blood pressure, a high saturated fat diet, high processed sugar, smoking and diabetes).

Alzheimers

Research shows that exercising increases the size of the hippocampus by 2% (the part of your brain that learns, has memory and emotion). As we age, the hippocampus shrinks by 1.5% a year above the age of 70, so exercise is very important for cognitive function and can help Alzheimers' sufferers.

Happiness

Not only do we have a sense of achievement, we feel fitter and healthier. We also get a surge of positive endorphins that boosts our mood and helps us sleep better at night, which lowers our risk of getting depression or anxiety by 50% than those who do not. Equally, it is a helpful tool for those who already have depression to lift their spirits. I have had so many clients who use outdoor activities as a means of an anti-depressant, with incredible results. Granted, if you are low in mood you won't feel like moving at all, but it's just one step at a time. The greatest athlete started their journey with just one step, and so can you.

Oxidative stress

When it comes to exercising your body, some oxidative stress is created because when you burn oxygen in your body it can produce free radicals. Oxidative stress accelerates cell ageing. Free radicals are unstable molecules in our body. This can result in some DNA damage with excessive Oxidative stress. Free radicals are a normal part of life, but can be an issue if the body cannot cope with the onslaught. This can happen when we endure high amounts of stress, pollution, infection or excessive exercise.

However, there are foods that can reduce oxidative stress. A study was undertaken of people exercising on a treadmill who were given watercress two hours before they trained. The result was that the group had fewer free radicals after the treadmill test than before. After two months of training on the treadmill and eating the watercress two hours beforehand, the participants had no DNA damage. So when you train, eat some watercress! All vegetables help fight free radicals, but it appears that watercress has super powers when it comes to oxidative stress and exercise.

So how should you train?

If you want to follow a particular plan, my award winning book and membership, 'The Body Rescue Plan' has a specific training programme to train your core stability muscles, increase your flexibility, improve endurance and strength through pilates, yoga, interval training and resistance work.

However, first things first, just get into the habit of moving- more!

Yoga

Yoga has a whole host of healing qualities, and will add many benefits to your health care routine in helping your body fight disease.

What I love about yoga is that not only are you strengthening and lengthening your body, but you are not using adrenalin in the process, so there is no pumping up and forcing an energy that perhaps you don't have that day. It's finding your inner chi energy to drive the postural session.

In addition, you are working on your breath, you are giving your organs an internal massage and you are improving the circulation in your body. Yoga is like a moving meditation, in flow state, at alpha level.

Studies show that yoga can help alleviate depression, help with digestive issues (more than traditional exercise can), increase strength and flexibility, improve breathing, improve health in many diseases and issues, and much more.

Yoga and Asthma

In a controlled study, 53 patients with asthma underwent yoga training, including breathing exercises, suryanamaskar, yogasana (physical postures), pranayama (breath slowing techniques), dhyana (meditation), for 65 minutes a day.

This group were then compared with 53 patients from another control group who had the same asthma, were the same age and sex, but they continued to take their usual drugs. There was a greater improvement in the yoga group in the weekly number of attacks of asthma, scores for drug treatment, and peak flow rate.

There are many different types of yoga, but there is something for everyone. I have had people come to my yoga classes from the age of five up to 86! I have had men come in, thinking it was going to be really easy and were shocked at how much of a workout they found it to be, and I have had frail old women come in and been surprised at what their body could achieve.

One of my clients, John, started yoga when he was 65. He was very inflexible and in a forward bend he could barely touch his knees, let alone his toes, but on his first try of a head stand he could it perform straightaway. Actually, there is an advantage to being a little stiff when doing a headstand. I find headstands difficult because I am so flexible and I wobble a lot.

I was 27 when I taught John, and at 65 his headstands were better than mine! But the other beauty about yoga is that it is non-competitive. What other people can do is irrelevant, it's about your own journey. The amazing thing about yoga though is you can improve for the rest of your life. My first yoga teacher was in her 80's!

My own exercise journey began as most people's do, at school. I know from speaking to many clients over the years that school can be the make or break of people's fitness, and for some it can put them off for life. I was naturally talented at physical endeavours like dancing, netball, hockey, swimming and athletics. However, I didn't enjoy competing in groups or teams, so had no interest in PE during the winter months. But when summer came, I flourished at athletics, javelin, discuss and sprinting. I excelled in, and even won, the school record for javelin throwing against 18 year olds when I was just 13.

I am highlighting this because there is always something for everyone in fitness. You just have to find what you enjoy.

Some people are only motivated in group sessions. Others need a personal trainer or friend to push them, and others only want to train alone.

Find your fitness passion!

Posture

If you have muscular pain in your body, it could be contributed to by poor posture. Bad posture is usually derived from our particular life style. Sitting at a desk all day and being on devices too much all result in misalignment of the spine. If you want to heal that part of you, you need to make a conscious effort to change what is causing this problem.

- If you use a laptop regularly at home, buy a separate monitor so your eyes are looking at the screen in alignment with your spine, rather than looking down, or get a separate key board and place your laptop higher.
- If you have a chair that causes poor posture, get a new one. There are specific ergonomic shops that sell orthopaedic furniture.
- Or get a standing desk.
- Work regularly on your posture, pulling your abs in every hour. Breathing will also help with this. If you sit all day, it's hard to pull your tummy in.
- Mobilise and stretch every few hours.
- Breathing correctly will also improve your posture.

What else can you do to improve your posture?

Sleep

Upon meeting clients for the first time, I generally find their most common complaint is that they are stressed and they lack sleep. The good news is there are plenty of ways we can actively improve our sleep, fairly simply, and there are also a lot of things we can stop doing that are making our sleep patterns worse.

Sleeping takes up a huge part of our lives. On average we sleep for 26 years! It is also where our body spends a big proportion of its time in repair and healing, so for our healing journey a good night sleep is vital. Many studies have researched sleep, and the general consensus is that we need around 7-8 hours sleep per night. In an adult, more than nine hours is not healthy, and less than seven hours is not healthy. In fact sleeping for seven to eight hours shows you are less likely to suffer a stroke. However, I would argue that whilst the length of sleep is important, the quality is more important.

There are four stages of sleep:

- Stage 1 N1 = 5% the lightest sleep, around 5-10 mins
- Stage 2 N2 = 45% heart rate starts slowing down, around 40 mins
- Stage 3 N3 = 25% the deepest sleep, delta, deep repair, around 20 mins
- Stage 4 N4 = 25% REM dreaming, heart beat increases, paralysed, around 20 mins

These four stages last between 60 to 90 minutes, each perform different duties and go in cycles throughout the night. Each stage is critical for healing and repair.

N1 is the start of our sleep journey and lasts about ten minutes. This is the lightest part of our sleep, and we can wake quite easily from it if we are disturbed.

N2 is where we spend the largest part of the sleep cycle. Our heart rate starts slowing down and our breathing becomes slower, with our body temperature and blood pressure dropping, this is getting us ready for N3.

N3 is the deepest part of our sleep cycle. It is very difficult to be woken up during this part of sleep. N3 is where our heart rate, breathing and blood pressure are at its lowest, our body is in deep repair and the production of cytokines are released which help reduce inflammation and fight infection. Cytokines relay messages between cells, and are integral in modulating your immune system. Without a decent N3 sleep your immune system is compromised.

N4 is also a deep sleep and where we start dreaming with rapid eye movement taking place. We are only in REM for 25% of our sleep time, and whilst we think we spend the whole night dreaming, we don't. Tissue repair and growth are happening at this stage.

If you don't spend enough time in stages N3 and N4, it can lead to mental health disorders, lowered core body temperatures and low immunity.

Immunity and sleep

As mentioned, cytokines which fight infection are released in N3 part of sleep, but a good night's sleep will also improve the action of the immune T cells as well. In order for T cells to work efficiently, they need a sticky substance called integrin. They literally stick to viruses and then destroy them. Sleep is important for this process because the hormones adrenalin and noradrenalin block the stickiness of integrins and these hormones lull in your sleep. Sleep = sticky T cell power.

So if you are not sleeping well, your T cells lose their ability to stick. You are then unable to fight disease as efficiently. Thus, the worse you sleep, the quicker you will get sick and the harder it will be to fight off illness.

Circadian rhythm and screen time

You probably know by now that your body needs darkness at night to induce sleepy downtime and that allowing bright screen time late into the evening affects your sleep. But did you also know that getting enough daylight in the day is also equally as important to help you sleep at night?

This is because your body runs on its own body clock, its circadian rhythm. Your circadian rhythm is vital to allow the cells and hormones that work in the day to work on their duties, and the ones that work at night whilst you are asleep to work on theirs. The circadian rhythm is influenced by light, darkness and when we eat. Your hormone melatonin regulates the cycle of awake and sleep.

As light and darkness are so integral to how we fall asleep, and how deep our sleep is, it's worth paying attention to. Get outside in the day, allow day light to hit your eyes, take off your glasses and allow the sun to penetrate your skin and face (do not stare into the sun). At night quit the screen time! Incidentally, as we get older, our eyes become weaker so we need more daylight and more darkness at night to instruct the release of melatonin.

Screens such as televisions, mobile phones, computers, or Ipads emit a blue light, and research shows us that this is particularly detrimental to our sleep.

According to Professor Rose Anne Kenny from the book 'Age Proof',

> *"The longer the exposure before sleep (to screens), the shorter the duration of sleep. Email checking has the most striking effect, reducing duration of sleep by one hour if exposure goes from none to four hours."*

The solution?

You can get glasses that block blue light which can improve melatonin levels, but then if you are stimulating yourself with screen time there are also other issues that will affect your sleep. Keep your phone out of the bedroom and have a downtime routine before bed that does not involve screens. It is not difficult, it's just a new habit to create. There is nothing productive about getting something done before bed if it affects your sleep as the next day you will have less productiveness.

Sleep apnoea and snoring

We learnt in the breath chapter in Stage 5 the relevance of nostril breathing, and how some people tape their mouths at night to improve their sleep. This can also help with snoring and therefore sleep apnoea.

Snoring is very related to sleep apnoea. These two conditions usually go hand in hand and should be considered a serious health issue. If you snore, take measures to help to prevent it with nose tape, mouth tape and other things from your pharmacy that can help.

Losing weight can also be a big consideration when it comes to snoring. Snoring also interrupts your sleep, and without it you will wake up feeling a hundred times better.

What foods to eat and avoid for sleep

Caffeine is an obvious food (or drug, I should say) to avoid if you want to improve your sleep. Studies show that it stays in our system for at least ten hours, if not more, and that if you do not want it to affect your sleep you should stop drinking it at least five hours before going to bed. However, in my own practice I have seen many thousands of people quit caffeine and transform their health and their lives.

The problem with caffeine is that people rely on it for energy, so it is not just the fact that it's a stimulant and has raised your energy artificially with a boost of adrenalin you don't actually need. Also, you haven't understood why you are tired in the first place, and in the first instance dealt with your body's needs. When our body says it is tired, it is usually because it needs nutrients, water or rest. The problem is we give it none of these and have a drink that strips us of nutrients, makes our sleep worse, and is a diuretic, so dehydrates us. The same goes for sugar. If you have to have caffeine, have it earlier in the day rather than later and drink more water to compensate.

However, I usually recommend having a green smoothie first thing in the morning so that your body starts the day with vital nutrition rather than something that messes with your blood sugars all day long. This green smoothie will also help you need less caffeine and sugar cravings too - another drug that will interrupt your sleep.

My clients report that having this green smoothie in the morning improves their sleep at night ten-fold in just a few days!

Green Goddess Smoothie

Ingredients

- ½ Avocado
- ½ - 1 tablespoon of wheat grass (or use green veg)
- ½ - 1 tablespoon of spirulina (or use green veg)
- 2 cups of coconut water
- 1 - 2 cups of frozen or fresh berries

Put it all in a blender and serve!

"*I am sleeping more soundly, but also more importantly for me I no longer have the afternoon slumps!*"
Beth Milner

"*I felt so much more energised and didn't suffer from the usual daily slumps!*"
Clare Kavanagh

In terms of when to eat, there are various studies to suggest that eating within an 8 to 12 hour time frame during the day is optimal for health. Therefore you want to go to sleep in a fasted state from about 7pm. The main reason is because you do not want to go to bed having to digest a heavy meal as it interrupts your sleep. This does not suit everyone though, especially if you have low blood sugar levels, and in any case eating some foods before bed can induce sleep.

Foods that bring on the production of melatonin and serotonin are:

- Bananas
- Almonds
- Kiwi
- Rice
- Milk
- Cottage Cheese
- Fatty Fish
- Tart Cherry Juice
- Porridge
- Vitamin D
- Omega-3

So if you need a late night snack, opt for these over something that will wake you up and be difficult to digest. I personally would not have porridge before I go to bed as it's very heavy, but half a banana suffices for me.

If you want to induce sleep without food, you can choose herbal teas.

Chamomile has an ingredient called apignen in it, which binds brain receptors to help you feel sleepy. You can have this as a herbal tea.

Lavender
You can drink lavender tea or use lavender oil on your skin or put a few drops on your pillow at night. Lavender is a very powerful anxiolytic (re-

lieves anxiety) and a sedative which then induces sleep. This is because it interacts with a neurotransmitter GABA which softens the nervous system activity, thus reducing anger and restlessness and helping you relax. It really works a treat too! I rub a little bit of oil on my hands and just under my nose every night and so does my daughter.

Other teas that also help you relax and improve sleep are:

- Passion Flower tea
- Valerian tea
- Lemon balm
- Magnolia Bark

When to exercise with sleep in mind

If you exercise at night you will stimulate your adrenalin hormone and feel over hyped for a few hours afterwards. If you have to exercise at night, make a conscious effort to wind down after, doing some deep stretches, deep breathing and having a warm bath in dim lighting, with lavender oil and a cup of chamomile tea.

Other reasons you can be over awake is the chatter in your head and too much energy in your body. Meditating can be a useful tool for teaching your body that it's now chill down time.

Improved sleep helps you mentally and physically improve your health, and can just take a few tweaks to increase the depth and length.

Nutrients
- Foods that heal

In all the sections in **the healed state** my aim is to make the information as easy to digest as possible. I have researched thousands of studies, studied many courses, read through many hundreds of books and have 26 years of experience in helping people heal - so I can sum up, and help you in an easy and effective way as possible. I want you to heal!

Nutrition is my passion. It has saved me and many clients from many hideous debilitating diseases and ailments. If you want a more detailed plan to boost your nutrients with delicious recipes you can sign up to 'The Body Rescue Plan.'

I have already brought to your attention how to feed your gut micro-biome, how to eat to help your breathing and even how to eat to feed your vagus nerve. This is a great start and even if you just focused on these things, they would have a dramatic effect on healing your body, resulting in more balanced hormones, balanced mood, better digestion, better skin and more energy.

When we look at what we put in our mouth, there are four things to focus on for healing:

- **Lowering inflammation** (avoiding toxins, adding anti-inflammatory foods)
- **Aiding your digestion** (feeding your micro-biome, avoiding toxic foods)
- **Giving you good energy** (nutrients in, toxins out)
- **Adding hydration** (choosing water based foods and water)
- **Tasting delicious** (never missing out on pleasure)

Really, that's it, because when you focus on these, they will have a knock on effect on the rest of your mind, body and soul.

The main focus I offer clients is not to look at calories, but to look at nutrients and if you want to lose weight, don't worry it will still happen!

Calorie counting is hopeless

The issue with most people is that they are nutrient poor, and that is why their body is not healing or losing weight in the way they want. So counting calories can be a hopeless task because it does not make you eat more nutritious food, if anything it makes you eat lifeless food that is flavoured with processed sugars and artificial sweeteners just so the fat can be sucked out and it can taste of something.

Picture this - you are eating a packet of crisps, plus a chocolate bar versus a vegetable risotto. They may have the same calories, but the junk snack will raise your blood sugar levels and drop them dramatically, so you crave sugar all day. It will affect your sleep so you crave food the next day, will affect your mood, will only temporarily satisfy you and has no nutrients, so your body is in a nutrient deficit, which means you will crave more sugar because you will be exhausted. Whereas the risotto will give you energy for a few hours, will replenish your body, help you fight disease, help you sleep and feed your muscles and cardiovascular system. The junk version is also addictive and can lead to other addictive cycles in your life.

So reading calories does not serve you.

Instead think about how to heal your body with nutrient dense foods that taste delicious.

Vegtables and Fruit

We all know fruit and vegetables are good for us, but if you want a power house of nutrients, think colour.

The colour in fruit and vegetables comes from phytochemicals which are natural bioactive compounds and these promote healing. The brighter the colour, the richer the plants are in vitamins, minerals, fibre and antioxidants. So think red onion over white onion, sweet potatoes (red) over white ones, red cabbage over white cabbage, red apple over yellow apple. Whilst the duller plants have nutrients as well, the colourful plants can boast over 100% more nutrients.

And we know that all plant based foods, particularly fruit and vegetables are high in fibre, which help your digestion and promote a healthy micro-biome.

If you want to feel better and look better, if you need help with your immunity or digestion you cannot ignore the food you eat. It's either healing you or causing you harm. Food has the ability to do both.

If you struggle eating fruit and vegetables or your children do, making smoothies, juices and soups is a great way to pack a punch with a large nutrient dish.

You want to have at least five servings of fruit and vegetables a day, so if you have to liquidise them to get them down your gullet, then do.

Green vegetables (broccoli in particular) are the highest nutrient vegetables you can have. In fact, you can reduce your cancer risk by up to 40% by eating three to five servings of cruciferous vegetables each week!

Common cruciferous vegetables are:

- Arugula
- Bok Choy
- Broccoli
- Brussels Sprouts
- Cabbage
- Cauliflower
- Collard greens

However, even better than broccoli, are broccoli sprouts. These are sprouts that germinate from seeds after a few days of watering and contain 100-400 times the content of sulforaphane than broccoli itself. Sulforaphane may help reduce the risk of cancer because it suppresses inflammation in our body.

Berries (blueberries and blackberries are the most nutrient dense) are the highest nutrient fruit you can have, which is why I have a green smoothie every morning. Incidentally, frozen berries have almost as many nutrients in as fresh ones!

When you eat more fruit and vegetables you will improve your digestion, skin, sleep, immunity, energy, reduce disease and fight disease.

Herbs and Spices

Herbs and spices are also highly nutritious, and make dishes taste tantalisingly more tasty. Rather than slathering on thick sauces that are packed with sugar and artificial garbage, use fresh or dried herbs and spices!

What is the difference between them? A herb is the green leafy part of the plant. A spice tends to come from the root, stem, fruit bark or flower of the plant.

Tumeric in particular has vast healing properties, so much so that there has been over 5000 published articles in medical literature about this exquisite spice. Turmeric has also been used for the last 4000 years in ayurvedic medicine.

Curcummin is the healing compound found in turmeric, and according to Dr Michael Greger in his book 'How Not to Die', he says *"We have seen how curcummin may play a role in preventing or treating lung disease, brain disease and a variety of cancers, including multiple miloma, colon cancer and pancreatic cancer."*

It is also good at treating rheumatoid arthritis, osteoarthritis, lupus and inflammatory bowel disease.

To eat turmeric you can add a teaspoon to your smoothie, add it to curries, or sprinkle on your salad. However, turmeric becomes much more absorbent in the body if you add a pinch of black pepper with it. This slows down the absorption rate and makes us absorb up to 2000 times more. So when having turmeric, always add black pepper too.

Turmeric is one of the highest anti-inflammatory foods on the planet, so any inflammation your body might be battling with (and we all do, daily) it will benefit.

Another easy way of having turmeric is to buy it whole from your supermarket (it looks similar to fresh ginger but is redder inside and smaller) and juice it (if you have a juicer), adding it to some fresh juice. I like a ginger, lemon and turmeric shot! I put them all through my juicer and then poor into ice cubes. I then have 2 ice cubes in my water daily. EASY!
Remember to add black pepper too!

Or just use powdered turmeric, black pepper and powdered ginger and juice some lemon.

Amla

What does it help? The highest antioxidant food on the planet is the amla plant. Rids heavy metals, good for memory, balances blood sugars.

How to use? You can have amla fresh (also known as the Indian gooseberry) or as a powdered herb. Add it each morning to the green smoothie I showed you and you will get 30% more nutrient hit from just a teaspoon!

Echinacea

What does it help? Helps boost immunity, especially against colds and viruses.

How to use? You can eat echinacea fresh, but for medicinal purposes it's better to have in tablet form because its more condensed.

Mint

What does it help? Aids digestion and freshens bad breath.

How to use? Add fresh to smoothies, salads, as a tea, in fresh drinks, with strawberries and sugar free chocolate.

Ginger

What does it help? Aids digestion and is anti-inflammatory.

How to use? Have fresh or powdered in smoothies, salads, curries, as a tea or with sushi. Also nice in sweet dishes like biscuits and cakes.

Chives

What does it help? Rich in antioxidants which improve heart health and fight cancer.

How to use? Have fresh sprinkled on soups, in salads, with fish, in sauces.

Basil

What does it help? Basil helps fight oxidative stress and inflammation in the body.

How to use? Have fresh or dried in tomato based dishes, in pesto, and salads. Also lovely with water melon.

Rosemary

What does it help? Helps alleviate muscle pain and boost immunity.

How to use? Use fresh or dried in fish, in stews and on roasted vegetables.

Coriander

What does it help? Lowers your blood sugar levels, promotes heart, brain, skin, and digestive health and helps fight infections.

How to use? Lovely in curries, soups and salads fresh or dried.

Cinnamon

What does it help? Is also a fantastic anti-inflammatory spice.

How to use? Use in sugar free biscuits and cake recipes, sprinkled on yogurt or porridge.

Cayenne Pepper

What does it help? Stomach infections and viruses.

How to use? Curries, chillies, dips, sauces or in hot water with a splash of lemon, ginger and garlic to help fight off colds and bugs.

Saffron

What does it help? Saffron makes you happy. Twenty four randomised controlled trials show it increases happiness as much as anti-depressants, without the negative effects. Anti-depressants can lower your libido, saffron raises it.

How to use? Saffron tastes sweet and floral, so goes with sweet and savoury foods. Nice in seafood, meat stews, and also in ice-cream! You can also add it to your smoothie. I have a delicious sugar free, vegan rice pudding recipe below using saffron.

Here are two delicious recipes from 'The Body Rescue Maintenance Plan' book using herbs and spices.

Vegan Saffron Rice Pudding

Serves 6
Ingredients

- ¼ teaspoon of saffron threads
- 8 oz / 225g / 1 cup Arborio rice
- 1 vanilla pod (split)
- 1 tbsp (or to taste) rice syrup, honey, or maple syrup
- Pinch of salt
- 2.75 pints / 1.6 litres / 7 cups almond milk

To serve:
Raspberries and blackberries

Preparation Method

- Toast saffron in a dry skillet for 30 seconds. Remove from the heat and crush into a powder with a spoon.
- Whisk together the crushed saffron and almond milk.
- Put all the ingredients apart from the milk into a saucepan.
- Cook the rice on the hob, adding the milk gradually, and stirring frequently. (It takes around 25 minutes.)
- Serve warm, with the berries on top.

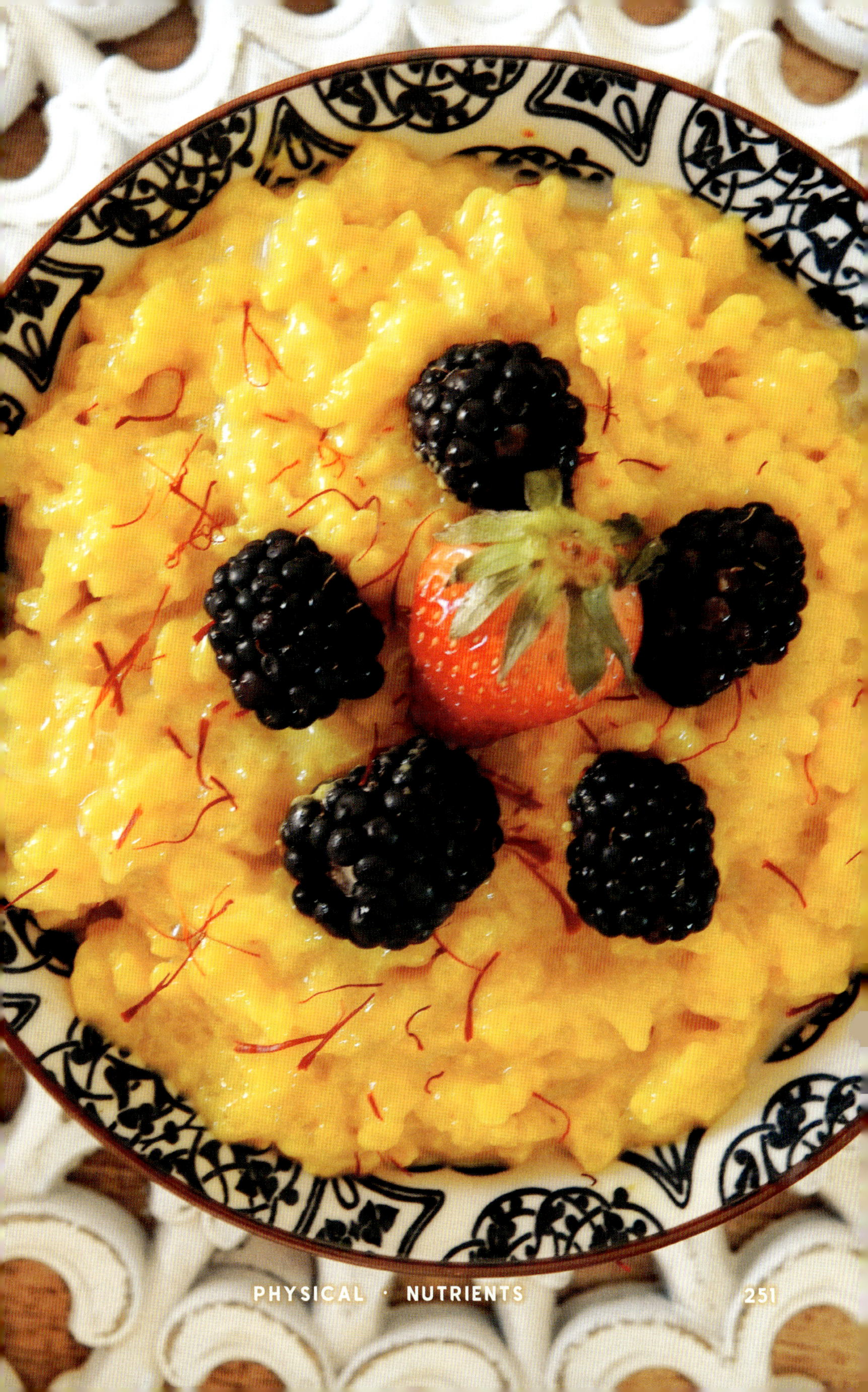

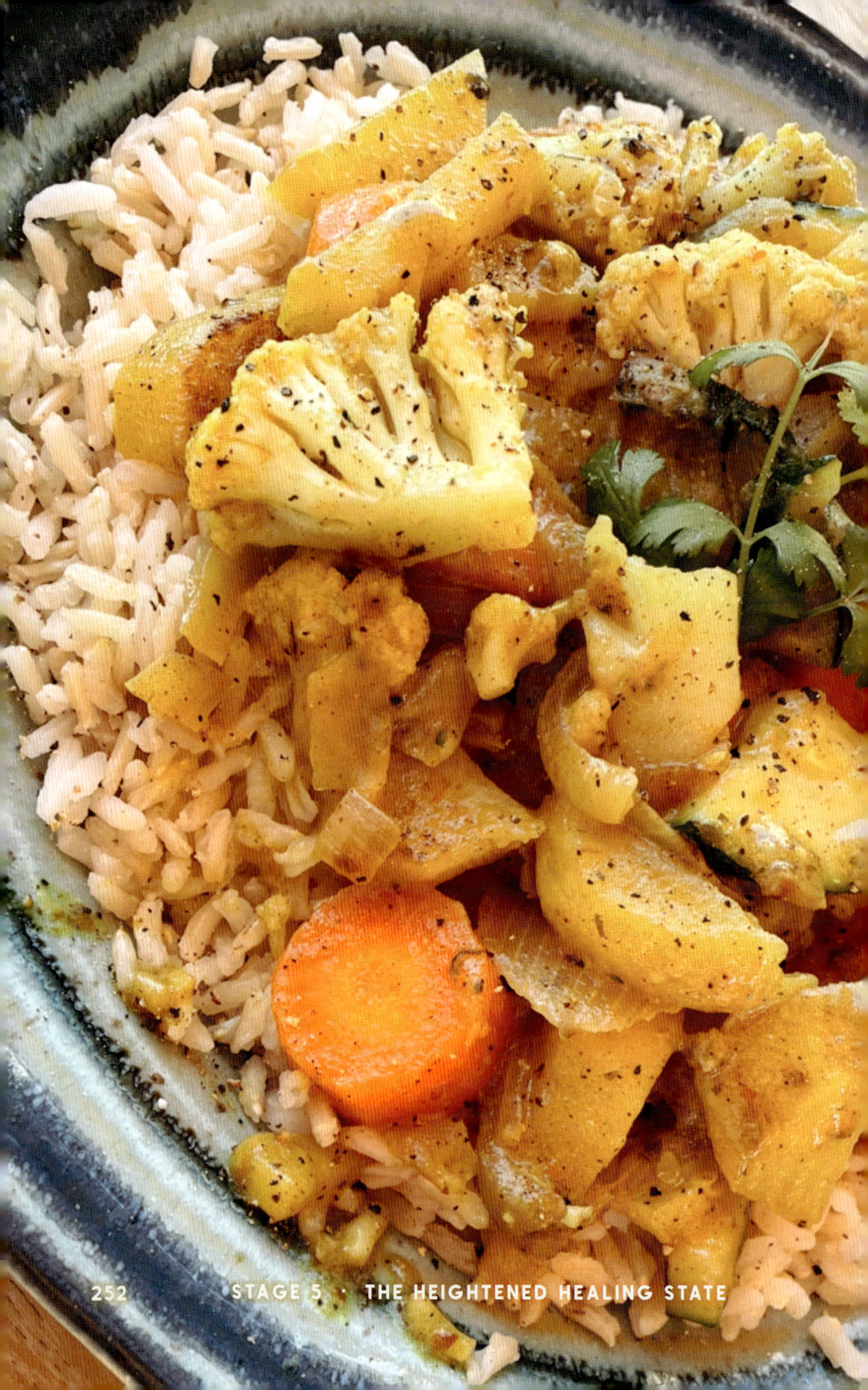

Vegetable Korma

Serves 4

Ingredients

- 1 tbsp coconut oil
- 1 dried red chilli, minced
- 2 onions, finely chopped
- 1 tsp ground coriander
- Pinch of ground black pepper
- 1 tsp turmeric
- 1 tsp garam masala
- 1 small cauliflower, separated into florets
- 2 carrots, cut into chunks
- 1 courgette, sliced
- 2 potatoes, peeled and cut into chunks
- 1 large can (400 ml) coconut milk
- Fresh coriander, chopped
- 10 oz basmati rice

Preparation Method

- The curry will take around half an hour to cook, so put the rice on to cook, timing it to be ready at the same time.
- Heat the oil in a saucepan and sauté the onions for 5 minutes. Add the chilli and spices and cook for a further minute.
- Add the vegetables and cook for 2-3 minutes, stirring to ensure they are evenly coated with oil and spices.
- Add the coconut milk and cook for a further 10-15 minutes, until the vegetables are tender.
- Garnish with coriander and serve with the basmati rice.

Other food groups

Carbohydrates - Gives you energy.
Eat whole grains over white processed rice, flour and pastas. Aim for around a fist size a day. Good carbs give you energy for a few hours, processed carbs will give you energy for 30 minutes and then send you crashing. So choose brown carbs - oats, millet and quinoa are particularly good.

Fats - helps you absorb Vitamin A, D and E.
Go for nuts and seeds as your main source of fats. Walnuts and almonds are the highest in nutrients. Walnuts contain alpha-linolenic and linoleic acids which are a natural anti-inflammatory for the body. Chia seeds are fantastic for your digestion and energy. Flaxseeds are high in Omega-3.

Protein - to build and repair tissue, bones, muscle cartilage and skin.
Legumes, eggs and fish are your best source of protein. Legumes will make you feel fuller for longer, so are great for weight loss. Lentils are rich in iron and folate and can also help to balance blood sugar levels and help with preventing weight gain.

Dairy - building bones, aids heart, muscles and nerve function.
Yogurt, cheese, milk and butter are high in calcium but so are green vegetables! Collard greens, bok choi, kale and broccoli are good sources of calcium!

Menopause
Due to menopausal hormonal changes, women's bones can weaken, sometimes leading to postmenopausal osteoporosis. You can get calcium from green vegetables, yogurt and calcium-fortified products like plant milks.

During menopause and post menopause women should consume 1200 mg of calcium a day (if you are not menopausal you need around 1000 mg a day).

- 1 cup broccoli is 42mg of calcium.
- 1 cup of raw spinach is 29 mg of calcium
- 1 tbsp of Poppy seeds is about 127 mg of calcium
- 10 whole almonds are 50mg
- 1 cup yogurt is 245mg
- 30g parmesan cheese is 300mg
- 120g tofu is 200mg
- 50g sardines (canned) is 200mg
- 6 dried Figs are 300mg
- 8 dried apricots are 50mg

So if you had six figs, two cups of yogurt, two tbsp seeds, two cups of broccoli and ten almonds a day you have your required amount of calcium.

Vitamin D

Your body needs Vitamin D to absorb calcium. You can find vitamin D in fatty fish like salmon, eggs and also via exposure to the sun.

Salmon is rich in both Vitamin D and Omega-3 fats, which are essential for menopausal women.

Vitamin D is also associated with reducing the risk of early menopause, it enhances the immune system and helps reduce depression, moodiness, and sleep problems.

It can also help with mental fog. Get in the sunlight!

Omega-3

Fats that contain Omega-3 fatty acids are particularly important to have during menopause, as research shows that Omega-3 fats help reduce hot flashes.

Studies have also shown healthy fats play a role in balancing mood disorders.

You can find these healthy fats in olive oil, avocado, fatty fish, nuts, and seeds - particularly flaxseeds. Flaxseeds contain Omega-3, fibre, B vitamins and phytoestrogens. A study of 140 women found decreased menopausal symptoms after three months of eating flaxseeds. Another study found an increase in eating flaxseeds reduced hot flashes.

Foods that harm

Processed Sugar

We will end the nutrition chapter and the physical part of Stage 5, with Sugar! Oh yes, my favourite subject.

If you did not know by now processed sugars are not good for you and it's a funny thing to say this now, as only a few years ago I would get responses like:

' We need sugar to live ' or *' I would die if I gave up sugar '*
' How do you get your energy if you don't have sugar '
' Sugar is natural, so no harm can be done '

Out of everything I have taught over the last 26 years to help heal my clients, by far the greatest thing, with the most dramatic affects is quitting sugar - and the healing is extremely fast too!

The reason processed sugar is not so good for us is because it:

- is addictive
- sends blood sugars through the roof and then make you crash
- makes you crave sugar over vital nutrients so you become nutrient poor
- robs you of nutrients just to process it
- affects your sleep
- affects your digestion
- ages your skin
- dehydrates you
- adds inflammation
- contributes to disease in your body
- makes you sick, ages you and kills you!

I started helping people quit sugar in 1996 after I experienced my own health issues as a child.

As a youngster I took a whole host of antibiotics for years due to bladder issues. By the time I was a teenager I had serious digestive problems, mental health issues and could barely focus on anything.

When I was 16 my elder sister who was studying to be a naturopath doctor suggested I try a series of colonics and quit sugar, which I did and It honestly transformed my life.

Suddenly I could focus again, suddenly I could actually go to the toilet every day, suddenly my skin was clear, suddenly I didn't feel depressed for no reason, suddenly I had amazing energy. It was an absolute revelation for me.

This was in 1988. There was zero information out there at the time, there were no cute sugar free snacks, I had to do a lot of the leg work myself. This led to a passion for mental and physical wellbeing and set my path in the wellness industry.

Why go sugar free?

I've been helping people go sugar free for the last 26 years and I've seen first-hand people improve their skin, their sleep, bloating, weight loss, joint pain in just a matter of days of quitting the white stuff.

Also hormonal issues such as hot sweats, bad skin, moodiness, fatigue, pain, symptoms reduce or disappear in just a matter of days.

Scientific studies have also shown that processed sugar is a toxin for our bodies. It can cause or exasperate disease, cancer, type 2 diabetes, heart issues and it's extremely inflammatory for the body.

As it's legal, we all think it's fine for us, and for some people it may be, but most people are in an addictive cycle, using it to wake us up, using it as a pacifier, using it when we are bored and when we are celebrating. And of course because it tastes so damn good!

This starts as a habit and leads to an addiction. The problem with using sugar in this way is that it becomes like a drug, which then weakens us, mind body and soul.

Sugar is both mentally/emotionally addictive and physically addictive.

I've helped 100,000s of people quit their addictive cycle with sugar and other toxic foods, I've helped the most hardened addicts who said they would die if they gave up sugar! They didn't die - in fact they have never felt so alive.

Quitting sugar not only helps rid you of disease and improves your energy and weight loss, digestive issues and hormonal issues. It also wakens up your senses. Imagine that- you are addicted to sugar because of the high you get when having it. It opens up your dopamine train.

But then every time that dopamine hit happens, your dopamine receptors weaken, which means you need more sugar to get the same high. Once upon a time you may have got a high from one piece of chocolate, now you need a truck load to be satisfied.

Sugar also dulls your senses. Your tastes buds change when you have it, you can't taste other foods as efficiently, so you need the strongest flavours in your mouth to become satisfied.

Within just five days of quitting sugar you actually really notice the difference in flavours, you become much more cultured in your cuisine.

And not only does this affect your taste, it affects all your senses.

Looking through life with an addictive lens means you don't feel anything deeply, except of course the deep feeling of loss and sadness when you don't have your sweet sugar.

You become on a loop.

Life is rich with abundant flavours, deep colours, beautiful aromas, enticing sounds and sensual things to touch. We don't feel any of those senses deeply when we are addicted to a drug. We just feel high when we have the drug and low when we don't have it- that's it. Every time we have that drug it weakens us and it also makes us prone to other addictions, our pattern has formed.

Now you may be reading this thinking that you don't actually have an addiction to sugar. In fact, you might not even like sweet flavours, but you just want to get healthier and that's fine too. Although you might not be addicted to processed sugar, the point is that sugar is in so much of what we consume.

Most packaged food, even if it's savoury, contains processed sugars. Sugar comes in many different guises, such as:

- Fructose
- Dextrose
- Sucrose
- Corn Sugar

In fact most things ending in 'ose'

When I'm suggesting you quit sugar, I'm talking about processed sugars which are also known by the above terms.

Artificial Sweeteners

I would also suggest you give up artificial sweeteners as they are equally damaging and also addictive. These have even more names:

- Sucralose
- Spender
- Aspartame
- Acesulfame K
- Saccharin

To name but a few.

Artificial sweeteners used to be considered safe because they were unable to affect the body. This is because your body can't physically digest them, so they exit out within the faeces.

However, there is now increasing evidence to show artificial sweeteners alter your gut microbiome, which as you now know causes an onslaught of physical and mental issues, if disrupted.

They also have cancer risks too. Current medical news states:

> *"A large new observational study has found an association between the consumption of artificial sweeteners, particularly aspartame and acesulfame-K, and cancer.*
> *The study found a 13% higher risk of cancer in general, with the highest likelihood of developing breast cancer and cancers related to obesity, for people consuming large quantities of artificial sweeteners."*

Artificial sweeteners are addictive and can also make you crave sugar!

Natural sweeteners

These are alright in moderation - I suggest about 1tbsp a day max. And also about 1 fist size of dried fruit a day maximum.

If you have issues such as diabetes or candida, (which is a fungus that lives off the sugar you consume), you might not want to have this much. However, I have seen with many previous clients that their overall sweet intake drops dramatically, even if they have fruit because it's white sugar that's addictive.

Natural sweeteners that have nutrients include:

- Honey
- Date syrup
- Yacon syrup
- Maple syrup
- Coconut sugar

Going sugar free is about nutrients in and toxins out.

When you switch to sweetening your body with foods that actually have nutrients in (processed sugar and artificial sweeteners have zero nutrients), you will actually crave sweet stuff in general less, even natural sweeteners.

That's the magic.

I often see sugar free plans suggesting you quit all natural sweeteners, all dried fruit, even all fresh fruit. Yes, these do have naturally occurring sugar in, but so do all plant based foods. But when you focus on nutrients in and toxins out, you naturally consume the right amount because your body doesn't crave the junk anymore because it it's satisfied.

Ahhh, that word 'satisfied!', how often do you feel that? I know, only when you've had a load of sugar, right?

Well, not any more.

Fruit is also high in fibre (processed sugar has no fibre) and because fruit is rich in nutrients, they fuel you effectively, so you don't crave unnecessary amounts . Who do you know that is addicted to fruit?

And by the way, no other mammal eats processed sugar, and there is no requirement for processed sugar in the human diet. Processed sugar gives no feeling of fullness and is acknowledged to be a major factor in causing obesity and diabetes both in the UK and worldwide.

What's wrong with processed sugar?

- It has no nutritional value
- It is toxic for the body
- It causes disease

What is processed sugars found in ?

- Some tinned food
- Most packaged foods
- Some bread
- Some chicken
- Some prawns
- Some smoked salmon
- Some drinks
- Most sauces

Eating the right foods to support going sugar free

I really recommend having my Green Goddess Smoothie most mornings to support you going sugar free. (in the sleep chapter)

Why does this work so well?

- Good fats fill you up!
- Greens are the highest nutrient vegetable
- Berries are the highest nutrient fruit
- Protein - makes you fuller for longer
- Coconut water - replaces lost electrolytes and great for hydration.

This works because you can crave sugar when you are tired, don't have enough nutrients, are dehydrated, don't feel full or don't feel satisfied.

This smoothie combats physical reasons why we crave sugar.

Worried about the sugar in fruit?

Don't be! According to Dr Michael Gregor MD, author of 'How Not to Die'

"Consuming sugar in fruit is not only harmless but actually helpful. Eating berries can blunt the insulin spike from high glycaemic foods, like white bread. This may be because the fibre in fruit has a gelling effect in your stomach and small intestine that slows down the release of sugars or because of certain phytonutrients in fruit that appear to block the absorption of sugar through the gut wall and into your bloodstream, so eating fructose the way nature intended, carries benefits rather than risks."

I have seen this myself thousands of times over when running large online groups with 7000 people in at a time. The feedback from the groups are that within five days of quitting processed sugar (but still having as much fruit as they want) is that the pain in their joints lowers or disappears, skin is improved, bowel movements improve, sleep improves and they lose around 5lb in weight. If fruit sugar and processed sugar responded the same in your body, then they would not notice any changes in five days- all they are doing is quitting processed sugar.

When people go on to give up sugar for 12 weeks or more on 'The Body Rescue Plan', they can reverse digestive issues, T2 diabetes, hideous skin conditions, autoimmune disease, reverse osteoporosis to osteopenia, lower cholesterol from high to low and so much more..

Jacqueline Ann who did The 'Body Rescue Plan' in 2018 said:

"This is my fifth day of feeling NO pain in my body!! Toxins no more!! Always had symptoms of fibromyalgia, was told I had chronic fatigue syndrome.. living my life in constant pain, headache, back pain, pain all over!! Completely gone!! I am pain free. I was living on over the counter medication and popping so many pills without even realising. It wasn't until we did the detox that I realised how many!! I feel alive.. full of energy.. happy.. NO anxiety!"

Gina Pearce also did 'The Body Rescue Plan' in 2018 and reversed her T2 Diabetes into remission, went from high to low cholesterol, lowered her high blood pressure and all whilst having an under active thyroid.

Eileen Brennan couldn't lose more than 10 pounds with every diet plan she had tried- and she tried everything! She had an under active thyroid and chronic IBS. On 'The Body Rescue Plan' she lost 2.5 stone and no longer has IBS.

Lesley Wood did 'The Body Rescue Plan' in 2020. She was 63 years old. She has reversed her T2 diabetes, gone from 13.9 stone to 11.3 stone, lowered her genetic cholesterol and has come off all meds, including statins.

"Today has been an amazing day for me. I had a call from my doctor today, He was giving me my blood results.... He was so pleased to tell me that my diabetes is in remission and as far as he is concerned my bloods are well within the normal level at a reading of 38, cholesterol figures improved... Liver and kidney function normal.... I cried. I keep saying it but so grateful in finding the BRP."

Eating without deprivation

My favourite recipe to share is my chocolate one! Yes, you can eat sugar free chocolate and it tastes amazing!

Body Rescue Chocolate

Ingredients
- 2 tbsp coconut oil
- 2 tbsp maple syrup
- 2 tbsp raw cacao powder

Preparation Method
- Melt ingredients together on a very low heat and poor into silicon moulds, or ice cube trays, or pour on baking paper or into Tupperware tubs and place in the freezer for 20 mins.
- Eat straight from the freezer.

You can have so much fun with this recipe, add nuts, dried fruit, add peppermint oil or orange oil – get creative!

Cacao

Cacao is very high in antioxidants, is antibacterial and immune stimulating. It improves your brain function, depression, decreases inflammation, fights cancer, helps asthma sufferers and may lower blood pressure. It also reduces bad cholesterol 'LDL.' Cacao is the less refined version of Coco. Coco has fewer nutrients so opt for cacao instead.

Processed Meats

The other food to consider reducing or quitting is processed meats. The World Health Organisation has classified processed meats as a Group 1 carcinogen- which means it can cause cancer. By eating the following, you increase the risk of getting bowel and stomach cancer in particular.

Processed meats are:
- Ham
- Bacon
- Salami
- Frankfurters

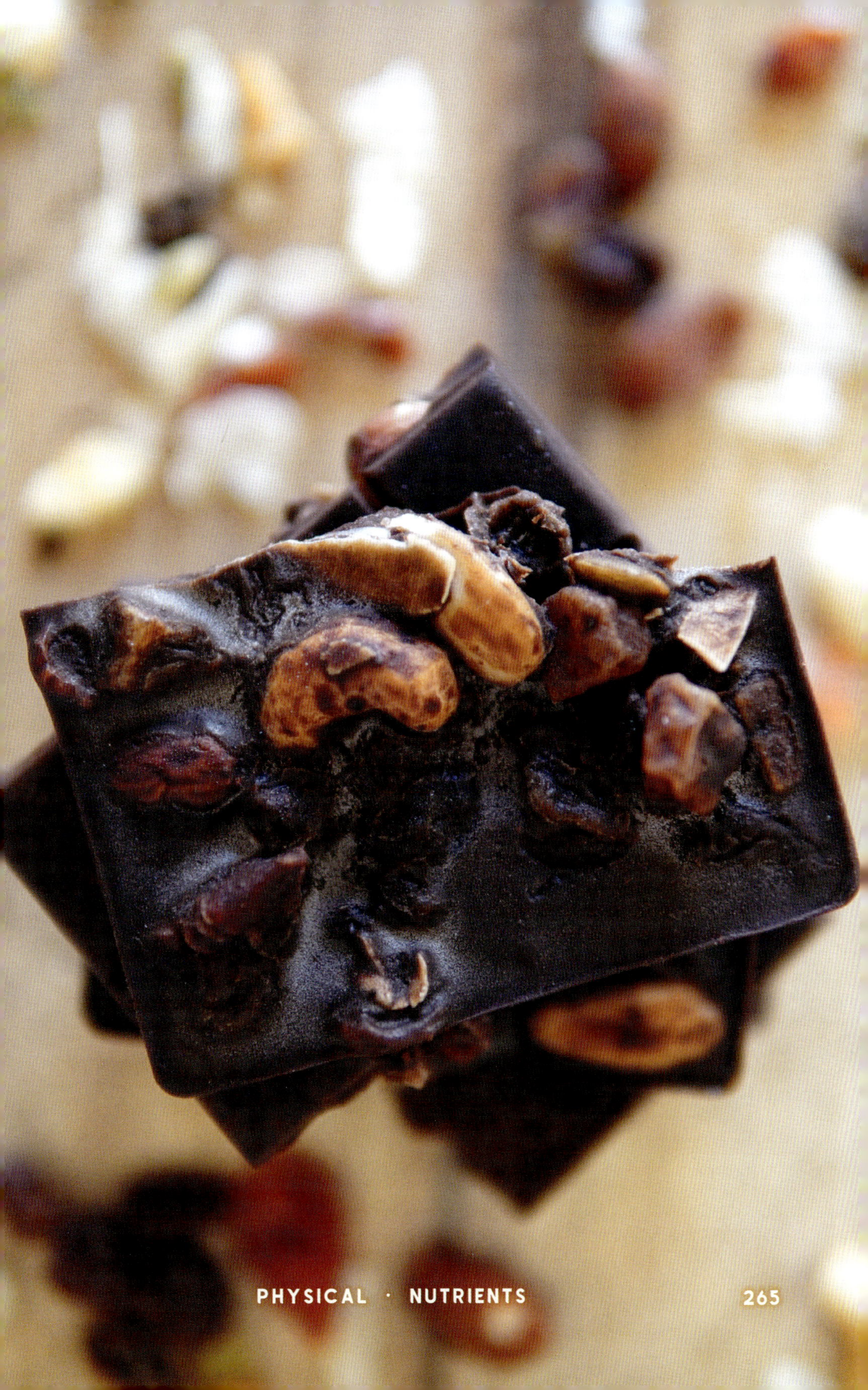

Foods that help heal

Anxiety & Depression	Cancer	Colds & Flu	Digestive Issues	Energy Boosting
Brazil Nuts	Beans	Avocados	Apples	Ashwangandha
Chamomile	Berries	Bananas	Beetroot	Cacao
Eggs	Broccoli	Berries	Chia Seeds	Fish
Fatty Fish	Carrots	Broth	Dark Green Vegetables	Flaxseeds
Lavender	Cayenne Pepper	Coconut Water	Fennel	Fruit
Leafy Greens	Cinnamon	Garlic	Fish	Ginger
Live Yogurt	Ginger	Ginger	Flaxseeds	Green Smoothie
Pumpkin Seeds	Legumes	Leafy Greens	Ginger	Leafy Greens
Saffron	Lemons	Live Yogurt	Live Yogurt	Live Yogurt
St Johns Wort	Nuts	Oatmeal	Miso	Nuts
Tumeric	Oregano	Salmon	Papaya	Oats
Vitamin D	Tumeric	Tumeric	Peppermint	Seeds

and prevent disease

Heart Disease Issues	Lung	Memory	Skin Issues	Sleep
Asparagus	Apples	Avocados	Almonds	Almonds
Beans	Beetroot	Berries	Avocados	Bananas
Broccoli	Blueberries	Broccoli	Baobab	Chamomile
Cacao	Brazil Nuts	Cacao	Broccoli	Chickpeas
Chia Seeds	Eggs	Eggs	Carrots	Fatty Fish
Fruit	Edamamae	Ginseng	Kale	Honey
Lentils	Garlic	Nuts	Kefir	Kombucha
Oats	Honey	Oily Fish	Pomegranate	Passion Flower Tea
Oranges	Kiwi	Peanuts	Salmon	Peanut Butter
Peppers	Lavender	Seeds	Tomatoes	Tart Cherry
Spinach	Peppers	Soy	Walnuts	Walnuts
Walnuts	Pumpkin	Whole Grains	Watermelon	Watermelon

PHYSICAL · NUTRIENTS

Mental

Psychiatrist, Dr Daniel Amen, studies the brain through brain scans as he believes that analysing only through words is not enough in his practice. He wants to not only see how the brain looks when the patient begins with him, but also how it looks after treatment to see the progression in the healing process. So this begs the question, is mental health, brain health?

Ways of ageing your brain and causing mental health issues are:

- Lack of blood Flow
- Ageing (lack of learning)
- Inflammation
- Genetics
- Head trauma
- Toxins
- Infections
- Immunity
- Diabetes
- Sleep issues
- Thyroid
- Low mood

Genetics can play a huge role in how our body repairs and heals- you are born with a pre-determined DNA that gets replicated as RNA. This then turns into proteins which govern every detail in how you look, function, and whether you are healthy or diseased. However, we are able to manipulate our genes to a certain point and are not completely controlled by their outcome. But equally, if we say with determination that something negative runs in our family we are affirming it even more so.

Bruce H. Lipton, author of 'The Biology of Belief' explains that our beliefs control our bodies, our minds, and our lives and that we are not determined by our genes, but by our responses to our environment.

"We are not victims of our genes, but masters of our fates, able to create lives overflowing with peace, happiness, and love... A cell's life is controlled by the physical and energetic environment and not by its genes. Genes are simply molecular blueprints used in the construction of cells, tissues, and organs. The environment serves as a "contractor" who reads and engages those ge-

netic blueprints and is ultimately responsible for the character of a cell's life. It is a single cell's "awareness" of the environment, not its genes, that sets into motion the mechanisms of life."

How we respond to our environment in our emotions makes our body physically change. If we perceive something as positive, we release positive endorphins which help our body heal. If we perceive things as negative, our Sympathetic Nervous System switches on and we go into a stressed state where we cannot heal. So how we think and feel has a direct correlation on how our body reacts, despite our genes. It is up to us then to interpret our environment to feed us balance.

There are ways we can help heal our brains even if we have genetic issues.

- Low levels of **Omega-3** fatty acids are associated with a smaller brain, so just by raising the amount of Flaxseeds or salmon can improve the quality of your brain function.

- **Curcumin (in turmeric)** decrease plaques responsible for genetic Alzheimer's.

- **Amla (Indian Gooseberry)** dramatically lowers cholesterol levels. (Cholesterol can reduce blood flow in the brain and there for cause memory issues). Studies have also shown that the high antioxidant levels in Amla that boost immunity and lower oxidative stress, also boost memory and can help other cognitive functions. It also balances blood sugar levels, which is relevant as Alzheimer's is now being referred to as Type 3 diabetes, because of the relationship between blood sugar and brain function. This is very relevant for Amla's healing powers for the brain.

Even with previous head trauma you can help heal your brain through improving sleep, exercising, losing weight, reducing stress levels and increasing nutrition.

Dr Amen also believes that increasing our happiness can be related to improving your hippocampus function in your brain.

Your hippocampus is in the medial temporal lobe behind the eyes, and deals with memory, mood and orientation. It can sustain damage through head trauma, stress, alcohol abuse and nutrient deficiency, but this can also be reversed to some degree and certainly can be improved in healthy people.

And it can be as simple as being kind!

> One study carried out MRI scans on two groups of people. The only difference between the groups was that one group volunteered and the other group were told to come.
> The volunteer group had grown their hippocampus more than the other group. So it appears that altruistic behaviour can improve brain function.

Aerobic exercise also helps promote hippocampal function.

Another study showed exercise increased the size of the hippocampus and enhanced memory retention.

Why does this matter? Because your hippocampus also regulates your mood, so if you look after it, it will look after you. You will be happier as a result.

Rewire the Brain

How to rewire your brain

We are creatures of habits. And those habits are often stemmed to feed our happy hormones.

Happy hormones are known as Endorphins, Dopamine, Serotonin, Adrenalin and Oxcytocin.

Cortisol is the unhappy hormone and kicks in when we are stressed.

You get a rush of happy hormones with different physical or mental applications.

- **Endorphins** when you exercise
- **Adrenalin** to mask pain
- **Serotonin** when you remember good times and get sunlight- this blocks depression.
- **Dopamine** when we are goal oriented
- **Oxytocin** when we feel the love and connection and eating cacao

You get a rush of cortisol when you are stressed.

One of the reasons we can be in an addictive cycle with certain substances or behaviours is because they can fire up all the happy hormones. It gives us a happy vibe and a rush of feel good hormones, which we then subconsciously remember and so every time we feel fear, sadness, pain, anxiety; we are programmed to use the drug (sugar, caffeine, alcohol, stress) to release the happy hormones once again.

How do you combat this?

You just have to do a little rewiring. It's not as difficult as you might think.

With something like sugar you have both a physical and mental addiction. Your body physically depends on the energy and the high, and you mentally depend on the feel good hormones to subdue your stress.

In order to create a new pathway, you have to be very, very conscious of what you want, and why, and then keep repeating the pattern towards it, until the new pathway has been created in your brain. Then you can once again turn on the happy hormones, but in a healthier way.

For instance, if every time you felt stressed you had a green smoothie, or you got up and danced or you meditated, your happy hormones would be released and eventually you will have rewired your brain to think that as cortisol is flooding through the system, you need that green smoothie for the happy release. It's a win, win. You feel happy, but also you don't have any negative side effects of the toxin you have replaced. You can also stimulate the vagus nerve as suggested in Stage 5.

What are your current habits when stressed?

How can you rewire your brain to create new habits when stressed?

Serotonin and oxytocin are also released when we are in a supportive group, or supporting others. Isolation and solitude can exasperate the lack of those feel good hormones, but even if you are in an online group your feel good hormones will still get released. Serotonin is also created in the gut, and the better our digestion and eating habits, the better the release of this hormone, which means we get less depressed.

We release endorphins when exercising. No matter how low you feel, even just a walk will pick up your mood, and when your mood is picked up you are less likely to arouse cortisol.

The three main feel good hormones you want to work on are:

- Serotonin
- Oxytocin
- Endorphins

Motivation versus routine

The second stage of mental is looking at what motivates you to actually want to heal.

There are two types of motivation for healing.

- Intrinsic
- Extrinsic

What Is Intrinsic Motivation?

Intrinsic motivation is when you do something that is healing for your mind and body because you find it rewarding. You are doing this particular activity because you find it stimulating and helpful within its own sake rather than wanting to do it for an external reward. So intrinsic motivation is self-rewarding.

What Is Extrinsic Motivation?

Extrinsic motivation is when you do something that is healing for your mind and body because you want to earn a reward or avoid a punishment. Therefore you are not necessarily enjoying this task or finding it satisfying, you are just to doing it for an external end result.

Which is better?

You might presume that intrinsic motivation is better than extrinsic, but actually both play a good part in our ability to motivate ourselves when we have to make choices for our health. For instance, movement over lethargy, or healthy foods over junk ones.

I use extrinsic motivation for my online groups, particularly with time frames. Creating scarcity means people know they have to complete something in a given time. Therefore they have to focus on it now rather than next week, next month or next year. We can put off healing our bodies because we have got so used to our particular routine, so sometimes we need some extrinsic motivation to say we have to do this now!

I do this in several ways:

- You have a start date
- You have a time frame to do the plan and each week you have to complete something
- You weigh in every Monday
- You are accountable in the group
- You share a recipe you have made in the group
- Praise within the group
- You get rewarded with discounts and gifts

This might motivate you to join a class, or make a commitment to something or someone, even a friend to be accountable to, so you see through your healing journey. Competition with others on a group can also be an extrinsic motivation too, but for others competitiveness is not motivating.

However, over rewarding can be problematic too. If you seek rewards for everything you complete, and get over saturated with competition and extrinsic motivation you can become overwhelmed.

There has to be a balance of intrinsic and extrinsic otherwise self-motivation can go out of the window. Only doing things for an external reward is not healing.

However, interestingly, praise and feedback can improve people's ultimate intrinsic motivation. I also find this with clients in that they will get to a stage where they will fly the nest on their own with all the tools they need to keep going.

Whether you are motivating yourself by intrinsic or extrinsic rewards, or both preferably, the ultimate goal is consistency. This becomes a pattern and a routine so that your life is mapped out with healing behaviours. Sometimes they are easy, like brushing your teeth each morning, and sometimes focus and determination are required, like preparing to exercise or cooking for the week. Regular routine versus sprucing it up a little with rewards can keep you going week by week.

I have seen a recent Tik Tok trend of people saying that you don't need motivation, you just need consistency. But something has to drive consistency and that is intrinsic and extrinsic motivation, coupled with a sprinkling of self-love and self-care.

- What motivates you to heal?
- What rewards can you offer yourself?
- What rewards can you go out and seek?

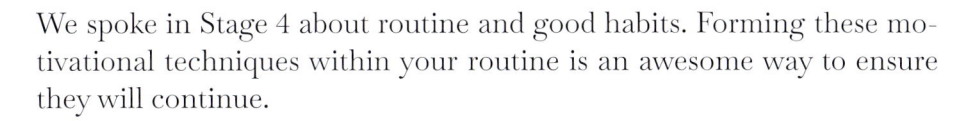

We spoke in Stage 4 about routine and good habits. Forming these motivational techniques within your routine is an awesome way to ensure they will continue.

What is your morning routine that has intrinsic and extrinsic motivation in?

What is your evening routine that has intrinsic and extrinsic motivation in?

When you stay focused on something, you attract it to you. So if you want more healing you focus on it and ways to have it. If you want less pain or destruction, you don't just push that away because you are then only giving it attention. You still focus on the healing.

However, sometimes it's easier said than done. Sometimes you wake up and your focus is chocolate, so then having intrinsic and extrinsic motivation and a routine becomes helpful.

Remember, if you are in the fight, flight or freeze response, ie you have switched on your sympathetic nervous system because of stress, your motivation will change. Get your vagus nerve stimulated first through some deep breathing or humming sounds, then get motivated again.

I love to watch my dogs and how they soak up life. They love routine and tell me when it is time to walk and eat- always at the same time each day. They also love spontaneity too, and will happily welcome an added bit of playtime, cuddles, walk or more food!

Emotional

Trapped Emotion

We have learnt that our body changes its state when stressed, going into fight-or-flight response (sympathetic) or when relaxed into rest, digest, feed and breed response (parasympathetic). With this our body also physically changes.

- In sympathetic you become tense, tight, sweaty, rigid, pulse racing
- In parasympathetic you are relaxed, lose, pulse calm.

In between these states you can get emotional, or at least you should.

A healthy nervous system switches between the two when one is required more than the other, but we should in theory be mainly in parasympathetic throughout the day.

So how can we trap emotions?

When we go into a very stressful state we get a surge of adrenalin and go about fighting the lion. When the lion flees, we then have to process the bodily changes to deregulate and go back to our chilled out state. The deregulation is the release of the adrenalin and it manifests typically through shaking, crying or even laughing.

In a very stressed state most mammals within the kingdom will have an after shock of shaking naturally. But, because us humans are a little more emotionally complicated, we may do nothing and this is where the trapped emotion lies. Because we have an ego, or mixed messages of the emotions we are allowed to show, or we are self-conscious and don't want emotions to be brought up, we can block this adrenalin release.

If we are in a public situation perhaps we don't want people to see we are emotional. We don't want them to see us shaking if we are on stage, we don't want someone to see us cry because it makes us look weak, or we think it inappropriate to laugh because perhaps we are at a funeral.

I know when I was younger I had a hard time crying and would block that emotion. Instead, I would sometimes laugh uncontrollably when stressed. I remember specifically when I was a young teen and my sister told me my Grandpa had died. I could not stop laughing. I was so embarrassed and had no idea why I was laughing, but I could not stop.

Now I know it was because I was upset, and had a rush of adrenalin, but because crying and shaking had been bypassed, laughing is what was left. I wasn't laughing because I found it funny that he had died, I was laughing to release the adrenalin caused from the shock.

If you block the emotion of shaking, crying or laughing after heightened stress you may block emotion internally within your body, and this can be physically trapped within you for years.

We can then manifest pain, issues and disease in our body as a result. Our body becomes like a pressure cooker, the more blocked we become, the more likely we stay in fight or flight too, which then sends us into exhaustion, causing more pain, disease and illness.

Equally, when we suddenly start releasing emotion and we don't know why, it can be because we have released the trapped muscular emotion that we previously blocked. This can happen through massage, exercise, yoga, meditation, even by listening to something triggering like music or certain words.

This can be managed and prevented by regulating our stress through vagal toning as discussed previously, but if you have already blocked emotion into something painful or physically destructive then there are also ways you can release that as well.

One of the ways can be through massage.

According to Mark Olson, PhD, LMT

> *"Emotions are constantly being generated — subconsciously or consciously — in response to the reactivation of memories or unsatisfied goals, The touch to X area is simply a reliable stimulus to reconstruct the pattern associated with that traumatic event."*

Exercise, massage, yoga and meditation can all help release blocked emotion, but even just simple shaking to simulate what your body would have done when adrenalised can also have huge benefits. Shaking sends a message to your body you are now safe, because it is mimicking the aftermath of shock.

If you are revisiting past trauma you may want support during this process.

Bradley Nelson DC, author of 'The Emotion Code' believes trapped vibrations in emotions cause tissues to vibrate at the same frequency. This is known as resonance.

He states:

> *"Each trapped emotion resides in a specific location in the body, vibrating at its own particular frequency. This may cause you to attract more of that emotion, creating a build-up or blockage."*

Emotions also play their part in how we physically hold ourselves and hold on to past or present emotional pain.

The spectrum of negative emotion is:

- Shame
- Guilt
- Apathy
- Grief
- Fear
- Anxiety
- Craving
- Anger and hate

The spectrum of positive emotions is:

- Trust
- Optimism
- Willingness
- Acceptance
- Forgiveness
- Understanding
- Love
- Reverence
- Joy
- Serenity
- Enlightenment

We can choose which emotion to hold onto throughout the day.

Louise Hay author of "You Can Heal Your Life "explains how thoughts create our experiences and that the key to healing is self-love.

> *"The past has no power over us. It doesn't matter how long we have had a negative pattern. The point of power is in the present moment. What a wonderful thing to realize! We can begin to be free in this moment!"*

Other ways to release trapped emotion:

- Tensing and releasing your muscles
- Crying
- Journalling
- Massage
- Stretching
- Breath work
- Floating in water
- Meditation
- Therapy

Another way I show clients how to release blocked emotion that has manifested into pain is to go through the body observing where the pain is, whether in a body scan meditation or just sitting with a pained area. I suggest placing your hand on that area and tuning in, taking deep breaths and then telling that area you are safe now. It is amazing how much physical tension we can release when we mentally tell our body that it is alright.

In Bessel A. Van Der Kolk's book: 'The Body Keeps the Score: Mind,

Brain and Body transformation in Trauma', *"Practicing mindfulness calms down the sympathetic nervous system, so that you are less likely to be thrown into fight-or-flight. Learning to observe and tolerate your physical reactions is a prerequisite for safely revisiting the past. If you cannot tolerate what you are feeling right now, opening up the past will only compound the misery and re-traumatise you further.*

We can tolerate a great deal of discomfort as long as we stay conscious of the fact that the body's commotions constantly shift. One moment your chest tightens, but after you take a deep breath and exhale, that feeling softens and you may observe something else, perhaps a tension in your shoulder. Now you can start exploring what happens when you take a deeper breath and notice how your rib cage expands. Once you feel calmer and more curious, you can go back to that sensation in your shoulder. You should not be surprised if a memory spontaneously arises in which that shoulder was somehow involved."

This is deep work, so please seek help if you need more support.

Placebo and Nocebo

The placebo effect is where health is improved in your body by the power of your mind, thus investing into the thought you will get better. Typically, placebo is referenced alongside clinical trials for drugs or treatments, even fake operations! The patient in the trial is told they will receive something that is potentially healing, but they could be given a placebo (they are not told either way and usually neither is the person administering the drug- this is called double blinded). What is fascinating with placebo is that around 40-50% of people are healed from many chronic conditions.

As discussed in Stage 2, patients can even get side effects from the drugs they are taking, even if they are in fact just a placebo sugar pill.

The power of the mind is still yet to be fully discovered, but what we do know is that you can wish yourself better given the right conditions. In the book 'Mind Over Medicine,' Dr Lissa Rankin explains that placebo can even work when the patient is being told that the pill is a placebo. This is more about the connection between the patient and the healer/medic giving the pill/treatment. Her conclusion through studying the effects of placebo for years is that it boils down to three things.

> 1. If you are naturally optimistic you are far more likely to receive a stronger placebo effect.
>
> 2. That your expectation is what makes or breaks how placebo works.
>
> 3. That support is everything when it comes to the power of our mind.

If we have a good practitioner or healer who makes us feel like we can achieve anything, we more likely will. Then if we can create other good support networks like yoga, church, marriage, family, AA meetings etc, we can take our healing to the next level. However, if it's a bad marriage, a church that judges you, a family that make you feel fear, etc, it will not work.

Dr Rankin also concluded that loneliness is worse for you than smoking and that the antithesis of a support network, ie: living in isolation- can kill you.

Ultimately, the overriding factor in how placebo works is feeling safe. When you are supported, you feel safe. When you feel safe, your fight-or-flight response switches off and your vagus nerve switches back on again. Placebo works when you feel safe and focused because safety is where your body heals.

The power of safety on healing your body is also explained in a very interesting study on a small town in Pennsylvania, called Roseto. Dr Stewart Wolf became intrigued with this town and its Italian immigrants because of their incredible resilience to death! Their death rates were 35% lower than the national average in the 1960s when the research began and there were virtually no heart attacks recorded in men under

65 years old (which at the time was the biggest killer in the US). There were also no suicides, drug addiction or alcoholism, very little crime and no one claimed welfare.

This 15 year study compared Rosetans to inhabitants of two neighbouring towns, Bangor and Nazareth. Despite a high rate of obesity in Roseto, and similar dietary, exercise and smoking habits, the inhabitants of Roseto seemed almost immune to heart disease.

So why were they so much healthier and living so much longer than their neighbouring towns?

The conclusion of the study was that they were healthier because of the old world values and the close knit culture that they had kept integrated in their town. This community spirit and unconditional support counteracts the fight-or-flight response, makes everyone feel safe and in turn lengthened their lives. The Rosetans all ate together, supported each other and many lived with three generations under one roof.

What is fascinating and also sad about this study is that the next generation of Rosetans, who went to universities in other towns, and brought back more modern ways of living, like TV dinners and less community values, became as sick as the national average. The next generation did not hold the elixir of youth anymore and the traditions of Roseta were lost in the new world.

The power of the mind can also create sickness in the body through the opposite of placebo- nocebo!

In 1997 I remember seeing this for myself when I first used to offer consultations in gyms. The consultation would consist of chatting with the client about their needs and then running some simple tests, taking their measurements, heart, blood pressure and a fitness test. It was seemingly basic to me, but to some of my clients it created terrible anxiety. I was warned by my educators that this is called 'white coat' syndrome. The moment that some people see a doctor's white coat they become anxious and their blood pressure goes through the roof. We did not wear white coats, but the uniform and environment did create this strange shock reaction in about 10% of the people I saw. I could tell it was happening because they would look pale, start to sweat, appear nervous and then their blood pressure would be unusually high. So I would take them out of the consultation room, walk them outside, do some breathing techniques until they realised they were safe with me, and then try again. If their blood pressure was still high, they would get sent to the doctor.

Nocebo is as real as placebo. If someone tells you are cursed, you will definitely fail, or any other knock on effect of negativity, you could absorb some of that which then could create a negative physical effect.

Playfulness, joy and wonder

Happiness is the meaning and purpose of life, the whole aim and the end of human existence.
Aristotle

As we have worked through the stages in **the healed state** to ultimately get into a healed state, this should have affected your happiness levels.

Happiness is a very personal barometer to work with, but if we are looking after ourselves living in a state of sensory observation and gratitude throughout the day, the chances are our happiness levels are raised.

Unsurprisingly happiness reveals physical health benefits too.

Scientific studies shows being happy gives you a

- Stronger immune system
- Stronger resilience with stress
- Stronger heart health
- Quicker illness recovery
- Better management of pain
- Even a longer life!

We explored this a little bit in Stage 3 when we looked at anger and forgiveness, but happiness also means you are far more likely to show acts of self-love. This has a knock on effect, it leads to more healing.

- A 2001 study showed that adults who were happier had a 26% less chance of experiencing a stroke.
- A 2003 study by Cohen et al exposed a group to the common cold virus who had previously rated their level of varying happiness and checked on them five days later to see who had contracted the cold. According to this study those who rated themselves happier were less likely to have caught the cold.
- A 2005 study by Zautra, Johnson & Davis found participants with chronic pain had less pain, the more happier they were.

The happier you are, the more engaged with happiness you will be also. So what makes you happier?

We can presume we will be happier when we have more material things, but by contrast we often hear people say 'money doesn't make you happy'. This is an irritating thing to hear when you are struggling to pay bills and becoming ill with stress, but the happiest people in the world are the not the richest, far from it.

Things that may make you happier are:

- Love
- A healthier body
- Gratitude
- Compassion
- Peace
- Music
- Good company
- Good food
- Nature
- Doing an act of kindness

What else makes you happy?

MENTAL · PLAYFULNESS, JOY AND WONDER

We may also think pleasure leads to happiness, but as discovered in the dopamine chapter of **the healed state**, pleasure can lead to less happiness if we are always in the pursuit of the pleasure itself, rather than being happy with our lot.

> *"The ultimate source of happiness is a mental feeling of joy, and not a wealth of material goods. The sensory pleasure material things provide is generally short-lived. Such satisfaction does little to allay anxiety and fear. On the other hand, mental joy sustains itself."* - Dalai Lama

Consciously tuning into joy takes practice and initially it may feel alien to you. You might not have a routine that is centred around a more joyful life, full of wonder. So when looking at your day, rather than thinking about where you can fit joyful activities, think about the majority of your day full of joy and where does everything else slot in. After all, this is what children do, we just lose it along the way being boring, responsible adults. Joy is sacred and should be protected at all costs.

This also means being consciously aware of all the distractions you have built up that are not making you happy, i.e. social media!

A study published in a scientific journal found that the more people went on Facebook, the less satisfied they were.

Remember when we talked about boundaries? Your 'time' fuelling your happiness should be your greatest boundary.

And remember when I said even fake smiling stimulated the vagus nerve to give you a feel good feeling?

Everything we have focused on so far in this book will create more happiness for you, but making a conscious effort to get the feel good factor can negate negativity as well.

The world is made up of energy, good and bad, positive and negative. We can't get rid of one or the other, but we can transmute these energies. So if we have had a bad experience that has made us unhappy, we can create a good experience to negate the bad emotion associated with the negative experience.

Allowing joy is allowing fun and playfulness in your life as we can forget to play. My daughter often asks me to play with her and often I have to refuse because I am working or busy, because I do have set times for work. However, I do break these too, because even though I don't feel like playing when I am in work mode, it's a fantastic mood booster and it re-energises me when I do. It also gives me a heart connection to my daughter and a feel good factor. I mean, as an adult have you ever played hide and seek in the middle of the day? It's hilarious, it's a dumb game that requires no skills, and yet it makes me giggle my head off when I am hiding, especially as I am so bad at it. On the other hand, my husband takes it very seriously, and my daughter loves the family bonding time- if she is happy, so am I.

Some of my clients who have come to me over the last two decades have showed up on their first visit with a seemingly perfect resume of fitness and diet.

They express,

"I eat well, I exercise every day, I do everything right, but I am still sick and over weight?"

When I work with clients I look at every aspect of their life, from fitness and diet, to relationships, sleep, self-love, home life, how they deal with pain and how much joy they allow into their lives. This then dictates to me how much stress is taking over their body and what prescription of joy is needed. If fear and shock can kill you in an instant, joy and laughter can bring you back to life.

Being in a state of joy also requires you to be in a state of awe and wonder. In fact, the word 'wonder', just pontificating about something that's possible, feels so positive.

Gay Hendricks, author of 'The Big Leap' explains this so well:
"Asking that question like how much love am I willing to allow in my life? How much good feeling am I willing to let myself feel? How much wealth am I willing to allow to come into my life? Those are really expansive questions, 'Wonder Questions'.

You put your mind and body, your creative spirit in a beautiful, dynamic tension because you're launching this question that says 'hmmn, here's something I really want to know...' and so when you ask a question like that, the answer becomes the life change that you really want to see and feel in yourself. I give so much credence to wonder questions because almost everything good that's ever experienced in my life has come out wondering like that."

Even the sound *"hmmmm"* takes away fear and stress from a question and allows an opening for joy. And remember noise resonated from *"hmmmm"* stimulates your vagus nerve. So precipitating a wonder question with a soft noise actually relaxes you and opens you up so you become a vessel for happiness and joy.

Hmmmm, I wonder how much more happiness I can fill my body up with?

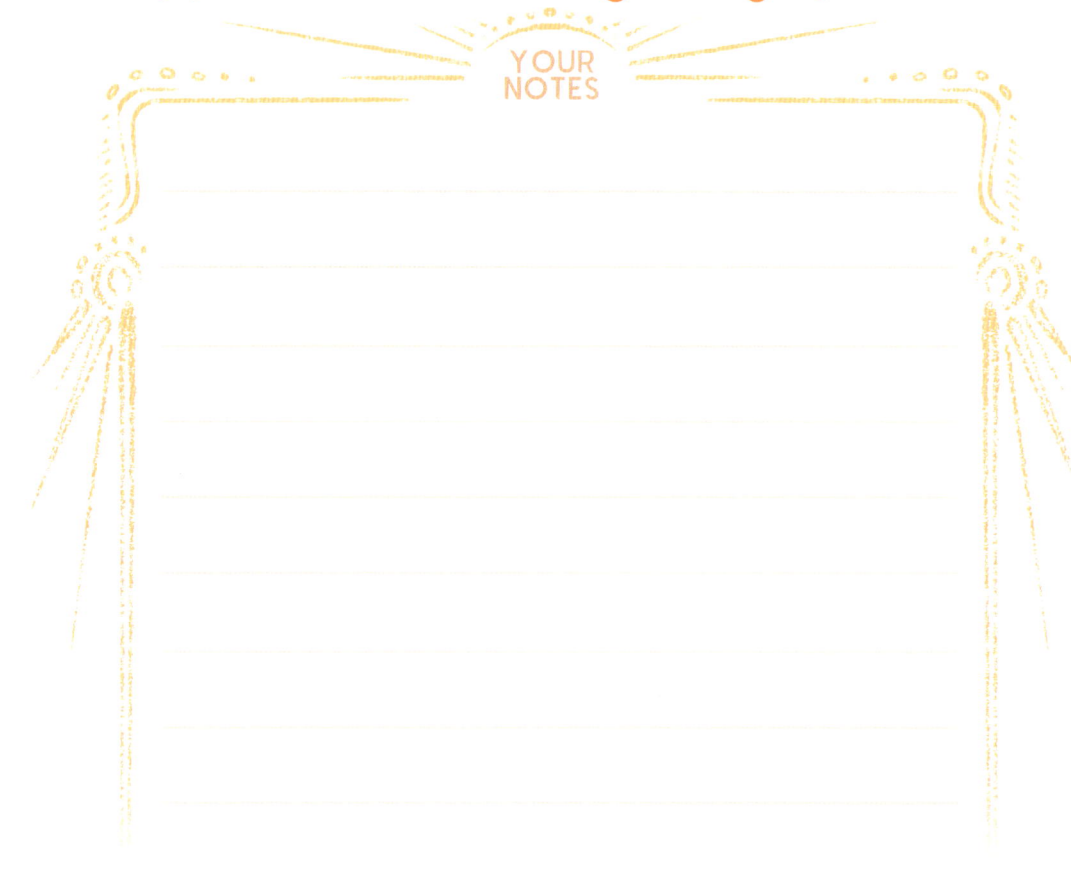

YOUR NOTES

Spiritual

So far in Stage 5 we have observed the Physical, Mental and Emotional aspects of healing ourselves. We now conclude the heightened healing state with the 'Spiritual'.

We have discussed many modalities throughout **the healed state** that lifts your 'spirit' and focuses more on healing through spirituality. There are two more prevalent areas I want to share with you that have helped me in my healing world.

In the many self-help books, courses and mentoring I have received over the years, there has been a running theme that spiritual energy, a spiritual belief system, heals. Even scientists agree that having a belief that we are somehow looked after, makes us feel safe, which you have learnt by now allows your body to thrive.

Spirituality looks different to everyone. Some may believe in God, others may believe in the power of the universe, but one thing we can all agree on is that life is a mystery and there are so many ways we can uplift our souls and lighten our spirit. It's worth taking the time to do so.

Meditation, praying, being in nature, being in flow, altruism, all help you get there.

The Heightened Flow State

In Stage 4 we spoke about the flow state, which is where your area of focus allows all distraction, pain, fear and anxiety to disappear, and you are in connection to heightening your senses for the thing you are focusing on.

You are totally in tune, absorbed and in love.

As we come towards the end of Stage 5, we are going to focus more on manifesting more healing into our lives, however that may look.

- We all manifest everything to us, whether intentionally or not

- We can manifest positive and negative energy, rich or poor.

- We can sometimes focus on one thing we want and get another, because actually that is what we need.

- We can get into a negative energy state, and focus on all the negative energies coming our way.

- We do have a choice in this. It's up to us what we want more of.

Do we want more healing, more of what makes our soul sing?

Or do we keep wanting to suffer, because that is all we know?

What are you most committed to? Whatever it is, you will get more of it!

I know you want to heal. You want those mountains in the road you have to climb to smooth out, so your pathway is a treasure chest of abundance.

So you can breathe each new exciting chapter in your life, without suffering consequences.

And so here we are feeling the good again, appreciating our life for all that it has given us, and we are ready to manifest our dreams.

I have coined the phrase 'Heightened Flow State' for raising the bar one step higher with the flow state.

This is actually a really fun exercise to do. It's very easy and it works miracles!

The heightened flow state is where you create a dream, wish or want in your mind's eye through a conversation that explains it has already happened. Whilst you are speaking, you are becoming really charged up and excited about what you 'have' already achieved, but actually in reality it hasn't happened yet. A kind of 'fake it before you make it', but with far more elegance and magic.

This exercise is easier to do with someone else, but you could also do it alone writing a diary, having a pretend conversation or even talking into a camera about 'what happened'!

You are not pretending something different happened in your past as of now, you are setting yourself in the future and then talking about the past between now and then.

> The reason why this is so powerful is that your body, mind and soul starts to believe it, and sends the vibrational message to your subconscious that all thoughts and actions go towards this vibration rather than towards the vibration of fear and self-doubt.

I have carried out this particular practice with many clients over the years with incredibly healing results. You can actually do it at any part of your journey, but because it needs a good charge of positive energy attached to it I have chosen to place it in Stage 5 so that some ground work has been covered beforehand.

One of the most joyful examples of my heightened flow state I can remember was about ten years ago whilst travelling to LA with my sister, Marie-Francoise.

My sister and I practiced this heightened flow state quite regularly. We used to do exercises in 'Cosmic Ordering' (which is what Law of Attraction used to be called!) and we would ask each other questions about where we lived, or what our house was like, or what we were doing in our business.

It would always be so fun and so charged with giggly, energetic and excited energy. A lot of healing can feel heavy, releasing, letting go, and focusing, but this way of manifesting is just dreamy and expansive, and at this stage in your healing the expansion wants to reveal itself to you.

Our first trip to LA was not pre-planned. It happened fairly quickly and spontaneously, but we both decided to go with a view to expanding our connections and just seeing what opportunities could be brought to us. My sister was a model and an actress looking to raise the bar in her work, and I was training celebrities and getting into the Press. It was a bit of fun with a bit of networking thrown in.

On our ten hour flight from the UK to LA, we decided to play the 'Heightened Flow State' game after watching the in-flight film 'Magic Mike!' My Sister and I were feeling giddy and silly by this point and it had put us in a hyper mood. We decided to pretend we were flying back to the UK at the end of our five day trip, so we were tuned into the vibration of how we wanted to feel by Day 5 and the experiences which had made us feel that way.

We started asking each other *'what happened on your trip?'* but then turned it into more of a conversation about *'OMG that was amazing when I was introduced to... and they helped me with... and we went to this party.... and I met this person ...'*

We were saying the most outrageous, obscure and totally unfathomable things we could think of that made us roar with laughter like we were drunk on life. Things we wanted to happen in our dreams, but ordinarily may not even vocalise. It felt so real and true because we were both in it together building the story up, and we were sitting on a long plane journey to make it feel real.

When we arrived in LA our energy was high, positive with a feeling of anything and everything is possible, and it really was. Pretty much everything we said 'happened' actually did happen, and the opportunities we were met with were extraordinary.

It is something we still talk about to this day. In fact, our senses were so heightened I even said at one point in LA that I feel like I am about to bump into an old friend who I used to train with at Pinewood on the Bond Movie set. He just manifested on the beach at Santa Monica in the rain five minutes later (I had no idea where he lived).

This charged energy is extremely powerful. It gets you into that flow state where all fear and worry gets pushed aside, and you get laser focused on what you will receive.

It's not '*I want this to happen*', but rather '*It's already happening, or has happened.*'

Your mind does not know the difference between real life and fantasy, in regard to how it should make your body feel.

There are many examples of this, but let's start with the obvious one to get your attention.

SEX!

If you read something arousing, or visualise something sexually stimulating – it's not actually happening to you, but your mind perceives it as happening and so your wonderful vagus nerve helps in giving you a sexual response to your nether regions as if to prepare you for sex.

The same thing happens if you read something emotional in a story. You may cry in response, even though it's not actually happening.

Or you may think of something scary, or watch a scary movie and all your hairs stand on end, your heart beats faster and you feel frightened, but again it is not actually happening to you. It's just fantasy.

So in that respect, our mind does not realise the difference between reality or not.

We can 'fake it till we make it', and our body can change in the process because our energy goes towards success and happiness rather than towards doom and gloom.

We can sometimes notice how strong our imagination is when we wake from a dream. It can feel so real we can wake up feeling attracted to or in love momentarily with a stranger. Or we can feel like we nearly had a car crash and we wake up in fear. But nothing has actually happened except the thoughts in our head.

So if we can turn that around, what possibilities are there for us beyond just getting better?

I will play the same game with you. Imagine that you are in the future, healed, feeling amazing and achieving your dreams.

No time for self-doubts, this is actually happening. Feel it in every fibre of your body and answer the questions out loud.

We are in the future, decide when this is.

- Hi, what is the date?
- How are you? How do you feel?
- What got you to feel so good?
- Can you teach me? I would love to learn?
- What else did you achieve beyond healing your pain?
- What else can you achieve?
- When will you achieve that by?

Notice how different you feel energetically after having answered these questions. This energy, this force, either gets us sick or well. Tune into this from now on and keep allowing this energy in every day!

This is your heightened flow state, this is for you and this will continue to heal you.

Goddess Energy

If you have played The Heightened Flow State game and also started tuning into the 'Flow State' you may already be experiencing different patterns of how you look and feel in your spirit realm.

Your Goddess energy may be revealing itself to you.

When you think of the word Goddess what energy does that display for you?

What kind of energy does she omit?

What would it be like for you to have some of that energy?

For me, quite simply it means that no matter what you look like, what age you are, no matter if you are big or small, wearing a dress or a plastic bag, whether you live in a mansion or a hut, this energy that exudes from you is bigger than any of that. So much so that that your Goddess energy is the biggest thing someone sees in you, over anything else.

Goddess energy, despite its name is not gender based, but rather a way to connect to your divine feminine energy that creates a harmony with your masculine energy.

We have been conditioned by the media and perhaps our upbringing to think that all this other 'stuff' is important and that it confirms our identity.

But what if it does not matter?

How does that then make you feel?

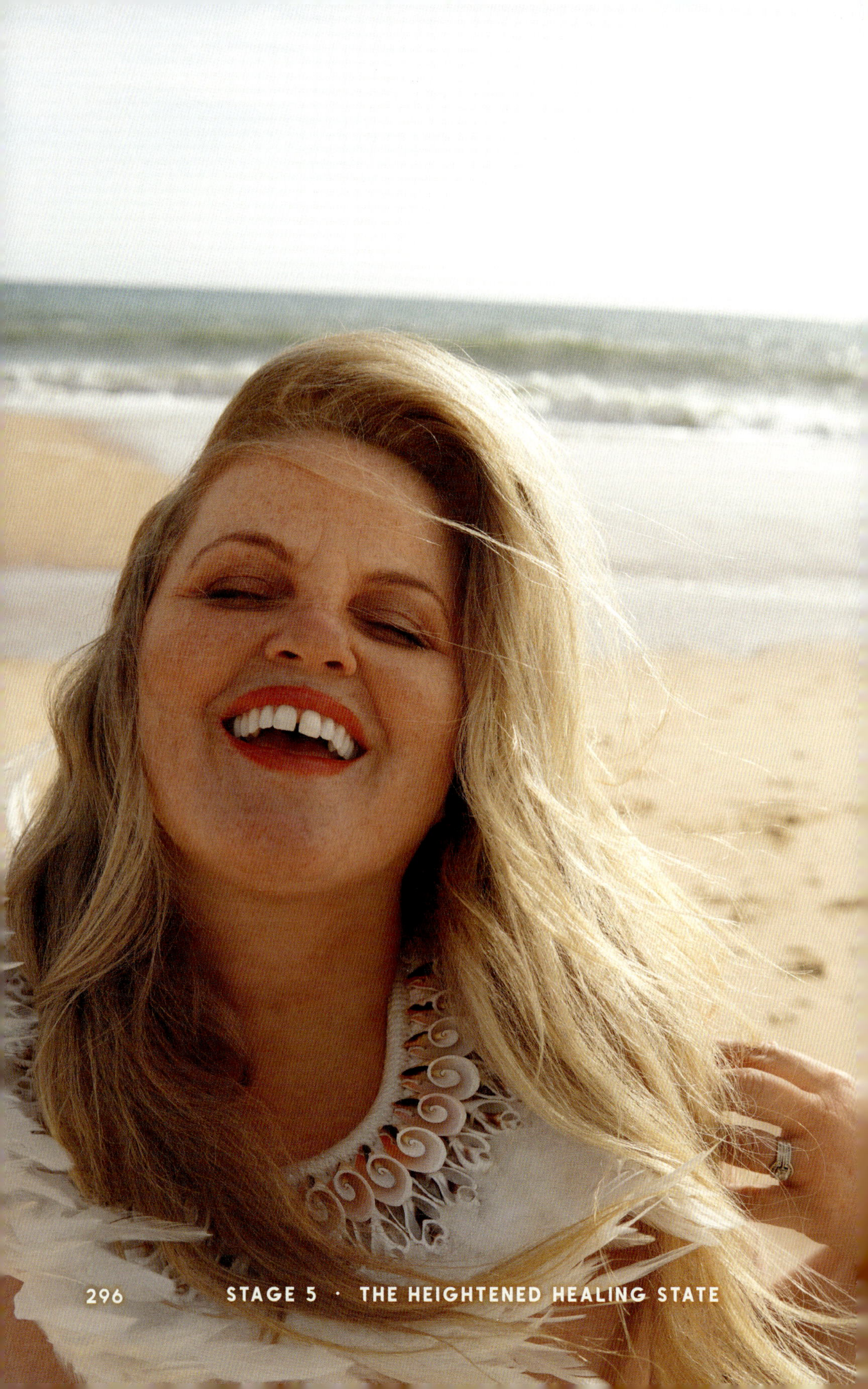

When I was five years old I was covered in warts. I was not really aware how hideous they looked until I joined the Brownies at the age of seven, and could sense people were starting to snigger and whisper. I knew they were asking my sister Suzie, who was two years older than me, 'Why does your sister look like that? Why is she covered in lumps?' I had the warts all over my hands, knees, arms, bottom and two on my face.

Unfortunately, the two on my face were on my nose. They were long and wiry, and one day at school I got told I had some bogeys on my face. When I explained they were warts I then got the nickname 'Bogey Face'.

However, I had resilience to the name calling because I was so young and unaware that my looks were of any importance. But my 'go-to' in how to react to this was, *"Well if I am going to look ugly, I'd better make sure my energy is what people see."* I remember this very clearly as just an exuberance that I could light up if I needed to.

Several years later, I had all the warts burnt off under an operation (because they got as resilient as my nature!). As a result I obviously became a little prettier and whilst I was appreciative of my good looks, it was not the thing I nurtured the most.

I know I have an energy that I can light up and I want you to know anyone can tune into that Goddess energy, including you!

We get so wrapped up in how we should look; make up, hair done, smelling the right way, driving the right car, saying the right thing even. But most of this is conditioned into you, rather than being true to who you are. In fact, trying to keep up with the 'Jones' can make us sick. We can end up never feeling enough, never feeling accepted, and being overly critical of ourselves and others so that nothing satisfies us at all. This attitude, this energy makes us ill because we never get there. We become a perfectionist of something that doesn't even exist. The perfection of you is YOU, it is already there.

Just as the trees blowing in the wind are confident in all their majesty, so can we be.

Perhaps you have already started to feel this when you tune into your senses and notice how beautiful they are when they are lit up.

Having to be something for someone else, having to be something you are not, having to be a certain weight before you love yourself, or let anyone else love you, are all signs you are not getting down with your Goddess energy.

How would it feel knowing that when you walk in a room you light it up?

How would it feel knowing that the energy of you is what people want to be around? They notice that before noticing how beautiful you are?

How would it feel knowing your very presence heals people and makes them feel so good?

Do you know anyone who has that Goddess energy?

What does it feel like being in their presence?

To feel this energy is like feeling a charge within you. You may know how that already feels when meditating, praying or being in the flow state, or the heightened flow state.

You may already feel this in other ways.

No drug, food, liquid or person is charging you. You are.

You are your own drug.

Going through the process of **the healed state** is a great way to get you to feel the feminine energy within, that power without effort. But the ultimate way to embrace The Goddess Energy is compassion and self-love.

Loving all your flaws and loving all of you.

People are blessed to be in the company of you because you are amazing. Do you know that yet?

Tuning into the act of self-love takes finding calming moments to be with you. When you have taken off so many layers of you throughout **the healed state** here you are. Here is the core essence of your beauty. You now choose when others see this and when you treasure 'you' moments for yourself.

Nature will light you up, your higher self will light you up, and you will light you up.

To ignite my Goddess Energy I …

- Go into nature daily. I feel the earth supporting me.
- Activate, release and charge in water.
- Move to music.
- Raise my sensual experience, through touch, taste, smell, sound and sight
- Receive healing from other therapists
- Listen to healing sounds
- Find quiet moments for me
- Give healing

I feel this journey is a personal one, which is why I am suggesting ways I do this rather than telling you to do it in that way too. You may find different ways of accentuating your divine Goddess, but when you do you will know, because your energy is heightened, you hold yourself differently, you care less about what people think of what you look like and you start attracting like-minded light energies. This in turn releases blocked, negative energy that may otherwise turn into disease.

It keeps you fluid, flowing, moving through healing waters rather than hiding, introverting into your imprisoned self.

Next we go into The Healed State

the healed state

STAGE 6
LIVING IN A HEALED STATE

A memory without the emotional charge is called wisdom

Dr Joe Dispenza

1. Recap

2. Process of being healed

3. Acknowledgement list

4. Pain as a motivator

5. The Healed State Barometer

6. STARRBEAM

7. STARRBEAM chart

Recap

Let's recap on everything we have learnt so far.

> **In Stage 1** you tuned into what you want to heal.
>
> **In Stage 2** you asked: Are you willing to give up what makes you sick?
>
> **In Stage 3** you tuned into if you are ready to receive healing.
>
> **In Stage 4** you sought to go out and seek forces that heal rather than forces that harm in your environment.
>
> **In Stage 5** you made changes in you that create healing.

In Stage 6, the final stage, you are now looking at living in a healed state.

Stages 1-5 covered the ground work, particularly in Stages 4 and 5 which looked at environmental and physical changes where we make our healing go through a journey. It is a process, not a quick fix; it doesn't happen overnight, but in time.

From here on in we are trying to achieve a process that stops self-sabotage, but at the same time also recognises the value and importance of the lower energy emotions when they come in.

For instance, being depressed or anxious, being in pain or experiencing vulnerability are not emotions that we want to be put aside; they are feelings to process and they are here to show us wisdom. If we ignore them, we could get ill again. When we feel these negative sensations and use them to give us value, rather than attaching a longevity of pain to them, we can then learn remotely, meaning we don't have to suffer long term. We can observe, process, and then when ready, ask that gift to leave us now. We don't have to attach or associate the rest of our lives being a victim of this past trauma or pain. It is not us; we are our core essence; we aren't our ancestors' pain and we aren't our past.

We are our present.

So before we start The Healed State stage- moving to the higher good, I want you to know that it's alright to dip sometimes, because this is where we can find wisdom. We are not looking for a perfect life without pain or issues, because life happens and throws many things in our way. We are looking for a way to manage all that we have so we can feel good, enjoy life and live in a state of bliss for the majority of the time.

Process of being healed

*Divine spirit within me,
move me in to the higher good*

When you cut your skin, it takes about three weeks to heal but if your mind is in a negative or depressed state it can take 60% longer. And that's just your mind.

- There is also making sure the cut is protected and doesn't get dirty or cut open again.
- There is also the management of looking after the cut until it is healed.
- Once it is healed there is also managing our own health in the foods we eat and the thoughts we think - we have to ensure our healing is proficient.
- Then there is also the awareness of not allowing that cut to happen again in the same way.

This is healing and being healed.

- What we put in our mouths
- What we allow ourselves to hear and see
- What thoughts we think
- How we move our body
- Who we surround ourselves with
- How we allow our body to rest

These are all ongoing processes that we live through every single day, allowing more healing or more destruction. It is completely our choice.

And initially perhaps your intention will need to be stronger to create the right ongoing choices because the habit hasn't quite formed yet.

Equally, we don't want to become so obsessed with healing ourselves that we don't allow for any negativity, toxins or pollution. Toxicity is everywhere. We can do our best to avoid it, but we can't live in a bubble. So when we give our body power, it can fight for us so we feel balanced.

Allowing for this continued behaviour is knowing your own light, feeling your core essence so you can live in bliss.

Living in a Healed State is not reacting as you once did in the past. It's having conscious awareness to be in love with yourself and allowing everything coming to you to be in love with you too.

Does the food that you eat love you?

Do the people around you love you?

Do your thoughts manifest into love?

Do your habits serve and love you?

Or another way to look at it is the reverse

Is the food that I am eating poison?

Do the people around me poison me?

Do my thoughts poison me?

Do my habits poison me?

It is pretty straightforward really, and it is keeping that simple state of being every day.

How can I show myself love even in trauma, or especially in trauma?

To continue your healing practice, the biggest issue you will be met with is a negative trigger. So it is a good idea to identify what your potential ongoing triggers could be and how you will manage them in a different way to how you managed them in the past.

If you want to live in a Healed State, continued forgiveness is inevitable. Someone may be attacking you every day, even just through a memory, so instead of truly living in a healed state you could be in a reactive state.

Forgiveness is not about being submissive. It's about releasing the negative impact that person has on your beautiful body and mind. The more you stew in anger, the more the core essence of you gets blocked and the less feeling and fun you have in your life.

Anger = lack of forgiveness

Living in a healed state is being conscious of your reactions and returning to your wholeness, your core essence.

Less reactions and more actions

Starting with your own vibration of how you want to feel today- i.e. that inner core you that you block endlessly can be vibrating far greater and higher.

So knowing how strong this high vibration will make you feel, wanting to maintain and grow it, will be the process.

I want to remind you that this power comes from you and the choices you make. All your body wants to do is fight for you, to protect you. It literally has an army of cells battling for you each and every day- why wouldn't you support that?

It's not really that difficult. In nature we have everything we need to support us so we can support our cells. Remember, there are simple restorative ways we can heal.

For example by eating:

- **Cacao** - You are growing new stems cells and new blood vessels.
- **Leafy greens** - You can lengthen the telemeters in your DNA, which protect you.
- **Blueberries** - You kill the killer cells that live within you.
- **Broccoli** - You can starve cancer.
- **Two apples a day** - You can lower the risk of lung cancer.
- **Seafood** - You can boost your metabolism.

We have gold dust all around us at our finger tips, waiting to heal us.

Acknowledgement list

So to start the Healed State Process, we are going to create an Acknowledgement list.

This is a really important step for your own accountability and ownership of how you could create destruction or connection to your healing in the future.

Your 'I acknowledge list' is asking what potential habits can I form, or have I formed, that I have got a high from, but then also ultimately lead to a low? We are observing the habits we formed in the past. It is not necessarily what you are doing now, although it could be.

Perhaps in the past you have let these habits or patterns creep in and then they cause an onslaught of issues thereafter.

By acknowledging this we are doing several things:

- We are being accountable for our actions and therefore not blaming anyone else. If we blame others, we become powerless to fix the problem because we believe only they can fix it. So, by honouring it is our problem to solve, we then find the solution i.e. we stop creating the behaviour that goes towards it.

- We can predict this may happen in the future and therefore fill the void it is trying to soothe, thus avoiding the problem.

- By being aware of our patterns and writing them down, we are far less likely to keep repeating them, or at the very least we can stop complaining about them to others, like it's something external to us.

Some of these patterns you may not even be aware of yet, and others are more obvious.

The question I am asking in the acknowledgment list are ...

1. 'I acknowledge'
This is your behaviour or habits you either do or have done that can cause you physical pain, interruptions with your sleep, negative behaviour, addictive habits, unhealthy weight gain/loss, injury, depression, anxiety and illness.

2. 'What is the high?'
This is acknowledging the high you get from the behaviour, it could be highs from food, being angry or being addicted.

3. 'What is the pain?'
This acknowledges that your actions, or lack of action (it could be stuff you are not doing) are causing physical, mental, emotional or spiritual pain, stress or illness. Or these actions are creating dependant behaviour that will eventually lead to addiction and or illness.

4. 'What can I do instead?'
This is understanding what high that activity is giving you, and what other behaviour you can put in place on a regular basis to give you a greater reward. Remember that short term highs generally give lows as well, i.e. addiction and pain. Long term highs lead to a path of healing and happiness.

5. 'What is my reward?'
This is understanding that changing your behaviour is not leading to a dull life of deprivation. It is leading to a life without so much pain and destruction, so you can feel and enjoy more.

Remember there is wisdom in pain. Pain can motivate you to change; it is telling you to stop the attitude going towards it, not to drown it out with noise, drugs, stress or to continue repeating the behaviour.

When writing your list, think of all areas or your life, relationships/friendships, work, exercise, eating, home, spiritual. Then think of patterns in those areas which have accumulated. It may be really obvious, or it could be a really small behaviour.

To help you tune into this and get started, ask yourself ...

What do I complain about repetitively?

When I see a client complain about something repetitively, it's a pattern that has accumulated from habit to addiction. Although initially perhaps it wasn't their fault that this 'thing' happened to them, how they react to it is in their own hands. They can take ownership of how to proceed.

Do they let it destroy them, or do they stop letting it happen again?

Sometimes we can gain energy by being a victim. Complaining can become addictive within itself, and if it's someone else's fault we don't have to fix it.

A client of mine, Jessica, complained continuously that she always had to do everything for everyone and never got anything in return. This is a common complaint, especially in women. And I get it, we all need to offload and complain if we are pissed off. But it's the habit of complaining that we are looking out for, not necessarily the odd complaining every now and then.

Jessica complained that she always helped people and often not only would they not help her back, but sometimes they would do something outrageously mean in return, slapping her generosity back in her face. This would send her into a depression and fill her with dread. She would then binge eat to satisfy her pain.

Jessica is a lovely person and did not deserve this reaction. She was not doing anything purposely to cause it. However, when we broke it down, we noticed she was subconsciously choosing ungrateful or rude people to be generous to. Jessica was somehow trying to seek and earn their love, but they could never reciprocate it.

When it came down to it, Jessica had been complaining about the same thing over and over again for the last 30 years. She was addicted to this pattern and nothing could change unless she changed. She then used that addiction to serve another addiction which was binge eating.

So, she had three choices:

1. She continued helping mean, ungrateful people and would continue complaining
2. She continued helping them, but did not complain herself
3. She stopped helping them.

When we unravel our behaviour and the things we complain about, having to stop moaning can mean having to own what is really going on inside. Being the victim repetitively means we can't change and we can't heal.

When Jessica stopped complaining she realised she didn't know how to receive love and generosity. She was uncomfortable with it because it made her feel out of control and vulnerable.

Having to help ungrateful people was a clever way of avoiding her own issues and also getting attention in another way. She could then use that to justify her own binge eating behaviour.

So we worked through the acknowledgement list to ensure she recognised her behaviour in the future.

So, lets write this acknowledgement list!

To help you with this list I have written down a few of my own that I have had to work on to help you understand what you may need to write.

My Acknowledgement List

I acknowledge?	What is the high?	What is the pain?	What can I do instead?	What is my reward?
I go on my phone at night in bed sometimes	Numb focus so I don't have to think about anything else.	• My neck aches • I sleep later and get lost down a rabbit hole. • I get less sleep because the light and information has messed with my sleep time. • Dulling my brain.	• Keep my phone out of the room • Connect with myself and my night time routine	• Better sleep • More contentment • More self-love and self-care
I don't have a green smoothie in the morning sometimes	Rebelling against routine gives me a kick.	• Cravings throughout the day. • Less energy • Eating more • Potential weight gain • Pains in joints	• Keep the kitchen tidy the night before • Put the food in the blender ready to blend for the morning	• More energy • Balanced mood • No cravings • Better skin • Calmer mood
I use the laptop too long sometimes	Rebelling against what I should do.	• Neck pain • Poor posture and back pain • Digestive issues	• Use my stand up desk • Set up my monitor • Use my orthopaedic cusion	• Less neck or back pain • More energy • Flatter abs

The interesting thing when I look at my list is that the highs are pretty pathetic in comparison to the pain I get in return, and then also in comparison to the rewards I could get instead with more positive behaviour.

Now it's your turn!

I acknowledge?	what is the high?	what is the pain?	what can I do instead?	what is my reward?

Pain as a motivator

We can be in a habit of learning through pain so we create more pain.

Christianne Wolff

Okay, a little bit about pain as the motivator!

If we get injured, we are in pain. This indicates to us to be careful about how to move our body till the pain subsides, and to be careful when next doing the activity that caused the pain. We also need to heal the pain.

Pain is a good motivator to fix the problem that caused it.

"I'm in pain, I no longer want to be in pain, what can I do to heal that pain and prevent it happening again."

However! Sometimes we can get addicted to pain as a motivator and then it does not serve us as well. Let me explain. Maybe you have put yourself in as much pain as possible before you get motivated to fix it?

Some examples are...

- You over indulge on junk food so much that you feel gross, fat, tired and unhealthy. Then when you are at your lowest ebb, you decide to finally make a change.
- Or you get warning signs to fix something in your body, maybe a small pain in your neck. You don't fix it until it is really painful and then you make a change.
- Or in a relationship- you only decide to seek help or leave when it is totally at rock bottom.
- Or you only get motivated to tidy up when you can't open the door because your house is so messy.
- Or you drown yourself in debt before you bother making more money.

The problem with this is we can fix ourselves to heal the pain, but as soon as we start to feel better again we are no longer motivated. We aren't motivated by feeling good, we are motivated by pain.

Learning to be gentle, and to listen quietly at what our body wants, means we can be consistent in our positive behaviour rather than always being motivated by pain.

However another scenario could be that we have amnesia to pain.

So, we were in pain, we sought to fix that pain and we then think '*Hey, I can now go back to my old behaviour because I am no longer in pain*' - forgetting how painful that old behaviour made you feel, and you are back to square one again.

So you can use pain as a motivator, but also then have pain amnesia all at the same time.

Yes, pain is a good motivator, but what we really want to look out for are the warning signs to motivate us, rather than the depths of suffering. The way we do this is to have a barometer check in each morning.

Being in pain also makes you present. How else can you feel presence?

This allows us to mood regulate. Mood dysregulation will lead to self-sabotage, so mood regulation is vital.

Small patterns lead to bigger ripples- in either direction!

The Healed State Barometer

Morning and Evening routine

As part of your **healed state** journey, I want to make it really simple for you by creating a morning and evening routine that only lasts five minutes or so. This is so we are well aware of the warning signs. We have a twice a day check in, making sure we are feeling alright. If we are not, we tend to that straight away rather than waiting for more pain. No more 'I'll take care of that later' attitude.

This check in process is easy to do if you just make it part of your daily habit and ritual, as simple as brushing your teeth. You do that each day, so why not do this too? In fact, creating a ritual that promises better health with its intention is a placebo within itself, and a ritual that invokes the spirit of you. Your soul's intention is an act of spiritual wisdom.

Morning Body Sweep

Each morning on waking up just spend five minutes or so asking your body how it is, go through your:

- ☐ Toes
- ☐ Feet
- ☐ Shins
- ☐ Calves
- ☐ Knees
- ☐ Back of the knees
- ☐ Quads
- ☐ Hamstrings
- ☐ Buttocks
- ☐ Groin
- ☐ Pelvis
- ☐ Genitals
- ☐ Womb
- ☐ Bladder
- ☐ Kidneys
- ☐ Liver
- ☐ Spleen
- ☐ Gallbladder
- ☐ Gut
- ☐ Heart
- ☐ Lungs
- ☐ Throat
- ☐ Chest
- ☐ Stomach
- ☐ Lower back
- ☐ Upper back
- ☐ Shoulders
- ☐ Arms
- ☐ Hands
- ☐ Fingers & thumbs
- ☐ Neck
- ☐ Throat
- ☐ Face
- ☐ Mouth
- ☐ Tongue
- ☐ Teeth
- ☐ Eyes
- ☐ Ears
- ☐ Scalp
- ☐ Brain
- ☐ Skeleton
- ☐ Skin

Then go through all your cells. Listen to the wisdom of your body.

With each area ask the following...

How are you?

What do you need today? (answer I want more of this and less of that)

Then if any of the areas are in pain, are tight, or feel toxic, say to them 'You are safe, I am listening to your needs' and breathe deeply in them.

Spend as little or as long as you like in this process but do at least five breaths in any areas that need energy.

Do the same process for your mind and spirit.

By doing this each morning, not only are you teaching yourself that you are important and your decision making that day will go towards you, but also you are preventing self-sabotage, pain amnesia and allowing more pain. The pain stops now, you get motivated by how good you feel, you want more and more and more of that.

You can listen to this sweep meditation if you wish or do it on your own.

Evening Routine Journalling

Your evening routine requires journalling. I would recommend you have a little ritual of having some aromatherapy oils in a steamer, or using a healing scent in the air, playing some soft music, or using crystals around you and then writing in your journal. Find a quiet place to sit down and write your thoughts. The journal wants to be a physical one, not on your phone or iPad. Go out and buy a beautiful book, or make one that has your energy in and around it. Remember, you don't want screen time at night as it will interrupt your sleep.

Here are six questions to answer each night

What am I grateful for today?

What did I find healing today for my mind?

What did I find healing today for my body?

What if anything caused me pain today?

How can I heal this pain for tomorrow?

What do I want for tomorrow?

With each question, practice your deep inhales and exhales so you are healing, releasing and not holding on.

REPEAT THIS DAILY

This is an ongoing process of healing.

Throughout the stages of **the healed state** you would have had some 'aha' moments, some exercises that connected with you that you can put to good use and make part of your routine. We are all on our personal journey and all have different things to heal.

We can all do the morning and evening routines to prevent self-sabotage and continue allowing the healing in.

But on top of that you can live by my STARRBEAM principles that I live by and teach my clients.

This is a simple acronym that reminds us to allow the good in our lives all day, every day.

You can choose to do this daily, hourly, or break it up into the week. Or use my chart on pages 312 and 313 as a focus to keep you motivated in this practice that will consistently make you feel healed.

This is your journey, this is your life, you control the narrative that is your story.

Make it a good one!

STAGE 6 · LIVING IN THE HEALED STATE

STARRBEAM

1 · Surrendering and Forgiveness
2 · Thankfulness
3 · Angelic flow state
4 · Relaxing with water and nature
5 · Reconnect - to God and yourself
6 · Breathe
7 · Eat Healthy Food mindfully
8 · Alpha level - meditate yoga
9 · Move your body kindly, joyously

STARRBEAM

	Monday	Tuesday	Wednesday
WEEK 1	• Eat Healthy • Self love meditation	• Eat Healthy • Self love meditation	• Eat Healthy • Self love meditation
WEEK 2	• Eat Healthy • Self love meditation • Move	• Eat Healthy • Move	• Eat Healthy • Self love meditation • Move
WEEK 3	• Eat Healthy • Self love meditation • Move • Total Play	• Eat Healthy • Move • Relax in water	• Eat Healthy • Move • Alpha level meditation
WEEK 4	• Eat Healthy • Self love meditation • Move • Total Play	• Eat Healthy • Move • Surrender/Forgive mediation	• Eat Healthy • Move • Total Play
WEEK 5	• Eat Healthy • Move • Total Play • Be in nature	• Eat Healthy • Move • Alpha level meditation	• Eat Healthy • Self love meditation • Move
WEEK 6	• Eat Healthy • Move • Total Play • Be in nature	• Eat Healthy • Move • Alpha level meditation	• Eat Healthy • Healing meditaion • Move
WEEK 7	• Eat Healthy • Move • Total Play	• Eat Healthy • Move • Alpha level meditation	• Eat Healthy • Relax in water • Be in nature
WEEK 8	• Eat Healthy • Move • Total Play • Be in nature	• Eat Healthy • Move • Be in nature • Give healing to animals / plants	• Eat Healthy • Move • Be in nature
WEEK 9	• Eat Healthy • Move • Total Play • Be in nature	• Eat Healthy • Alpha level meditation • Give healing to animals / plants	• Eat Healthy • Move • Be in nature • Alpha level meditation

Chart

	Thursday	Friday	Saturday	Sunday
	• Eat Healthy • Self love meditation	• Eat Healthy • Self love meditation	• Eat Healthy	• Eat Healthy
	• Eat Healthy • Move	• Eat Healthy • Self love meditation	• Eat Healthy • Move	• Eat Healthy
	• Eat Healthy • Move • Be in nature	• Eat Healthy • Move • Flow state meditation	• Eat Healthy • Move • Reconnect	• Eat Healthy • Surrender/Forgive mediation
	• Eat Healthy • Move • Surrender/Forgive mediation	• Eat Healthy • Move • Be in nature	• Eat Healthy • Move • Reconnect	• Eat Healthy • Surrender/Forgive mediation
	• Eat Healthy • Move • Be in nature	• Eat Healthy • Move • Flow state meditation	• Eat Healthy • Move • Reconnect • Relax in water	• Eat Healthy • Surrender/Forgive mediation
	• Eat Healthy • Move • Be in nature	• Eat Healthy • Move • Flow state meditation	• Eat Healthy • Move • Reconnect • Relax in water • Be in nature	• Eat Healthy • Surrender/Forgive mediation
	• Eat Healthy • Move • Recieve healing	• Eat Healthy • Move • Flow state activity	• Eat Healthy • Move • Reconnect	• Eat Healthy • Surrender/Forgive mediation
	• Eat Healthy • Move • Healing meditaion	• Eat Healthy • Move • Flow state activity	• Eat Healthy • Move • Reconnect • Relax in water • Be in nature	• Eat Healthy • Surrender/Forgive mediation
	• Eat Healthy • Move • Recieve healing • Alpha level meditation	• Eat Healthy • Be in nature • Flow state activity	• Eat Healthy • Reconnect • Relax in water	• Eat Healthy • Surrender/Forgive mediation

STARRBEAM CHART

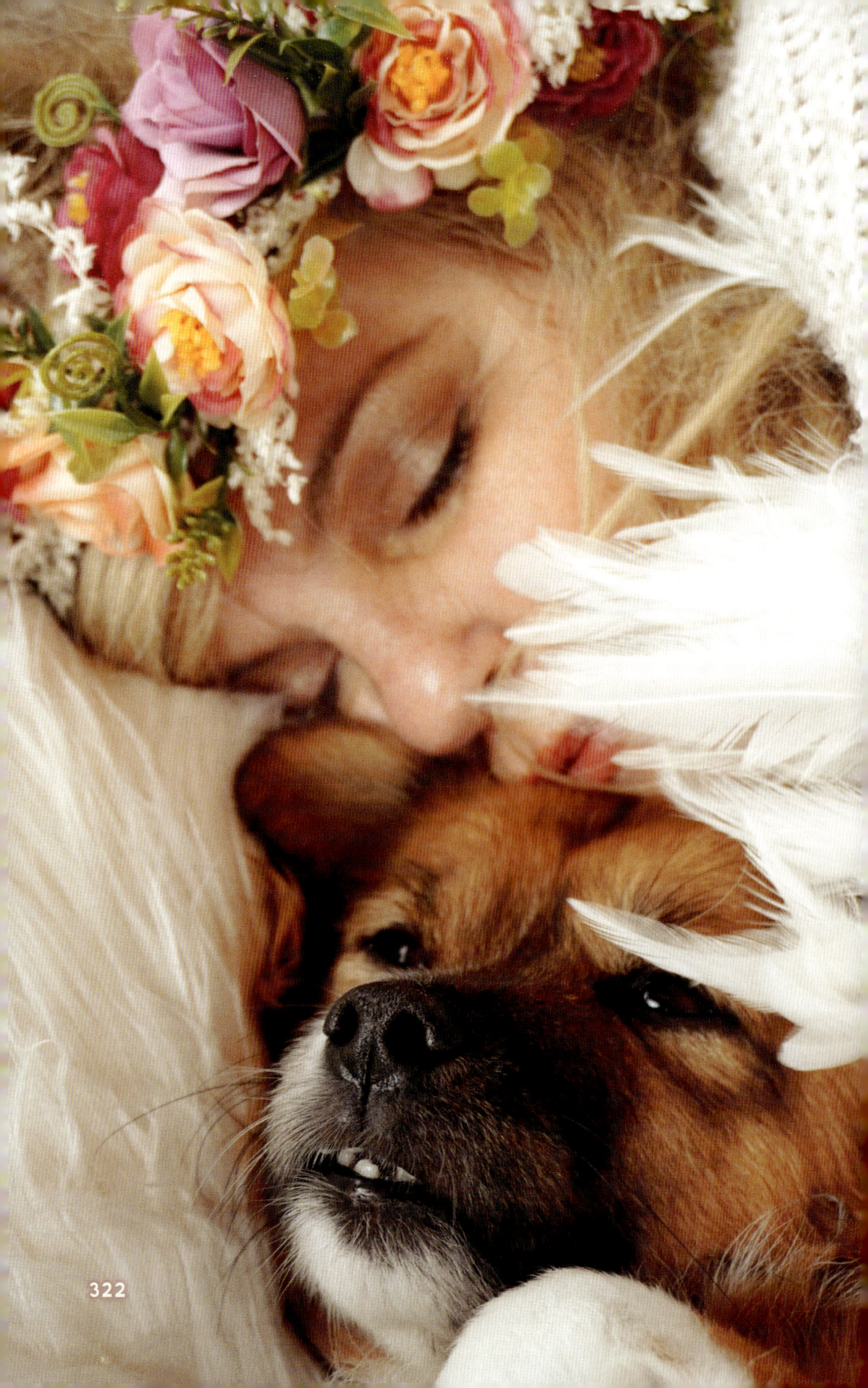

If you sit quietly
after difficult news,

if in financial downturns
you remain perfectly calm;

if you can see your neighbours
travel to fantastic places
without a twinge of jealousy;

if you can happily eat
whatever is put on your plate;

if you can fall asleep after a day of running around without a drink or pill;

if you can always find contentment
just where you are.

You are probably a dog!

Jack Kornfield

Congratulations on going through all the stages of healing for The Healed State!

I'm so proud of you for getting this far and you should be very proud of yourself also. Even if you have only embraced some of my ideas, your emotional, mental, physical and spiritual wellbeing will improve.

You can revisit any of the stages at any time and listen to the meditations regularly to help you also. This can be done in any order, just by flicking through the book you will feel supported and safe. I have designed the colours, images, drawings and words to allow you into the world of feeling healed.

Remember life is not linear and there can be many disruptions to your healing process, enjoy the journey and make it a consistent one. To help you frequent this journey, keep The Healed State book in a place you can feel a connection to restoring your energy, perhaps create a meditation area, an alter, or just a shelf with a candle and a journal.

You can also use my Healed State Affirmation Cards along with this book, to allow comfort, support and intention on your life journey.

We also have The Healed State journal here also so that you can commit every day to the process of allowing good energy in and releasing out the old.

Allow all the vibrancy of colour around you to continue to enrich your life!

Until next time!

With love and healing,

Christianne xx

ABOUT CHRISTIANNE

Christianne is a multi award winning best selling author of many health and wellness books in The Body Rescue Plan series. She has been a healer for over 30 years, running her own practice in the UK before moving to Portugal with her husband Robbie, daughter Angelique and rescue dogs Bula and Pablo.

Christianne is a leader in healing through nutrition, mindset, meditation, exercise and yoga. She also runs wellness retreats, courses and online memberships, whilst appearing regularly in the national media.

www.thebodyrescueplan.com

IN THE PRESS

Woman and Home magazine
"Christianne uses spiritual and relaxation practices, combined with healthy recipes and mindset to heal old patterns."

Soul and Spirit Magazine
"Christianne Wolff has a handy spiritual tool for you with meditations for those guilty of excesses."

Sunday People
"Turbo charge your immune system with Christianne Wolff."

The Daily Mirror
"Christianne has Tasty recipes packed with immune boosting foods."

REFERENCES

American Society of Agronomy. "Common antibacterial triclosan found in most freshwater streams".
ScienceDaily, 25 May 2016.
http://www.sciencedaily.com/releases/2016/05/160525121602.htm

Austelle, Christopher W et al. "A Comprehensive Review of Vagus Nerve Stimulation for Depression".
Neuromodulation: Journal of the International Neuromodulation Society. Vol. 25,3, 2022, pp 309-315. doi:10.1111/ner.13528

Balanzá-Martínez, Vicent, and Jose Cervera-Martínez. "Lifestyle Prescription for Depression with a Focus on Nature Exposure and Screen Time: A Narrative Review".
International Journal of Environmental Research and Public Health Vol. 19,9 5094, 2022. doi:10.3390/ijerph19095094

Barrett, Bruce et al. "Meditation or exercise for preventing acute respiratory infection: a randomized controlled trial."
Annals of Family Medicine. Vol. 10, No 4, 2012, pp 337-346. doi:10.1370/afm.1376

Blum, Winfried E H et al. "Does Soil Contribute to the Human Gut Microbiome?".
Microorganisms Vol. 7,9 287, 2019. doi:10.3390/microorganisms7090287

Cherednichenko, Gennady et al. "Triclosan impairs excitation-contraction coupling and Ca2+ dynamics in striated muscle".
Proceedings of the National Academy of Sciences of the United States of America, Vol. 109, 35, 2012, pp 14158-14163. doi:10.1073/pnas.1211314109

Cetisli, Nuray Egelioglu et al. "The effects of flaxseed on menopausal symptoms and quality of life."
Holistic Nursing Practice. Vol. 29,3, 2015, pp. 151-157. doi:10.1097/HNP.0000000000000085

Clark, Ian and Landolt, Hans-Peter. "Coffee, Caffeine, and Sleep: a Systematic Review of Epidemiological Studies and Randomized Controlled Trials."
Sleep Medicine Reviews. Vol 31, 2017. doi:10.1016/j.smrv.2016.01.006

Dallam, George et al. "Effect of Nasal Versus Oral Breathing on Vo2max and Physiological Economy in Recreational Runners Following an Extended Period Spent Using Nasally Restricted Breathing."
International Journal of Kinesiology and Sports Science. Vol 6, 22, April 2018. doi:10.7575/aiac.ijkss.v.6n.2p.22.

Debras, C. et al. "Artificial sweeteners and cancer risk: Results from the NutriNet-Santé population-based cohort study."
PLOS Medicine. Vol 19, 3, 2022, e1003950.
https://doi.org/10.1371/journal.pmed.1003950

Emoto, Masaru. "The Hidden Messages in Water".
Atria Books, 2005

Erickson, Kirk I et al. "Exercise training increases size of hippocampus and improves memory".
Proceedings of the National Academy of Sciences of the United States of America. Vol. 108,7, 2011, pp 3017-3022. doi:10.1073/pnas.1015950108

Executive Board 115. "R6: Antimicrobial resistance: a threat to global health security".
Resolutions and Decisions. 2005.
https://apps.who.int/iris/bitstream/handle/10665/20247/B115_R6-en.pdf?sequence=1&isAllowed=y

Fülling, Christine et al. "Gut Microbe to Brain Signaling: What Happens in Vagus...,"
Neuron, Vol 101, 6, 2019, pp 998 – 1002.
https://doi.org/10.1016/j.neuron.2019.02.008.

Gøtzsche, P C. "Niels Finsen's treatment for lupus vulgaris".
Journal of the Royal Society of Medicine. vol. 104,1, 2011, PP 41-42. doi:10.1258/jrsm.2010.10k066

Halden, Rolf U et al. "The Florence Statement on Triclosan and Triclocarban".
Environmental Health Perspectives, vol. 125, 6 064501. 2017. doi:10.1289/EHP1788

Harrison, Pam. "Forgiveness Can Improve Immune Function".
Medscape, 5 May 2011. https://www.medscape.com/viewarticle/742198

Hirshberg, Caryle and O'Regan Brendan. "Spontaneous Remission: An Annotated Bibliography".
Institute of Noetic Sciences, 1993

James, Peter et al. "Exposure to Greenness and Mortality in a Nationwide Prospective Cohort Study of Women".
Journal of Environmental Health Perspectives. Vol. 124, 9, 2016. https://doi.org/10.1289/ehp.1510363

Jiang, Shu-Ye et al. "Negative Air Ions and Their Effects on Human Health and Air Quality Improvement".
International Journal of Molecular Sciences. Vol. 19, 10 2966. 28 Sep. 2018. doi:10.3390/ijms19102966

Ju, Yang et al. "Effect of Dietary Fiber (Oat Bran) Supplement in Heart Rate Lowering in Patients with Hypertension: A Randomized DASH-Diet-Controlled Clinical Trial".
Nutrients Vol. 14, 15 3148. 30 Jul. 2022. doi:10.3390/nu14153148

Kaminer, D et al. "The Truth and Reconciliation Commission in South Africa: relation to psychiatric status and forgiveness among survivors of human rights abuses".
British Journal of Psychiatry: the journal of mental science. Vol. 178, 2001, pp 373-377. doi:10.1192/bjp.178.4.373

Kenny, Rose Anne. "Age Proof: The New Science of Living a Longer and Healthier Life".
Lagom. 2022

Kerek, Orlena, Host. "What Should I Eat to Lead a Long and Healthy Life? With Dr Alan Desmond".
Fit and Fabulous Podcast, Episode 100, iTunes, 17 Nov 2020.
https://www.drorlena.com/blog/plant-based-diet-dr-alan-desmond

Komisaruk, B. R., and Whipple, B. "Brain Activity Imaging During Sexual Response in Women With Spinal Cord Injury".
In J. S. Hyde (Ed.), Biological substrates of human sexuality. American Psychological Association, 2005. https://doi.org/10.1037/11196-005

Lee, H M et al. "Forced vital capacity paired with Framingham Risk Score for prediction of all-cause mortality".
The European Respiratory Journal, Vol. 36, 5, 2010, pp 1002-6. doi:10.1183/09031936.00042410

Li, Qing. "Effect of forest bathing trips on human immune function".
Environmental Health and Preventive Medicine.vol. 15,1, 2010, pp 9-17. doi:10.1007/s12199-008-0068-3

Lin, I. M. et al. "Breathing at a rate of 5.5 breaths per minute with equal inhalation-to-exhalation ratio increases heart rate variability".
International Journal of Psychophysiology, Vol 91, 3, 2014, pp. 206 -211. https://doi.org/10.1016/j.ijpsycho.2013.12.006

Liu, L., Lu, Y., Bi, X. et al. "Choline ameliorates cardiovascular damage by improving vagal activity and inhibiting the inflammatory response in spontaneously hypertensive rats".
Scientific Reports. Vol 7, 42553, 2017. https://doi.org/10.1038/srep42553

Manippa, Valerio et al. "An update on the use of gamma (multi) sensory stimulation for Alzheimer's disease treatment".
Frontiers in Aging Neuroscience. Vol. 14 1095081. 15 Dec. 2022. doi:10.3389/fnagi.2022.1095081

Mate, Gabor. "When the Body Says No: The Cost of Hidden Stress".
Vintage Canada, 2004

McMurry, L M. "Triclosan targets lipid synthesis".
Nature, Vol. 394,6693, 1998, pp 531-532. doi:10.1038/28970

Mehta, Ria et al. "Evidence for the Role of Mindfulness in Cancer: Benefits and Techniques".
Cureus. Vol. 11,5 e4629, 2019. doi:10.7759/cureus.4629

Mol, Maartje B A et al. "Heart-rate-variability (HRV), predicts outcomes in COVID-19".
PloS One, vol. 16, 10 e0258841. 28 Oct. 2021. doi:10.1371/journal.pone.0258841

Nagarathna, R. and Nagendra, H. R. "Yoga for bronchial asthma: a controlled study".
British Medical Journal (Clinical Research Ed). Vol 291:1077, 1985. doi:10.1136/bmj.291.6502.1077

Naveen, G H et al. "Positive therapeutic and neurotropic effects of yoga in depression: A comparative study".
Indian Journal of Psychiatry. Vol. 55, Suppl 3, 2013: S400-4. doi:10.4103/0019-5545.116313

Newman, Kira M., "Six Ways Happiness Is Good for Your Health."
Greater Good Science Center, 28 July 2015.
https://greatergood.berkeley.edu/article/item/six_ways_happiness_is_good_for_your_health

Oliveira, Raquel and Arriaga, Patrícia. "A systematic review of the effects of laughter on blood pressure and heart rate variability".
HUMOR, Vol. 35, no. 2, 2022, pp. 135-167.
https://doi.org/10.1515/humor-2021-0111

Panchal, Saharsh et al. "Impact of Himalayan Singing Bowls Meditation Session on Mood and Heart Rate Variability".
International Journal of Psychotherapy Practice and Research, Vol 1, No 4, 2020, pp 20-29. https://doi.org/10.14302/issn.2574-612X.ijpr-20-3213

Petruson, B, and K Theman. "Reduced nocturnal asthma by improved nasal breathing".
Acta oto-laryngologica. Vol. 116, 3, 1996, pp 490-492. doi:10.3109/00016489609137878

Radboud University Nijmegen Medical Centre. "Research on 'Iceman' Wim Hof suggests it may be possible to influence autonomic nervous system and immune response".
ScienceDaily, 22 April 2011.
http://www.sciencedaily.com/releases/2011/04/110422090203.htm.

Rankin, Lissa. "Mind Over Medicine: Scientific Proof That You Can Heal Yourself".
Hay House Inc, 2020

Redwine, Laura S et al. "Pilot Randomized Study of a Gratitude Journaling Intervention on Heart Rate Variability and Inflammatory Biomarkers in Patients With Stage B Heart Failure."
Psychosomatic Medicine vol. 78,6, 2016, pp 667-676. doi:10.1097/PSY.0000000000000316

Rubin, Gretchen. "Life in Five Senses: How Exploring the Senses Got Me Out of My Head and Into the World".
Crown, 2023

Schorr, Melissa. "Antibacterial Soaps Concern Experts".
ABC News, 7 Sept 2000.
https://abcnews.go.com/Health/story?id=117985&page=1

Schulze, Hendrik et al. "Immunomodulating Effect of the Consumption of Watercress (Nasturtium officinale) on Exercise-Induced Inflammation in Humans".
Foods (Basel, Switzerland). Vol. 10,8, 30 Jul. 2021. doi:10.3390/foods10081774

Schünemann, H J et al. "Pulmonary function is a long-term predictor of mortality in the general population: 29-year follow-up of the Buffalo Health Study".
Chest Vol. 118, 3, 2000, pp 656-664. doi:10.1378/chest.118.3.656

Shinichi Sunagawa et al. "Structure and function of the global ocean microbiome".
Science Vol 348,1261359. 2015. doi:10.1126/science.1261359

Triana Barbara E. G. et al. "Mouth breathing and its relationship to some oral and medical conditions: physiopathological mechanisms

involved".
Revista Habanera de Ciencias Médicas, Vol 15, No 2, 2016, pp 200 – 212. http://scielo.sld.cu/pdf/rhcm/v15n2/rhcm08215.pdf

Ulrich, Roger S. "View Through a Window May Influence Recovery from Surgery.".
Science 224, 1984, pp 420-421. doi:10.1126/science.6143402

Val-Laillet, D. et al. "Chronic vagus nerve stimulation decreased weight gain, food consumption and sweet craving in adult obese minipigs".
Appetite, Vol 55, 2, 2010, pp 245-252.
https://doi.org/10.1016/j.appet.2010.06.008

Watson, Nathaniel F et al. "Recommended Amount of Sleep for a Healthy Adult: A Joint Consensus Statement of the American Academy of Sleep Medicine and Sleep Research Society".
Sleep. Vol. 38,6, 2015, pp 843-844. doi:10.5665/sleep.4716

WebMD Editorial Contributors. "Health Benefits of Amla (Indian Gooseberry)".
Nourish by WebMD. 14 Sept 2022,
https://www.webmd.com/diet/health-benefits-amla

Witte, Laura et al. "Floatation Therapy for Specific Health Concerns. A review of the research on this increasingly popular intervention".
Natural Medicine Journal, 7 April 2021.
https://www.naturalmedicinejournal.com/journal/floatation-therapy-specific-health-concerns

Wolters Kluwer Health. "Mindfulness-based stress reduction helps lower blood pressure, study finds".
ScienceDaily. 15 October 2013. http://www.sciencedaily.com/releases/2013

INDEX

A

Addiction	35, 41-42, 45-48, 258-259, 309 - 310
Adrenalin	190, 201, 237, 239, 243, 271, 276-277
Alcohol	34, 70, 152, 213, 270-271
Alpha Waves	142
Anxiety	7, 9, 103, 129, 137, 149, 165, 169, 200, 232, 286, 289, 308
ASMR (Autonomous Sensory Meridian Response)	193, 223
Ageing	98-100, 134, 185, 232, 268
Aromatherapy	148-149, 177, 317,
Autonomic nervous system (ANS)	203, 209
Avoidance	67
Ayurveda, Ayurvedic Medicine	149-150

B

Backley, Steve	103
Body Rescue Plan, The	12, 121, 167-169, 232, 263
Boundary Setting	61, 68-69, 181
Breath work	198-209, 224-225
Breathing	98-100, 200-209, 233, 235, 237-239
Brown, Brene	90

C

Cacao	153, 154, 163, 182, 184, 264, 271, 306
Caffeine	10-11, 177, 213, 239-240
Cancer	42, 49, 52, 59, 86, 124, 134-135, 230, 246-247, 249, 260, 264, 306
Ceremony	181-182
Choline	213
Chromotherapy, Colour Therapy	131-132
Cortisol	93, 100, 148, 177, 190, 201, 271-271,

D

Depression	124, 149, 152, 165, 168-169, 173, 271,
Derks, Peter	123
Domagk, Gerhard	58
Dopamine	44-48, 53-54, 258, 271

E

Emoto, Masaru	179

Endorphins	53, 123, 269, 271-271		Anti-inflammatory	185-186, 222, 237, 247-249, 264
Exercise	23, 71, 150, 164, 204, 223, 229-234, 243, 270-271		Intention setting	53, 150, 179-182, 315

F

Faecal Microbiota Transplantation (FMT)	169-171
Fat	34, 111, 138, 152, 213, 231, 245
Flow State	92, 128, 136-145, 233
Heightened Flow State	289-295
Forest Bathing	148
Forgiveness	8, 89-96, 279, 305

G

Gratitude	229, 283-284, 133-135, 182
Guided Meditations	18-19, 24-30, 53, 95, 101, 107, 316
Gut health	59, 152-153, 164-166, 169-171, 211, 244, 260-262

H

Heart rate	99, 192, 199, 204, 209-210, 226, 229, 236-237
Heart rate variability (HRV)	212-213, 224, 227-229
High Fibre	153, 213
Hof, Wim	174, 207
Homeostasis	40, 46-48, 69
Human Microbiome Project	164
Hygiene	57-58
Hypothalamus	120

I

Inflammation	36, 167-168, 176, 237, 256-257, 268

K

Khalsa, Dharma Singh	99

L

Laughter	123-124, 224
Lembke, Anna	45-46
Levy, Stuart	60
Limbic Brain	45, 190
Libido	124, 250
Longevity	99-100, 176, 201, 230

M

Mate, Gabor	68
Meditation	87-88, 98-105, 122, 128, 133-134, 142, 145, 180, 209, 223-224, 233, 277-279, 289
Microbiome	132, 152-171, 209, 211-213, 229
Mindfulness	133-135, 145, 174, 209, 280
Mindset work	41, 98, 101, 105
Moon Bathing	149-150
Motivation	45, 273-275

N

Nature	71, 122, 126-128, 135, 143-150, 152, 172-173, 193-194, 209, 284, 289, 299
Nestor, James	205-206
Nightingale, Florence	57-58

Nitric oxide	150, 205, 231	Self-Care	24-29, 67-71, 119, 181
NK Cells	148	Self-Love	67, 119-120, 279, 284, 287, 298-299
Nocebo Effect	52, 104, 280-282	Self-Sabotage	8, 13, 54-55, 195, 302-303, 314-318

O

Omega-3 fatty acids	212-213, 242, 254-256, 269
Owen, Amy	95
Oxidative stress	232, 249, 269
Oxytocin	87-88, 203, 272

P

Parasympathetic nervous system	204, 209-210, 212-213, 224-225-229, 276
Phytoncides	148-149
Pineal Gland	99
Placebo Effect	52-53, 85, 103-104, 280-283
Pleasure	45-47, 120-129, 133, 143, 244, 286
Polyphenols	153-163
Porges, Stephen	22
Probiotics	152, 166-167
Psychoneuroimmunology	68

R

Rankin, Lissa	52-53, 69, 124, 281
Recipes	156-163, 214-221, 264
Release	90-94, 278-279, 299
Rosenberg, Stanley	225

S

Schroth, Katharina	203
Scoliosis	203
Second Brain, The	164-165

Self-Care	24-29, 67-71, 119, 181
Self-Love	67, 119-120, 279, 284, 287, 298-299
Self-Sabotage	8, 13, 54-55, 195, 302-303, 314-318
Self-Worth	11, 62, 120
Semmelweis, Ignaz	58
Senses	37, 39-44, 122-124
Heightening the senses	39, 126-129, 131-133, 289
Serotonin	164-165, 203, 242, 271-272
Sex	39, 47, 124-125, 137, 203-204, 209, 212, 293
Sleep	142, 185-186, 194, 206, 211, 230, 236-243
Smudging	182-184
Sound bath	101, 182, 192, 223
Sound healing	189-195, 209
Spiritual Hygiene	61-68
Stress	7-9, 11, 53-54, 68, 98-101, 120-123, 136-138, 148-149, 168, 173-174, 199, 207, 209-212, 222-230, 269-272, 275-277, 283-284, 287-288
Sugar	34-37, 42, 46-47, 70-71, 121, 152-153, 166-169, 213, 245, 256-263, 271
Sunbathing	150
Surrender	89-96, 319
Sympathetic Nervous System	93, 203-204, 207-212, 225-227, 276
Fight-or-Flight	44, 93, 190, 201, 209-210, 223, 226, 229, 280-282

T

Tolerance	47
Triclosan	58-60
Triggers	48, 54-56, 193-195, 305

V

Vagus Nerve — 40, 165, 209-227, 229, 244, 275, 281, 288, 293

Vagal toning — 212-213, 222, 224-226

Validation Seeking — 62, 64-65

Vibration — 13, 94, 108, 179, 189-193, 278, 291-292, 305-306,

Visualisation — 103-104

W

Water — 122, 126-129, 144-145, 172-179, 191, 213, 319
- Cold Water Therapy — 174-177, 209, 223
- Float therapy — 279
- Negative ions — 140, 149, 173-174
- Water memory — 179-180

Weight loss — 62-65, 178, 222, 230, 254, 257-258

Williamson, Marianne — 88

Y

Yoga — 199, 200, 204, 209, 223-224, 227, 229-235, 277-278, 281, 319

If you want to keep in touch, follow me:
@thehealedstate on Instagram and Facebook
@christiannewolff on Youtube
Or listen to **The Christianne Wolff Podcast Show** on iTunes

Christianne Wolff is the author of 4 other paper back books which are:
- The Body Rescue Plan
- The Body Rescue Detox Recipe Book
- The Body Rescue Vegan Plan
- The Body Rescue Maintenance Plan

You can also subscribe to my memberships on
www.thebodyrescueplan.com